Victorian Occultism and the Making of Modern Magic

Palgrave Historical Studies in Witchcraft and Magic

Series Editors: **Jonathan Barry, Willem de Blécourt and Owen Davies**

Titles include:
Edward Bever
THE REALITIES OF WITCHCRAFT AND POPULAR MAGIC IN EARLY
MODERN EUROPE
Culture, Cognition and Everyday Life

Alison Butler
VICTORIAN OCCULTISM AND THE MAKING OF MODERN MAGIC
Invoking Tradition

Julian Goodare, Lauren Martin and Joyce Miller
WITCHCRAFT AND BELIEF IN EARLY MODERN SCOTLAND

Jonathan Roper (*editor*)
CHARMS, CHARMERS AND CHARMING

Alison Rowlands (*editor*)
WITCHCRAFT AND MASCULINITIES IN EARLY MODERN EUROPE

Rolf Schulte
MAN AS WITCH
Male Witches in Central Europe

Forthcoming:
Johannes Dillinger
MAGICAL TREASURE HUNTING IN EUROPE AND NORTH AMERICA
A History

Soili-Maria Olli
TALKING TO DEVILS AND ANGELS IN SCANDINAVIA, 1500–1800

Laura Stokes
THE DEMONS OF URBAN REFORM
The Rise of Witchcraft Prosecution, 1430–1530

**Palgrave Historical Studies in Witchcraft and Magic
Series Standing Order ISBN 978–1403–99566–7 Hardback
978–1403–99567–4 Paperback**
(*outside North America only*)

You can receive future titles in this series as they are published by placing a
standing order. Please contact your bookseller or, in case of difficulty, write to us
at the address below with your name and address, the title of the series and the
ISBN quoted above.

Customer Services Department, Macmillan Distribution Ltd, Houndmills,
Basingstoke, Hampshire RG21 6XS, England

Victorian Occultism and the Making of Modern Magic

Invoking Tradition

Alison Butler

Lecturer in History, St. Francis Xavier University, Canada

First published 2011 by
PALGRAVE MACMILLAN

Palgrave Macmillan in the UK is an imprint of Macmillan Publishers Limited, registered in England, company number 785998, of Houndmills, Basingstoke, Hampshire RG21 6XS.

Palgrave Macmillan in the US is a division of St Martin's Press LLC, 175 Fifth Avenue, New York, NY 10010.

Palgrave Macmillan is the global academic imprint of the above companies and has companies and representatives throughout the world.

Palgrave® and Macmillan® are registered trademarks in the United States, the United Kingdom, Europe and other countries.

ISBN 978–0–230–22339–4   hardback

This book is printed on paper suitable for recycling and made from fully managed and sustained forest sources. Logging, pulping and manufacturing processes are expected to conform to the environmental regulations of the country of origin.

A catalogue record for this book is available from the British Library.

A catalog record for this book is available from the Library of Congress.

10   9   8   7   6   5   4   3   2   1

20   19   18   17   16   15   14   13   12   11

Printed and bound in Great Britain by
CPI Antony Rowe, Chippenham and Eastbourne

Contents

Acknowledgements

Most of the research for this book was conducted in England between 2000 and 2007. Further research took me to Ireland, while the actual written product took shape in Canada. I am therefore extremely grateful for the support and encouragement from individuals and institutions in all three countries. First and foremost, I would like to thank Ronald Hutton for his critical supervision of the initial stages of this project and for his continued advice and encouragement. Owen Davies and James Thompson offered invaluable help by encouraging me to clarify my arguments and flesh out key points. David N. Bell set me upon this fascinating path of research and I am indebted to him for his generous guidance and support.

My work on this project was initially funded by the Social Sciences and Humanities Research Council of Canada and the Rothermere Trust. I would also like to acknowledge St Francis Xavier University for providing me with the funding that enabled me to share my research and receive critical feedback at various national and international conferences in 2007–10.

Some sections of this book began as conference papers and selected material from the fourth and seventh chapters was first presented at the Canadian Society for the History and Philosophy of Science, London, Ontario, in 2005; the Victorian Interdisciplinary Studies Association of the Western United States, Boulder, Colorado, in 2007; the Northeast Victorian Studies Association, Toronto, in 2007; and the first international *Societas Magica* conference, Waterloo, Ontario, in 2007. I was fortunate to have the opportunity to avail myself of the scrutiny of my work and the subsequent encouragement and beneficial suggestions offered by colleagues at these meetings.

Portions of the sixth chapter originally appeared in 'Making Magic Modern: Nineteenth-Century Adaptations' in *The Pomegranate: The International Journal of Pagan Studies* 6, II, 2004: 212–30. I gratefully acknowledge the permission of Equinox Publications to reprint some of this material. Some of the material in the fourth chapter also found initial form in journal publications and I wish to thank the following for permission to reproduce copyright material: *Limina Collective* for 'The Intellectual Origins of the Victorian Occult Revival' in *Limina* 9, 2003, 78–95; Mandrake of Oxford for 'The Importance of Barrett's *Magus*' in

Journal for the Academic Study of Magic 1, 2003, 7–32; and Anthem Press for 'Anna Kingsford: Scientist and Sorceress' in David Clifford *et al.* (eds) *Repositioning Victorian Sciences: Shifting Centres in Nineteenth-Century Scientific Thinking* 2006, 59–69.

Research for this book was carried out at the Bodleian and Radcliffe Science Libraries at Oxford University, the British Library, the Warburg Institute, the Wellcome Institute, the University of London Library, the National Library of Ireland, the University of Toronto and the Bristol Central Library. I greatly appreciate the helpfulness of the staffs at these libraries, particularly the Bristol Central Library and the National Library of Ireland. I am also indebted to R.A. Gilbert for his generosity in sharing his research and for some enlightening conversations. I would also like to thank the people at Palgrave Macmillan who have helped bring this research to publication; they include Owen Davies, Ruth Ireland and Sally Daniell.

Throughout this project, friends and family have been unstinting in their help. I am grateful to Emma Butler for her constant encouragement. Finally, my thanks and more go to John Cook for his selfless support and to Stella and Russell for their patience and inspiration.

Introduction

In 1887 the famous microbiologist and chemist, Louis Pasteur, was recovering on the French Riviera from an unknown illness. What he did not know was that he was actually recovering from an attempt on his life. The would-be assassin was hundreds of miles away in London celebrating the partial success of her occult efforts to murder the scientist. By Anna Kingsford's reckoning, Pasteur would have been victim number three in her mission to rid the world of what she called 'those demons of vivisection'. Her method? Magic. Kingsford, in two of her previously successful attempts, and in her attack on Pasteur, projected a magical force of destruction against her victims.

Two questions emerge upon hearing of this incident. Why did Kingsford want to kill Pasteur and why did she use magic? The first is easy to answer. Kingsford was obviously violently opposed to the practice of vivisection and believed that by silencing the scientists engaged in this form of experimentation she could also stop the practice itself. It would seem logical to conclude that if enough people died while experimenting on live animals, other vivisectors might hesitate to continue this practice and such 'demons' might hold back on using this form of experimentation. The second question, however, 'Why use magic?' Is a far more complicated one that requires much examination and explanation. Why would a student of medicine, in an age of progress, scientific advancement and secularization, rely upon such seemingly supernatural means to produce a very physical effect?

Kingsford represents a marginalized segment of Victorian society involved in occultism. This book is about people like her and about the literature they relied upon and created in their magical endeavors. Despite Kingsford's position as a scientist, her scientific activities and beliefs in no way conflicted with her magical beliefs. This conflation of science and sorcery is characteristic of Victorian occultists and is a key feature in the nineteenth-century revival of magic. Kingsford, as a scientist, mystic, spiritualist, and social activist was one of the most remarkable individuals responsible for the emergence of a new occultism in Victorian Britain. In her various roles and interests, however, she was quite typical of the thousands of men and women dabbling in esoteric interests during the period. Nineteenth-century science and magic were not exclusive of each other, much like in any other historical period. Rather they enjoyed or endured a completely complicated relationship. Many scientists in fact straddled the realms of science and the occult with little difficulty. Much recent scholarship has demonstrated the readiness of nineteenth-century scientists to investigate the seemingly supernatural. Historian Alex Owen situates medical psychologists including Pierre Janet, Charles Richet, Albert Freiherr von Schrenk-Notzing, William James and Freud, at séances, either as participants or observers.[1] In her book on the German occult, Corinna Treitel exposes the strong ties between experimental psychology and occultism in the late nineteenth and early twentieth centuries and identifies several famous scientists from the fields of astrophysics, mathematics and psychology as occult particpants.[2] Despite the ability by some Victorians to traverse both the realms of science and the occult, not all Victorians were able to reconcile the scientific with the spiritual so easily. Many turned either to science or to certain esoteric forms of belief to make sense of this new age of secularization. It was a marginalized minority, however, that turned to occultism and applied scientific method to their experiments. As one of the more influential individuals belonging to this minority, Kingsford believed that through magic she could direct her will to produce physical results. This magic relied upon the notion of correspondences between the visible and the invisible – a notion fully developed much earlier by Renaissance scholars and magicians. Kingsford was also influenced by the French occultists whose work helped to develop the importance of the power of the individual will when coupled with that of a divine one. This power would come to be a signature feature of British occultism in the late nineteenth century.

As a middle-class Victorian woman with both a scientific and spiritual background, influenced by Renaissance and French occultism, Kingsford embodies the key features of the dominant occult organization of the era, the Hermetic Order of the Golden Dawn. The men and women who belonged to this society practised a unique form of ceremonial magic, one which drew upon an established magical tradition yet incorporated new elements resulting in a transformation of Western magic, the effects of which are still felt today.

The so-called revival of occultism at the end of the nineteenth-century has been explored from other angles. Most of these examinations have taken the form of concentrated histories of specific secret societies and certain key individuals while others have focused on examining this 'revival' as a departure from secularization and rationalism. More recently, scholarly examination has focused on the role of occultism in the development of modernity.

In *The Place of Enchantment: British Occultism and the Culture of the Modern,* Alex Owen argues for the rationality of fin-de-siècle British occultism and its pivotal contributions to the modern preoccupation with subjectivity.[3] Corinna Treitel observes occultism's role in the development of the German modern.[4] In his look at nineteenth-century French occultism, David Allen Harvey examines the political role of Martinism within the context of French nationalism.[5] Most of the recent scholarship on nineteenth-century occultism in Britain, France and Germany contributes to a current challenge to debunk the long-standing equation of modernity with disenchantment.[6] While such attempts have largely been successful in reinstating an appreciation of an enchanted modernity, this scholarship fails to address another equally taxing task in the study of occultism. In linking occultism so strongly with modernism, minimal attention is given to occultism's lineage and its roots in the history of Western magic. Studies that so firmly position and contextualize occultism within the advent of modernity are simply falling into a familiar trap for historians and that is to see magic as a static phenomenon, occurring within a particular time period and therefore limiting the search for origins within a certain geographical place and era. While many such studies seek to rescue magic and occultism from the label of irrationality, by merely arguing for its rationality within a given time and place, they once again provide an excuse for an occult worldview – 'it made sense at that time.' This ignores the prevalence and proliferation of occult practices and beliefs throughout the Western world, both past and present. It is time to stop apologizing for magic.

This book seeks to steer clear of such apologies by positioning Victorian occultism not only within the context of its own era but also within that of a continuous tradition of Western magic. With such a dual focus this examination is not so much preoccupied with what Victorian magic signifies, as where it came from. In contrast with other studies on British occultism, this book positions the nineteenth-century fascination with magic within a wider historical context in order to demonstrate how Victorian occultists transformed the magical tradition they inherited and how the significance of occultism evolved throughout the century. Nicola Bown, in her review of Owen's *The Place of Enchantment,* argues that the sharp distinction of occultism as modern and the focus on the fin-de-siècle obscures a broader history of nineteenth-century magical interests. This current volume seeks to broaden this history by establishing both the occult revival's 'real' origins in the greater nineteenth century and its 'invented' or 'invoked' origins within the larger scope of history.[7]

Thus, this book is concerned with providing an historical analysis of Victorian occultism by revealing the people, institutions, texts and traditions responsible for its emergence. By exploring primary documents that, until now, have not been examined from an academic perspective, this book proposes that Victorian occultists played a radical role in transforming Western magic.

As such, this book seeks to explore the history of Victorian occultism and will focus on the individuals and traditions responsible for the formation of the Golden Dawn as the culmination of Victorian magical innovation. Through such an examination of late nineteenth-century magic, we will further explore its role in transmitting a refashioned Western magical tradition into the twentieth century and beyond and we will establish the nature and significance of this refashioning.

With such goals in mind, the book opens with a detailed examination of Victorian occultism in the form of the magic practised by the Golden Dawn. The first few chapters are concerned with uncovering the origins of the Order itself and the magical practices and beliefs of its members. The first chapter deals with the former while the second explores the magical and esoteric traditions that provide the framework for Victorian occultism with a particular focus on the textual evidence left behind by Golden Dawn magicians. In the third chapter, the focus narrows with an analysis of the influence of several key nineteenth-century esoteric traditions on the structure and rituals of Victorian magic. The fourth and fifth chapters deal with the actual men and women engaged in practising occultism and the textual sources and collections which helped to shape their practices and beliefs. Victorian magic's legacy is the subject of the sixth chapter while the final chapter looks at the social and cultural context of British occultism. In such a manner, the book begins with a microscopic view and, on its path of exploration, draws back to incorporate a broader cultural perspective. Such a structure is preferable in teasing out the origins of Victorian magic. While this magic was certainly influenced by the culture in which it emerged, its roots lie in older traditions, both invented and historical. Recent research into nineteenth-century occultism has focused on the role of the occult in the development of modernity and as such has been concerned with demonstrating the reciprocal influence of occultism and the culture in which it was practised. The goal of this book is not to deny the importance of this contemporary influence, but rather to provide a greater historical context by demonstrating that Victorian magic is but one chapter in a larger study: that of the Western mind's fascination with magic. The book's structure facilitates this by first establishing the historical influences on Victorian magic and then discussing how its structure and format was shaped and enabled by its cultural climate.

At this point, a definition of magic must be settled upon for the purpose of this book. In the context of this study, magic is a particular way in which an individual interprets and participates in existence. This particular way is based upon an ordering of the universe which enables the individual, once he/she has knowledge of this ordering, to interact directly with the universe and to manipulate aspects of this universe through the appropriate correspondences and through the use of the individual's will and imagination. This interaction and manipulation may or may not involve intermediary beings and such beings may or may not be supernatural. This definition will serve to encompass most of the magic encountered in this book.

Two other terms which need to be addressed and which will feature frequently in this book are occultism and esotericism. Victorian magic falls under the auspices of both terms and therefore a person or society engaged in magical activity may be referred to as magical, occult or esoteric. The term 'occultism' dates from the nineteenth century and implies the study and/or practice of the occult or 'hidden' sciences which include ceremonial magic, alchemy, astrology, and cabalistic magic. Such sciences stood in direct opposition to the mainstream science of the day, that of materialism. In the nineteenth century, one could be an occultist without being a magician. The same holds true for the term esoteric. An esotericist need not be an occultist or magician but to be a Victorian magician or occultist involved the study of esoteric traditions. For something to be esoteric there must be a hidden knowledge behind a system or tradition of thought. When we speak of Victorian magic, we speak of a system of practice and belief that is not only magical but esoteric and occult. As a mix of various occult sciences, late nineteenth-century magic is interchangeably referred to throughout this book as both Victorian magic and Victorian occultism. Many of the traditions and societies which informed Victorian occultism involved a hidden body of knowledge and are thus referred to as esoteric.

This book seeks to discover the founding influences behind the rise of this occultism. In doing so, considerable time will be spent in examining the key players. Such a social history would be incomplete, however, without considering the crucial role of textual influences. The magic we refer to when speaking of a nineteenth-century occult revival is a 'high' or 'learned' form of magic. As such, it is heavily reliant upon texts. Not only for the purposes of transmission of a magical tradition but for the expression of it also.

Britain has long been a place of magic. What has been called magic can be found in the practices and beliefs of pre-Christian Britain and in the histories and invented traditions of British druidry and paganism. The kind of magic this book focuses on however is a different sort of magic; a magic that is text-based and therefore has a more elitist history. Ceremonial magic relies upon magical texts or *grimoires* and is naturally historically associated with literacy. The increase in literacy in the nineteenth century, the focus on self-education, the proliferation of public libraries and the rise of the middle class resulted in the erosion of this elitist status of ceremonial magic to some degree. In current practice, however, we still see some differentiation between individuals and groups who practise text-based magic and those who are less concerned with practising magic 'by the book'. And while the shape-shifting nature of magic in general enables this more intellectual manifestation to both adapt and be adapted by other traditions, it does have a history of its own.

1
A New Order

At the turn of the century, Victorian Britain witnessed a revival of interest in magic and the occult. All sorts of respectable men and women were dabbling in dubious pastimes such as ritual magic and attempting to communicate with the dead. Medical doctors donned ceremonial dress and wielded wands in magical ritual; an accountant and a tea heiress astrally projected themselves to other planets; actors and poets gathered together to transmute evil into good. Such gatherings were by no means unusual. Throughout the latter half of the nineteenth century such individuals gathered together in groups to practise and study magic for a variety of purposes including communicating with one's guardian angel, healing the sick, interplanetary travel, and even murder. However, while certain individuals did seek such objectives in their pursuit of occult knowledge, the average Victorian magician was seeking something far less sensational but just as radical. Men and women across Britain were joining magical societies in an attempt to evolve into their 'true selves'. They believed that ancient wisdom passed down over the centuries through cabalistic, Hermetic, alchemical and occult sources held the key for individuals to gain access to their divine beings. And despite the seeming extreme nature of these endeavours, what these men and women were doing was actually quite in keeping with Victorian social and cultural interests. The scientific doctrine of evolution and the more social doctrine of self-betterment tied in nicely with this dominant goal of occultism. And so by the end of the century more and more men and women of all classes were participating in a wide range of esoteric activities. These activities and the knowledge required to engage in them were provided through the increasing number of societies and organizations dedicated to discovering and nurturing the occult powers of the individual. Some of these groups were secretive or exclusive, while others, such as the Theosophical Society, were quite well known to the British public and as equally open. Theosophy, spiritualism, and a variety of pseudo-scientific interests were well integrated into society. Along with such mainstream organizations and interests, more secretive and esoteric interests were also flourishing, feeding on the same social desires and interests that characterized Victorian culture. Occult societies and esoteric branches of the more established and prominent organizations provided, to some degree, a place for those interested in learning more about magic in the Western tradition. Some societies went even further, providing not only a place to learn about magic, but a place to practise it as well. It was not until 1888, however, that men and women throughout Britain had the opportunity to have their occult desires quenched by what proved to be Britain's first school of magic, focused on teaching the techniques of ritual magic to interested initiates. This society was the Hermetic Order of the Golden Dawn and was the most significant and influential occult organization of its era, and, arguably, of the last two centuries. Its role in synthesizing pre-existent magical traditions and producing a modern magical system that would survive throughout the Edwardian period and well into the twentieth and twenty-first centuries makes it the defining occult society in recent Western history. The Golden Dawn also served as a hub for much of the occult and esoteric activity taking place in the late nineteenth century as its members were affiliated with several other contemporary esoteric societies. The Order represented the culmination of both British and French occult innovation and scholarship of previous centuries. Therefore, when we speak of Victorian occultism, we are talking about the magic practised and refined within the Golden Dawn.

Emerging in a society accustomed to the secretive nature of Freemasonry, the ghostly realm of the spiritualists, and the mysticism of the Theosophists, the Golden Dawn stood out as a society for practising magicians. Its organization found precedence in other nineteenth-century Rosicrucian societies such as the *Fratres Lucis* or the Order of the Swastika, and the *Societas Rosicruciana in Anglia* (*Soc. Ros.*). As we will see later, earlier occult societies such as the Royal Order of Sikha , the Sat B'Hai , the Hermetic Brothers of Egypt and the Society of Eight also influenced the Golden Dawn. While there certainly were nineteenth-century precedents for such an occult organization, the Order was the first magical society to institutionalize magical learning and create an actual school of magic.

From 1888 to 1901, hundreds of men and women were initiated into the Order at five different temples: the Isis-Urania Temple in London

(1888), the Osiris Temple in Weston-super-Mare (1888), the Horus Temple in Bradford (1893), the Amen-Ra Temple in Edinburgh (1893), and the Ahathoor Temple in Paris (1894). Among these hundreds were the Order's three official founders, William Wynn Westcott, Dr William Robert Woodman, and Samuel Liddell MacGregor Mathers. These three were joined by men and women from all walks of life including such famous personalities as William Butler Yeats, Florence Farr, Annie Horniman, Maud Gonne, Mina Bergson, Arthur Machen and the notorious Aleister Crowley.

The first Golden Dawn temple, the Isis-Urania temple in London, proved to be the most popular and the most controversial, attracting more initiates than its sister temples and attracting many of the Order's more prominent members. One of its first initiates was Mina Bergson, a student at the Slade School of Fine Art and sister to the well-known philosopher Henri Bergson. The Order welcomed men and women from all classes and professions in its hierarchical system of initiation and Mina was quickly joined by 50 further would-be magicians, most of them male and already entrenched in Masonic tradition.[1] By 1896 the Order had initiated more than 300 members at its five temples.[2] The Golden Dawn offered instruction in a program devised by MacGregor Mathers and Westcott that was essentially a synthesis of the entire Western magical tradition broken up into different stages.

Initially the Golden Dawn had one order, the first or outer order, and its teachings were based on the cipher manuscript, a suspicious document that Westcott claimed contained the teachings of a German occult order. In 1891, a second, or inner order formed within the Golden Dawn and these teachings were based on personal communications between MacGregor Mathers and the supposed secret chiefs of the Order. The precedent for such secret chiefs is found in many esoteric societies, but most pertinently for the Golden Dawn, in the Theosophical Society's 'Mahatmas'. Such figures were beings with superhuman powers who encouraged and helped mortals to establish esoteric and occult societies and who passed on wisdom and knowledge normally inaccessible to human beings. In establishing himself as the link between the Order's secret chiefs and the rest of the Golden Dawn, MacGregor Mathers succeeded in wresting all power away from the other founders, one of whom, Woodman, was soon to pass away and cared little about such matters of authority, and the other, Westcott, was ill prepared to compete with the creative genius and ambition of MacGregor Mathers. MacGregor Mathers also succeeded in making this Second Order the nucleus of magical ritual and practice in the Golden Dawn, designating the First Order as primarily concerned with imparting esoteric and magical theory to its members.

MacGregor Mathers' claims to correspondence with secret chiefs soon led to his downfall as members of the Golden Dawn evolved from naïve initiates to suspicious adepts. The Order, in its original form, self-destructed in 1900 in the midst of a scandalous court case and general insurrection. What the Order left behind, however, has proved to be indestructible. The magical system of the Golden Dawn continues to be practised by hundreds of thousands of magicians around the world.

What is known of the founding of the Order and of those responsible has been well documented.[3] The three founders, Westcott, MacGregor Mathers and Woodman, were previously acquainted with each other through their esoteric and occult interests. William Wynn Westcott was a London coroner by profession and a Freemason who was fascinated by occultism. He was born in Leamington, Warwickshire in 1848. His father was a surgeon and both of Westcott's parents passed away when Westcott was nine years old. His uncle, also a surgeon, took him under his wing and Westcott followed in his uncle's and father's professional footsteps, studying medicine at the University of London and joining his uncle's practice around the age of 23. Westcott was appointed coroner for North-East London in 1881 and held that position until 1918. Prior to this appointment, Westcott had gone into seclusion for two years to study cabalistic philosophy, and Hermetic, alchemical and Rosicrucian writings.[4] He joined the *Soc. Ros.* in the early 1880s. This society was of utmost importance in the establishment of the Golden Dawn as it was the organization through which much magical knowledge and interest was transmitted from the occultists of the early and middle part of the century to the actual founders of the Order, as all three co-founders shared membership in the *Soc. Ros.* The society was founded in London in 1865–66 by two esotericists and occultists: Robert Wentworth Little and Kenneth Mackenzie. It was an esoteric society of Freemasons interested in studying occultism with an emphasis on cabala and Masonic symbolism, all under a clearly Christian orientation.[5] Westcott went on to become the society's Supreme Magus from 1891 to 1925 and laid out its purpose as follows in a lecture he prepared on the history of the Rosicrucians.

> To afford mutual aid and encouragement in working out the great problems of Life, and in discovering the Secrets of Nature; to facilitate the study of the system of Philosophy founded upon the Kabbalah and the doctrines of Hermes Trismegistus, which was inculcated

by the original Fratres Rosae Crucis of Germany, A.D. 1450; and to investigate the meaning and symbolism of all that now remains of the wisdom, art and literature of the ancient world.[6]

In this same lecture, Westcott tells the story of the society's formation. Apparently, Little had found some old rituals in the storerooms of a Freemason's hall and brought them to Mackenzie's attention with the intention of forming an esoteric group. Mackenzie had earlier received Rosicrucian initiation and was granted the authority to form the society (to which Westcott refers here as an 'allied English Masonic Rosicrucian Society of a less esoteric character than the Continental system') while living in Austria with a certain Count Apponyi.[7]

Westcott was also familiar with the teachings of the Theosophical Society. He presented several lectures to its membership and was an honorary member of the Hermetic Society. This latter society was an offshoot of the Theosophical Society. It was founded by Dr Anna Bonus Kingsford and focused more on Western esotericism, whereas the Theosophists were guided by supposed Eastern doctrines. Westcott learned much from his memberships in a variety of esoteric societies and from his association with the Theosophical Society about how to establish a secret order. The Eastern focus and lack of exclusivity of the Theosophists and the lack of concentration on ritual magic in the Hermetic Society left an opening for Westcott to fill. He used his knowledge and experience as a Theosophist, a Freemason, a member of the *Soc. Ros.* and as an accomplished student of the occult to formulate the initial thought that sparked the beginning of a new order and a new brand of magic. After co-founding the Golden Dawn in 1888, Westcott concentrated his energies predominantly upon his new society. The Order provided Westcott with the opportunity to pursue an area which fascinated him, cabalistic magic. He did not, however, withdraw from his duties in other esoteric groups. In particular, he remained quite involved in the *Soc. Ros.* and, as mentioned above, went on to serve as its Supreme Magus. In fact, after the initial establishment of the Golden Dawn, Westcott's role in that organization became increasingly less necessary and instrumental. It was MacGregor Mathers who quickly achieved status within the Order as the ultimate authority despite the original plans for three equal chiefs. Westcott did not appear to have the ability, or the desire, to challenge MacGregor Mathers' authority and when accused by MacGregor Mathers in 1900 of forgery and deception in the establishment of the Order, Westcott retreated to the security of his earlier occult associations. He occasionally resurfaced in Golden Dawn affairs when the Order began to splinter into differing factions, but finally departed from the occult world in 1918 when he retired to South Africa to live with his daughter. He died in July 1927.

Mystery and intrigue surround the establishment of the Golden Dawn, as is appropriate for a secret society of magicians. Westcott apparently discovered ancient manuscripts written in cipher which were given to him by a Reverend Adolphus F.A. Woodford. Westcott recorded a meeting with Woodford about the manuscript in which Woodford says he showed it to the influential mid-century occultist Kenneth Mackenzie, of whom more will be discovered later in this book. Mackenzie was apparently quite surprised and had never seen such a manuscript before. In Westcott's entry, Woodford claims that he received the manuscript from France and that it had once been in the possession of the famous French occultist and darling of British esoteric circles, Eliphas Lévi.[8] Another account claims that the British occultist Frederick Hockley deposited these manuscripts in a Masonic store-cupboard before his death which is where Woodford found them.[9] Upon deciphering the text Westcott discovered that it contained five mystical rituals similar to those practised in Masonic lodges. According to one account, the code was created by the fifteenth-century German abbot and occultist, Johannes Trithemius of Spanheim and examples of this cipher were readily available in manuscript in the collection at the British Museum.[10] Among the leaves of the manuscripts Westcott also discovered the address of a certain Fräulein Sprengel, a supposed German Rosicrucian adept. Westcott wrote to this woman and received instructions from her to form an English branch of her occult order, *Die Goldene Dämmerung*. This led to the establishment of the Isis-Urania Temple of the Hermetic Order of the Golden Dawn in 1888. Westcott then asked MacGregor Mathers and Woodman, who were fellow occultists and members of the *Soc. Ros.*, to join him as chiefs of the new order. Westcott also commissioned MacGregor Mathers to compose new rituals in accordance with those discovered in the cipher manuscript to add to the Golden Dawn's corpus.

It did not require modern scholarship to cast doubt on the authenticity of this cipher manuscript. The Golden Dawn was scarcely up and running when its own members indicated they felt they were being duped. Arthur Edward Waite joined the order in 1891 and made his own copy of the founding cipher manuscript in the early 1900s. He suspected that the manuscript was not as old as Westcott asserted, but rather of quite recent origin. He based his suspicions upon two facts. First, the manuscript included ancient Egyptian material, which was incomprehensible until hieroglyphs were deciphered in 1822. Second, the manuscript contained allusions to the compatibility of the tarot with the cabalistic Tree of Life, a comparison that first occurred in the writings of Eliphas Lévi in 1856.[11] Modern scholarship has confirmed Waite's suspicions. Golden Dawn historian Ellic Howe examined various types of writing paper in England and Germany in the nineteenth century. He sought professional advice in examining the grammar used in correspondence between Sprengel and Westcott and found that Sprengel's German was ridden with the common mistakes made by English-speaking people. Based on this and other inconsistencies, Howe presents the following alternative explanation behind the founding of the Golden Dawn. Westcott forged the letters from Sprengel using foreign writing paper. To compose the manuscript, he enlisted the help of an employee of German ancestry who worked for a surgical supply company in which Westcott held financial interests. Extensive research attempting to verify the existence of a Fräulein Sprengel proved equally inconclusive and Howe argues that both she and the manuscripts were fabricated by Westcott.[12] Through his association with esoteric societies and occultism, Westcott was well aware that every secret society needs a tradition from which to grow and secret chiefs from whom to take guidance. Westcott conveniently disposed of his fabrication by having Fräulein Sprengel grant the Golden Dawn autonomy and then die. That Westcott made up this German correspondence is further supported by MacGregor Mathers' own accusation in 1900 that Westcott had forged these letters and had then, in turn, pledged MacGregor Mathers to secrecy. Regardless of origin or authenticity, Westcott enabled the Hermetic Order of the Golden Dawn to have all the proper credentials, namely an obscure manuscript encoded with esoteric and ancient rituals and a foreign Rosicrucian order looking for a successor. Westcott, MacGregor Mathers and Woodman were in business.

While it was Westcott who developed the original structure of the Golden Dawn through invention and appropriation, it was the extraordinarily talented MacGregor Mathers who bestowed mind and spirit upon the order and transformed an esoteric society into an association of practising magicians. Westcott conceived the notion of the order and provided it with an appropriate history and tradition, but for it to take shape as a living and growing organism it required nourishment. MacGregor Mathers furnished this with the rituals he created, the addition of other occult systems through his translations, and with the leadership (sometimes disputed) that he provided to the Order's members. Westcott understood from the beginning that the Order needed more spirit and substance than that which he could offer. He immediately turned to MacGregor Mathers requesting his assistance in overseeing the Order and in composing more rituals based on the cipher manuscript. Westcott already had an appreciation and awareness of MacGregor Mathers' occult abilities, charisma and talent and he was probably aware of his own inadequacies as a magician. Westcott recognized that his personal primary interest was in acquiring magical knowledge as opposed to practising it.

As is fitting for a man of magic, the details concerning MacGregor Mathers' birth and death are hazy, providing fodder for the myth of immortality that surrounds legendary occultists. MacGregor Mathers' birth certificate states his full name as 'Samuel Liddell Mathers', the 'MacGregor' was to be added later. He was born 8 January 1854 in West Hackney, Middlesex. His father, William, was a merchant's clerk who died while MacGregor Mathers was quite young. The young Mathers continued to live with his widowed mother, Mary Ann, until her death in 1885. There is some debate over MacGregor Mathers' education. While there was indeed a Mathers who attended Bedford Grammar School during the time of MacGregor Mathers' youth, Ithell Colquhoun in her biography argues that MacGregor Mathers' mother would not have been able to pay the school's fees. Furthermore, Colquhoun argues that the mediocre marks on record for this Mathers do not reflect the magical MacGregor Mathers' intelligence. Therefore, she suggests that this Bedford Mathers was a cousin whose schooling our MacGregor Mathers adopted for his own later in life.[13] Other sources however argue that the Bedford Mathers and Samuel Liddell were one and the same.[14] Such an account is also verified by MacGregor Mathers' wife, Moina Mathers (Mina Bergson) who also claims that her husband specialized in Classics during his stay at the Bedford Grammar School.[15]

MacGregor Mathers' esoteric education began, predictably, with initiation into Freemasonry. He joined the Freemasons' Hengist Lodge in Bournemouth in 1877 at the age of 23. He achieved the level of Master Mason and it is upon this document that he first demonstrated his desire to pass himself off as something, or someone, other than he was. Here he used the title 'Comte de Glenstrae' and so began his self-determined lineage with the Macgregor's of Glenstrae.[16] MacGregor Mathers later joined the *Soc. Ros.* at the invitation of Westcott and Woodman and as part of this initiation, he took the name 'S Rioghail Mo Dhream' (Royal is my race), the motto of the MacGregor clan.

Through his association with the *Soc. Ros.*, MacGregor Mathers met all the right people to nourish his magical ambition. He was highly thought of by mid-century occultists such as Kenneth Mackenzie and his contemporary and soon-to-be collaborator, Westcott, whose varied interests in all types of occult knowledge, especially cabala, expanded the horizons of the British occult revival. Through these associations, MacGregor Mathers also became familiar with the ideas of the Theosophists and their brand of Eastern occultism. One particularly influential person in MacGregor Mathers' life was Dr Anna Bonus Kingsford, a medical doctor and mystic. Kingsford was president of the Theosophical Society's London branch in 1883 and later went on to found its Hermetic Lodge, which eventually splintered off in its pursuit of Western Hermeticism. Her influence on MacGregor Mathers and the Golden Dawn will be examined thoroughly in a later chapter.

MacGregor Mathers' interest in occult matters shaped his life and personality but another passion of his, however, played an almost equal role. He had a keen interest in war and military tactics and, at one point, signed up with the First Hampshire Infantry Volunteers. Combining his skill at translation with his military interests, in 1884 he published *Practical Instruction in Infantry Campaigning Exercise*, a translation of a French manual that he adapted to British military requirements.[17] A year later he followed this translation with *The Fall of Granada: A Poem in Six Duans*.[18] His occult and military interests also combined with a competitive and energetic nature, as displayed in his skill and zeal as a boxer and fencer. MacGregor Mathers believed that an occultist should strive for intellectual and physical fitness, and both in mind and body he exhibited a desire to lead and to win.[19] This desire, harnessed to his intelligence and creativity, eventually led him to the position of supreme authority within the Order.

What can be reconstructed from the sketchy historical information is that MacGregor Mathers, like Westcott, was influenced by Masonic structure and symbolism. He also had a yearning to recreate his own past and a desire to establish a new identity for himself, one of a higher social status than that into which he was born and one of a romanticized Scottish flavour. Masonic lodges and esoteric societies provided a perfect environment in which to create a different identity through the drama of initiation and the use of mottoes as new names for individuals. The process of elevation of status via initiation into higher levels in the lodge or society also suited MacGregor Mathers' aspiration to rise above his original station in society. His occult ambitions and desire for knowledge were expressed in his translations of obscure esoteric texts and his synthesis of magical rituals for the Order using the knowledge he gleaned from the shelves of the British Museum, the Bibliothèque

Nationale and the Bibliothèque de l'Arsenal. His intelligence and creativity are found in the legacy he left in his written work and in his living work, the Hermetic Order of the Golden Dawn.

Without Westcott, MacGregor Mathers' life may have taken a very different path. Westcott not only introduced him to the idea of forming a magical order, but he also provided the financial support for MacGregor Mathers to carry out his translations. If it had not been for Westcott's support, MacGregor Mathers would have been unlikely to have become the talented magician he was destined to be; but without MacGregor Mathers, the Golden Dawn would have been a very different society. Westcott recognized MacGregor Mathers' talent, although he might not have been fully aware of his colleague's ambitions. Both Westcott and Woodman commissioned MacGregor Mathers to make the first English translation of Knorr von Rosenroth's *Kabbalah Denudata* (1684) which was itself a translation of a staple of the Hebrew cabalistic canon, the *Zohar*. The resulting text, *The Kabbalah Unveiled*, was published in 1887 in London.[20] The next work Westcott required resulted in MacGregor Mathers being invited to join Westcott and Woodman as one of the three founding chiefs of the Golden Dawn. Westcott needed more rituals than those provided in the cipher manuscript in order to fuel the society's occult needs and he knew MacGregor Mathers was his man. Westcott's faith was not unfounded and MacGregor Mathers set about this task with ambitious enthusiasm. In creating the founding texts of the Order, MacGregor Mathers fashioned the essence of the Golden Dawn. The concept of synthesis, the tradition upon which the Order was based, and the original founding manuscripts were all borrowed elements. What MacGregor Mathers contributed was what made the Golden Dawn a living, breathing and, most importantly, growing body of magical adepts. Without his direction and creative genius there would have been little to differentiate the Order from the other esoteric societies operating throughout Britain at the end of the century. The Order would simply have existed as an offshoot of the *Soc. Ros.* with an emphasis on cabalistic and ceremonial magic. Instead, it not only revived the Renaissance process of esoteric synthesis which was so essential to the occult tradition, but it also stepped back further into the history of magic in its incorporation of older magical texts and rituals. MacGregor Mathers was also responsible for the addition of even more recent magical systems such as the Enochian magic of John Dee, as we shall see later.

In 1892, after producing the rituals and attracting some initiates, including his future wife, Mina Bergson, MacGregor Mathers created a second order within the Golden Dawn called the Rose of Ruby and the Cross of Gold (*R.R. et A.C.*) in 1892. The third chief, Dr Woodman, had died a year earlier, leaving Westcott and MacGregor Mathers to run the Order. MacGregor Mathers had already begun to assume command both in the administration of the original, or First, Order and in the creation of the Second Order. The Second Order was open to initiates by invitation only, that is, by the invitation of MacGregor Mathers, as Westcott had very little to do with this extension of the Golden Dawn. At the time there were already several initiates in the original Order. Some of the more prominent members included Reverend W.A. Ayton and his wife who were among the first to join in 1888, along with Mina Bergson. The wife of Oscar Wilde, Constance Mary Wilde, also joined the Isis-Urania Temple in its opening year. Medical doctor, Edward Berridge joined in 1889, and Annie Horniman, tea heiress and friend and fellow student of Mina Bergson at the Slade School, joined the same year. The actress Florence Farr signed up in 1890, at the encouragement of William Butler Yeats, who claimed he joined in 1887 although that date seems a little early. He is also responsible for introducing Maud Gonne to the Order in 1891, the same year Arthur Edward Waite became a member.

With the First Order well under way and a burgeoning roster of Second Order initiates, MacGregor Mathers pulled up roots and moved to Paris, arguably the birthplace of nineteenth-century occultism. The move was financed by the ever-generous Horniman and in Paris, the two Matherses established the fifth Golden Dawn temple, this one dedicated to the Egyptian goddess, Hathor. MacGregor Mathers immediately set to work creating new rituals for the new temple, the Rites of Isis.

Following the Matherses' move, the Golden Dawn in its original form began to fall apart owing to personality conflicts and disillusionment. With MacGregor Mathers gone, Annie Horniman took on the role of leader at the Order's London headquarters. Horniman continued financing the Matherses while they lived in Paris with the failed hope that Moina would pursue her art studies. In 1896, shortly after Horniman withdrew her funding of the couple's Parisian lifestyle and following an internal dispute between Horniman and another member of the Golden Dawn concerning magical doctrine, MacGregor Mathers suspended Horniman from the Order for making mischief and meddling in the society's affairs. The suspension was met with outcry from other members who petitioned to have her readmitted.[21] From here on in, the Order descended into mutiny and rebellion. Generally the source of the bickering was a lack of agreement on various methods and formats of magical practice. At the onset of the Order's troubles, while things were still somewhat stable, MacGregor Mathers published his translation of yet another magical text, *The Book of the Sacred Magic of Abra-Melin the Mage*, with financial help from Golden Dawn member Frederick Leigh Gardner, who, to some extent, had stepped in to fill the place of benefactor left empty by Horniman's dismissal.

It was MacGregor Mathers' announcement in 1900 that the founding documents of the Order, the cipher manuscript, were forged that created a most serious disturbance among initiates. MacGregor Mathers' defamation of Westcott was in defence of the true origins of his Second Order. Westcott had retired from the Order three years earlier citing personal and professional reasons. He explained some of these reasons in a letter to Gardner:

> the reason is a purely personal one, owing to my having recd. an intimation that it had somehow become known to the State officers that I was a prominent official of a society in which I had been foolishly posturing as one possessed of magical powers – and that if this became more public it would not do for a Coroner of the Crown to be made shame of in such a mad way. So I had no alternative – I cannot think who it is that persecutes me – someone must talk.[22]

Howe suggests that the 'someone' was MacGregor Mathers. Certainly he had grown to see himself as the natural leader of the Order, and he had no use for any earthly equals. Westcott served no further purpose for the Golden Dawn: administratively, magically or financially.

In a letter written to Farr, who had assumed many of Westcott's duties upon his 'retirement', MacGregor Mathers tells of the alleged forgery in order to make the point that Westcott could not have had anything to do with the founding of the Second Order, given his deception concerning the First Order's establishment.[23] MacGregor Mathers was responding to a letter from Farr which has unfortunately disappeared so it is difficult to know what it is that Farr wrote to provoke this attack on Westcott's character. Historian Alex Owen, however, claims Farr had written to MacGregor Mathers stating her wish to resign from her Second Order duties in order to work more closely with Westcott.[24]

This news of deception dropped like a bombshell on the British temples of the Golden Dawn. Members began to question the Order's authenticity and authority. An investigation into the matter held by members of the Second Order into the legitimacy of the founding documents of the Golden Dawn proved fruitless as some of the key documents had apparently gone missing from the Order's archives. The Order itself began to decentralize as disillusioned members either left entirely or regrouped in a fashion dictated by their own conception of what structure the Order should take. The seeds of doubt planted by MacGregor Mathers' accusations, the dismay over Horniman's dismissal and the physical distance between the Order's sole remaining founder and his followers made for unstable ground. And things did not improve.

In Paris, MacGregor Mathers was outraged that members had undertaken this investigation without his authority and sent his avenger, Aleister Crowley, to the Second Order's London headquarters at Blythe Road to reclaim MacGregor Mathers' authority. Crowley had received his controversial initiation into the Second Order in Paris a few months earlier, an initiation not recognized by the London members. Crowley's attempt to quash the revolt and retake the headquarters failed, resulting in the Second Order cutting all ties with MacGregor Mathers and electing an executive committee to run the Order's affairs. This committee included Farr, Yeats, and the newly readmitted Horniman. In response to this mutiny, Dr Berridge, one lone member loyal to MacGregor Mathers, set up shop with a new Isis-Urania Temple. The problems met in London, however, were not seen elsewhere in Golden Dawn temples across Britain as the Horus Temple in Bradford and the Amen-Ra Temple in Edinburgh remained under MacGregor Mathers' authority. The Osiris Temple in Weston-super-Mare had become moribund, never having attracted more than 12 members and resigning its charter in 1895.[25]

On to this turbulent scene came the opportunistic and fraudulent characters calling themselves Mr and Mrs Theo Horos. Their appearance proved disastrous to the already fragile and fractured Order. Mrs Theo Horos claimed to be none other than the infamous Anna Sprengel and the Matherses, among others, believed the story. The Horoses were really Frank and Editha Jackson, an American couple who were accomplished con artists, preying upon people interested in the occult, deceiving the naïve into providing for them financially and sexually. In 1901, after the two had already duped the Matherses into accepting them into the Golden Dawn fold, a London court found the couple guilty of fraud and sexual assault. As revealed in the case, the couple had been using a magical society, the Order of Theocratic Unity, as a front to attract their victims. The scandalous trial received huge publicity and the Golden Dawn was tarnished through association. The Jacksons claimed affiliation with the Golden Dawn and when the scandal broke the Order received much unwanted attention. After some details of the Golden Dawn rituals in the possession of the Horoses were mockingly read aloud in court, several members jumped ship and the Order never fully recovered. It was not only the sensational and criminal aspects of this event that irrevocably damaged the Order, which, for various reasons, was slowly destroying itself in any case, but also the exposure of the Order's mysteries, the telling of its secrets through the publicizing of supposedly secret rituals.

This scandal and previous in-house disagreements resulted in the end of the Order. What was left of the Golden Dawn had already been divided into two camps: MacGregor Mathers, his Paris temple and a few British diehards on one side, and most of the members of the Second Order lead by Yeats, Horniman and Farr on the other. The Horos trial dissipated any vestiges of the original Golden Dawn. Farr left the Order in 1902, turning to the Eastern spirituality offered by the Theosophists. She ended her days in Ceylon where she died from cancer in 1917. Horniman left the following year focusing her impressive management and funding capabilities on Yeats and his Abbey Theatre in Dublin. Thus ended the magical careers of two of the most powerful Golden Dawn women.

MacGregor Mathers carried on his occult activities adopting a new name for his order, the Alpha et Omega, while the London faction took on the name Morgen Rothe. By 1903 two other societies emerged from the ashes under the leadership of former Golden Dawn members. The *Stella Matutina* was under the leadership of Robert William Felkin and Arthur Edward Waite headed up the Independent and Rectified Order. Felkin later moved to New Zealand bringing with him the magic of the Golden Dawn. Meanwhile, with only a very small part of his very big ego bruised by the battle of Blythe Road, the *enfant terrible* of British occultism, Aleister Crowley, established his own version of the Golden Dawn in 1907, the Argentinum Astrum.

The final blow for MacGregor Mathers came with Crowley's devastating rejection of both him and his creation, the Golden Dawn. Crowley had been MacGregor Mathers' protégé and champion in earlier skirmishes with defiant members, but in 1910, in an act of betrayal, Crowley published large portions of the Order's rituals in the occult journal *The Equinox*. MacGregor Mathers duly brought Crowley to court, winning his suit while enduring public ridicule and mockery. MacGregor Mathers returned to Paris in 1912 and carried on with his occult work, translating *The Grimoire of Armadel* and initiating men and women, Americans in particular, into Golden Dawn magic.[26]

The results of such initiations saw the emigration of Golden Dawn magic to America in the form of actual temples and in the establishment of the Masonic *Societas Rosicruciana in America*.[27]

MacGregor Mathers died in Paris in 1918, but of what, no one is sure. Yeats related his death to a street brawl and bouts of depression. MacGregor Mathers' wife claimed an illness lasting three months took his life and yet another source attributed his death to the Spanish influenza. His death certificate cites no cause of death,[28] a suitably mysterious end for one who sought such mystery during his life.[29]

Much has been discussed and examined concerning two of the Order's founders and their influence in shaping the immediate history of the Golden Dawn. There has been little mention of the third chief, William Robert Woodman, of whom the least is known. Woodman died shortly after the Order was founded and little historical documentation remains to indicate his having exerted much influence on the structure or magic of the Order. Like Westcott, Woodman had studied medicine and was a member of the *Sos. Ros.*, succeeding its founder, Robert Wentworth Little, as Supreme Magus in 1878. In Westcott's lecture on the history of the Order to members of the Golden Dawn, he makes reference to manuscripts written by Woodman which are in the 'Library of the Second Order'.[30] Yet, none of these manuscripts has surfaced and an examination of the Westcott Hermetic Library, the library of the Golden Dawn, turns up no entries by Woodman.[31] While he shared Westcott's enthusiasm for cabala, astrology, the tarot and alchemy, it is unknown whether he, like the other two chiefs, had any dealings with the Theosophical Society.[32] Woodman was a mentor to both of his junior colleagues, encouraging their cabalistic studies, and was described by the London occult book publisher, John Watkins, as 'the moving spirit in the founding of the Golden Dawn.'[33] Apart from this particular comment and occasional references by Westcott and other members of the Order, Woodman left little by which he can be known better. Given the charisma, ambition and creativity of the other founders, it is difficult to accept that Woodman is as inconsequential as the paucity of available material on him suggests. It is not unlikely, however, that Woodman was chosen for his status and seniority as a long-time *Soc. Ros.* member and a respected character in occult circles. His presence as a third chief may have provided balance to the youth and inexperience of MacGregor Mathers. And of course, a third chief was required for the proper Rosicrucian symbolism. Nevertheless, it is undeniable that all three founders, including Woodman, would have made a significant contribution, some more than others, to the magic of the Golden Dawn.

Victorian magic, as shaped and refined by the magicians of the Golden Dawn, has had an immense influence on Western magic as practised worldwide by a variety of groups including Western mystery followers, pagans, wiccans and druids to name a few. Most, if not all Western magical societies, rightly or wrongly, either trace their origins back to the Golden Dawn, or proudly proclaim their reliance on the Order for their magical doctrine. Current societies claiming Golden Dawn lineage include a non-profit Florida organization called the Hermetic Order of the Golden Dawn, and an EU and Canadian society of the same name. There is also the Esoteric Order of the Golden Dawn, self-proclaimed guardians of the 'true' Golden Dawn mysteries, and the Open Source Order of the Golden Dawn, a group of mostly pagan magical practitioners. It is now possible to become a magician of the Golden Dawn online through the variety of societies spread across the globe claiming to be the inheritors of the original.

Why this Victorian magical formulation proved to be so influential can be revealed by looking at the actual magic practised within the Order. Such an analysis requires uncovering the history of nineteenth-century occultism and, to point us in the right direction, a close look at the individuals, societies, and textual sources of these magicians will prove fruitful. A good place to begin is with the paper trail, the textual evidence left behind by the men and women of the Golden Dawn.

2
A New Magic

The magical legacy left behind by Victorian occultists was formulated from a hodge-podge of esoteric subjects. Some of these had become closely entwined much earlier in the history of Western magic while others were brought into the fold during the nineteenth century owing to the efforts of British and French occultists including Golden Dawn chief, Samuel Liddell MacGregor Mathers. Victorian magic is heavily reliant upon the idea of invented tradition. The various esoteric traditions incorporated into late nineteenth-century occultism were very much influenced by this process and Golden Dawn magic itself was the result of its creators engaging in the practice of inventing tradition. Part of this practice involved the most striking characteristic of Western magic, its reliance on the method of synthesis. The close relationship between magic and synthesis and magic and invented tradition dates back centuries, and is witnessed most significantly during the days of the Renaissance magi. In order to understand the importance of this synthesis and invented tradition in the formulation of Victorian occultism, we must look to the origins of this process. Leaving nineteenth-century Britain for the moment we must now examine the Western magical tradition inherited by Victorian occultists so we can better understand the building blocks of British magic.

The system of magic established and developed in the Renaissance provided the ideal basis for the assimilation of many currents of esotericism. This magical synthesis began with scholars such as Pico della Mirandola, Johannes Reuchlin and Heinrich Cornelius Agrippa. Victorian magic owes its origins largely to this resulting magical system. While the various strands that formed this synthesis, such as Hermeticism, Neoplatonism, cabala, demonic magic and natural magic, predate the Renaissance, it was during this particular era that they were brought together to form an influential system of magic, the effect of which has continued to influence Western magic to the present day. This system is predominantly characterized by the addition of Jewish mysticism in the form of cabala to an already eclectic jumble of esoteric systems of thought that were being rediscovered by scholars. The key figures behind this synthesis are found in fifteenth-century Florence, a time and place in which such pursuits were encouraged and financially supported through the patronage of the Medici.

During the fifteenth and sixteenth centuries, some Renaissance scholars, who were well versed in Greek, had greater access to works by Plato and the Neoplatonists. The enthusiasm for such ancient learning was in part due to a trend in intellectual thought to search in original sources for solutions to religious, philosophical, and scientific quandaries. Early humanists in the fifteenth century discovered in the works of Plato a link between paganism and Christianity. The philosophy of Plato was deemed to be similar to monotheistic theology in that it interprets pagan polytheism as functions or members of one divinity.

In 1450 Cosimo de'Medici entrusted the establishment of his Platonic Academy to Marsilio Ficino, a physician, priest and soon-to-be Renaissance magus. Ficino was given the task of translating many of the newly discovered works by Plato, which had been previously unavailable in the West. Ficino's patron interrupted this initial undertaking by asking his translator to begin work upon a newly discovered esoteric Greek manuscript believed to be of great antiquity. This was the *Corpus Hermeticum*, thought to be written by the great (or thrice great) Hermes Trismegistus, a mythical Egyptian sage. It was believed that this text predated Moses and Plato and was in fact a source for both, thus providing a convenient bridge between theology and philosophy.[1] The texts which composed the *Corpus Hermeticum* were not as old as Renaissance scholars believed and were written in second-century Egypt. Ficino's Latin translation was produced in 1471 and its influence on Renaissance Neoplatonism helped shape the occult philosophy that Ficino and his contemporaries went on to establish. This influence is obvious in the works of Ficino, for his scholastic work was not restricted to translation. He was the first Renaissance scholar with an adequate knowledge of Greek to attempt to uncover the mysteries of classical paganism. He developed his own philosophical and religious system, which presented a sophisticated view of pagan theology within the constructs of Christianity, Neoplatonism and Hermeticism.[2] It is in his *De Vita Coelitus Comparanda* that Ficino as magus makes his presence known.[3] Ficino presents his magic as a blend of natural and spiritual magic. Ficinian magic was structured upon groups of sympathetic relationships between all things in the universe based on astrological characteristics, which could be manipulated by tapping into these relationships through an astral influence with the appropriate incantation, invocation or even music. While Ficino's magical theory is largely Christian and spiritual and centres on the Neoplatonic ideal of a world spirit and a living cosmos, he did believe that demonic magic existed and that it could be worked through the invocation of planetary demons. Ficino advocated the practice of non-demonic magic based upon this world spirit and affecting the human spirit. He warned of the risks of demonic magic, however, which, although it could be used in a proper and just manner, held potential danger for the human soul.[4] Ficino's magic was a synthesis of the ideas found in the Platonic, Neoplatonic and Hermetic texts he translated, with Christian theology – a union of ancient paganism with Christianity. It provided the perfect receptacle for the next addition of esoteric thought to infiltrate Renaissance esotericism.[5] Ficino's cofounder of the Neoplatonic movement, the philosopher Giovanni Pico della Mirandola, introduced Jewish cabala into this magical, Hermetic, Neoplatonic, and Christian synthesis, believing that this form of Jewish esotericism confirmed the Christian faith.

Cabala refers to the mystical and esoteric teachings of Judaism, believed to have been given by God to Moses as the oral and esoteric portion of the Law and which could be used to interpret the secret meaning of the written Law.[6] The mystical goal of cabala is to apprehend through contemplation and illumination, that which is beyond the grasp of the intellect, namely God and creation. This contemplation takes place through the use of symbols and metaphors.

In the Middle Ages cabala developed into a theosophical system that could be classified into two complementary forms, speculative and practical. Speculative cabala attempts the interpretation of the fundamental structures of cabala and their symbolism based on the ideas of Neoplatonic and Aristotelian philosophy. These structures include the notion of an unknowable God existing outside of creation and ten sephiroth, which are emanations of the God's identity. These ten sephiroth can be interpreted as ethical symbols, elemental symbols, astrological symbols, planetary symbols, mathematical symbols and, most importantly, as constituting different paths with which to reach the unknowable God or Ein-Sof. Practical cabala consists mostly of what could be termed 'white magic'; magic carried out through the power of sacred names, such as those of God and the angels, in order to affect the physical world.[7] Such magic is not prohibited but restrictions do exist to prevent an individual from practising magic for personal gain. Another kind of magic also exists within cabala which uses a variety of combinations of Hebrew letters. This type of letter combination was frequently used in conjunction with the more practical magic.[8] In general, magical practice within cabala was a mixed affair and over the course of history, the fine line between what was considered proper magic and that which was considered evil or 'black' (carried out in order to harm others, or for personal gain and carried out through the help of demonic powers) became blurred. Such black magic was associated with demonology and other forms of sorcery which disturbed the natural order and created connections between things that should not be connected.[9] As a result of the lack of clarity between 'white' and 'black' magic, the literature of practical cabala contained a mixture of both.

Such was the state of Jewish cabala by the time Christian intellectuals became aware of its tenets and appeal. It was the nature of Renaissance Neoplatonism to look to ancient sources and exotic places for the answers to philosophical and theological dilemmas, passing over the tomes of commentaries supplied by medieval scholars. Jewish cabala was a perfect fit for what Renaissance scholars were looking for, an ancient and authoritative source that bridged the gap between Christianity and Judaism by originating with Moses. Cabalistic ideas were easily disseminated into fifteenth-century Florentine cultural circles not only because of this particular intellectual environment but also because of a wider circulation of print that enabled cabalistic texts of the thirteenth century to be readily available to Renaissance scholars.

Pico started his cabalistic studies in 1486, learning the techniques of cabala from Spanish Jews six years before their expulsion from Spain.[10] This atrocity served only to spread cabala further as it travelled with the exiles into Italy, France, Germany and England. Pico believed that cabala confirmed the Christian faith and he applied it in such a fashion in his writings. He was not the first to express interest in Hebrew studies. The academy with which he was associated, Ficino's Platonic Academy in Florence, supported the study of Hebrew and lobbied for its acknowledgement as a third historic language of the West, alongside Greek and Latin. Pico's purpose in his Christian appropriation of cabala was not to convert Jews, but simply to achieve a synthesis between cabalistic techniques and Christianity. He used practical cabala and the combination of letters to prove that Jesus was indeed the Son of God. Pico also found in the cabala convergences with other systems of thought embraced by Renaissance scholars. He found that cabala supported the theories of Pythagoras, Plato, Hermes Trismegistus and the Neoplatonists. As a result, Pico furthered the synthesis and presented the argument that cabala was the proper companion of the natural magic expounded by Ficino. He packaged his novel ideas in his famous 900 theses which he brought to Rome for public debate. Seventy-two of these concerned cabala, others dealt with magic drawing from Hermetic, Orphic, Platonic and Neoplatonic sources. Some of his more interesting magical conclusions are that no other science assures us more of the divinity of Christ than magic and cabala, and that to operate magic is nothing other than to marry the world.[11] This relates to Pico's understanding of natural magic as being inextricably linked with astrology and Hermeticism. The stars and planets are part of the interdependent and inter-influential system of the macrocosm and the microcosm, therefore, in order to effectively operate magic, the power of the stars and that which is above must be harnessed with the power of the natural world below. Pico understood natural magic as the union of the sky with the earth, a marriage of the world.[12] The ecclesiastical authorities rejected most of his propositions as heretical. Pico's subsequent apology, published in 1487, contained one of his most famous works, *Oration on the Dignity of Man*.

Both speculative and practical cabala played a role in Pico's synthesis. The doctrine of the sephiroth and the art of combining letters comprised the speculative component and it was this which Pico used in his presentation of cabala as the divinely revealed interpretation of the Law. Practical cabala came into play as a science that supported Ficinian natural magic and even vindicated it from accusations of demonism. Renaissance scholar Frances Yates demonstrates that Pico believed cabala could be used to capture the power of spirits and angels and, because of the good and holy nature of cabala, this kind of magic was also good and holy and would likewise attract only good and holy spirits and angels. However, she also notes that there still remains danger for the unholy magician who could run into spiritual dangers.[13]

The Christian cabala that Pico helped establish was unique in its attempt to synthesize the various traditions and to build relationships and correspondences between each tradition. Ficino's Hermeticism and Neoplatonism established a vision of the world as interconnected by a series of correspondences which could be magically manipulated within the realm of one unifying world spirit. Pico continued Ficino's work and expanded upon it by looking to cabala to reinterpret Christianity and by establishing the resulting occult philosophy. Not only in his

particular synthesis, but also in his actual process of synthesizing, Pico
was to affect the future of Western magic. He not only shaped the form
of future magical theory but also provided it with the method in which
it would continue to adapt and survive.

Influenced by Pico's work, the Christian Hebraist and humanist
scholar, Johannes Reuchlin, furthered this association of cabala with
Christianity and brought it even more into the arena of public awareness,
moving Christian cabalistic studies from Florence to Germany. One of
the more prominent scholars of the German Renaissance, Reuchlin
was purportedly encouraged to study cabala following a conversation
with Pico in 1490 while on a diplomatic visit to Florence.[14] Pico urged
Reuchlin to further his already sound grasp of the Hebrew language in
order to better understand the intricacies of cabala and how it could
be used as a natural ally of both Christianity and of magic. Reuchlin
believed that cabala contained Christian elements which supported the
doctrine of the Incarnation and that the combination of Hebrew letters
could be used to assert that the world was divided into three historical
periods which corresponded with the divine names of God. He developed this theory in two influential books, *De Verbo Mirifico*, 1494 and
De Arte Cabalistica, 1517. Both books took the form of dialogues, the
former between a Greek, a Jew and a Christian, and the latter between a
Pythagorean philosopher, a Jewish cabalist and a Moslem. The first book
furthers the importance of cabala and its relevance to Christianity, reas-
serting much of what Pico presented in his cabalist conclusions, while
the second was intended as an apology for the Christian study of cabala
and is considered the first full exposition on cabala by a non-Jew.

Despite Reuchlin's more scholarly approach, for unlike Pico he was
not trying to create a brand new religious and philosophical synthesis,
his cabalistic works carry on Pico's emphasis on the influence of cabala
on magic. In *De Arte Cabalistica*, the third section of the book deals with
angel magic in practical cabala; the first two deal with messianism and
the relationship between cabala and Pythagoreanism respectively. This
angel magic involves contacting a celestial world of 72 angels associated
with the sephiroth and ten angelic spheres, through letter combinations
of the Hebrew alphabet.

Reuchlin's continuation and expansion of Pico's Christian cabala is
important because it brought cabala into a new geographical and intellectual forum. Furthermore, Reuchlin's expertise as a scholar of Hebrew
enabled him to access much more cabalistic literature than Pico had had
at his disposal, thus providing Christian cabalism with a larger corpus.
Reuchlin wrote the definitive Renaissance texts on Christian cabalism.

Pico had merely provided the seeds with which to germinate his synthesis in the form of his conclusions. This is not to diminish Pico's importance as the founder of Christian cabalism. Without Reuchlin, however, the path and duration of Christian cabala would have differed greatly. Both Pico's and Reuchlin's writings led to greater awareness and knowledge of cabala by incorporating it within the leading intellectual developments of the time. Most importantly, the natural magic of the Renaissance had gained an influential ally in cabala, and one that was used to having magical affiliations. Cabala brought a new symbolism and mythology to Renaissance magic.

The final chapter on Renaissance magic must close with the most notorious Christian cabalist whose name has been unjustly tarnished through numerous unflattering historical and literary depictions. Heinrich Cornelius Agrippa of Nettesheim has yet to be adequately redeemed from the libellous character placed upon him by history as a black magician. It was Agrippa who provided the definitive magical textbook which contemporary magicians still consult almost 500 years later. *De Occulta Philosophia*, published in 1533, is important for yet another reason. In this text Agrippa brings together magical belief and practices from the Middle Ages with the new cabalistic magic of Pico and Reuchlin. When those Renaissance magi were creating their synthesis, they looked past magic's immediate history in favour of the magical notions expressed in such intellectual structures as Hermeticism, Neoplatonism and other perceived ancient sources. It is Agrippa who combines them all neatly in the three books that make up *De Occulta Philosophia*.

Agrippa was a physician who had also studied alchemy, astrology, philosophy and theology.[15] He taught in various universities and gave public lectures on Reuchlin's *De verbo mirifico*. A true Renaissance man, Agrippa's travels and varied careers took him to Spain, France, Italy and England as he took appointments as physician, professor, political advisor and historiographer. He associated with scholars such as the magical theorist Trithemius, abbot of Spanheim, and the great humanist, Erasmus. Like Ficino before him, Agrippa sought to redeem magic from the bad reputation people were inclined to believe and to spread. This attempt took shape in his encyclopedic three-book compendium in which Agrippa freely expounds upon theories developed by Pico and Ficino without naming them.[16] His named sources are primarily medieval and include Albertus Magnus, Avicenna, Roger Bacon and Peter of Abano. In this mixture of medieval and more contemporary Renaissance sources, Agrippa brings together older medieval traditions of magic and the new magical synthesis of the Renaissance. He also introduces Florentine Ficinian magical theory into the intellectual circles of northern Europe, for his predecessor Reuchlin had focused largely upon Pico's Christian cabala.

In *De Occulta Philosophia*, Agrippa's cabalistic, Hermetic and Neoplatonic understanding of the universe is demonstrated in his presentation of three realms, elemental, celestial and intellectual, and the structure of his work reflects this order in its three-book format. The first deals with natural magic and aims to show that many magical effects are produced naturally. It is here that Agrippa presents and explores Ficinian magic, the influences and correspondences of planetary and talismanic magic. This book is not devoid of demonic magic. In this first book, however, its presence is minimal. Evidence of spiritual and demonic powers is present in chapter LX for example, 'Of madness, and divinations which are made when men are awake, and of the power of a melancholy humor, by which spirits are sometimes induced into men's bodies'.[17] The second book contains more material dealing with spiritual and demonic magic in its treatment of celestial and mathematical magic. An example of this emphasis can be found in chapter XLII, 'By what ways the magicians, and necromancers do think they can call forth the souls of the dead'.[18] The third book is a ceremonial and cabalistic magical guidebook instructing upon areas of demon invocation, compelling angels and evil spirits to assist in magical operations, and the use of magical and divine names. Chapters XXXII, 'How good spirits may be called up by us and how evil spirits may be overcome by us', and XXXIII, 'Of the bonds of spirits, and of their adjurations and castings out', give proof of this.[19]

Throughout this book Agrippa maintains the same attitude towards safe magical operations as did Ficino and Pico before him. He fully supports the theory that cabala makes magic safe through its divine influence, that it also strengthens it and protects the magician from demons and damnation. In this fashion the magic advocated by Agrippa is not black magic despite later accusations made against him. His first serious condemnation came from the Renaissance demonologist and lawyer Jean Bodin. In his *De la démonomanie des sorciers*, published in 1580, Agrippa is depicted as a black magician spurred on in his evil pursuits by a demon masquerading as a black dog. Agrippa was not the only one to be attacked in Bodin's treatise. Pico and Johann Weyer, a disciple of Agrippa, are called evil magicians for their incorrect use of cabala. Bodin's work was primarily produced as an enquiry into the perceived rise in witchcraft. He believed that Pico, Agrippa and Weyer were instrumental in agitating the demons, which, once provoked by this blasphemous use of cabala, proceeded to possess witches. This dark image of Agrippa had been building over time but its existence in print, thanks to Bodin, an influential character in his day, was irrevocably injurious to Agrippa's character. Subsequent literary representations of Agrippa as found in Marlowe's *Doctor Faustus*, and Mary Shelley's *Frankenstein* are coloured by this perception of him as an evil sorcerer. Marlowe's Doctor Faustus decides to be 'as cunning as Agrippa was, whose shadows made all Europe honor him' in his decision to study magic.[20] In Shelley's *Frankenstein*, the main character enthusiastically reads Agrippa, much to the dismay of his father who calls such work, 'sad trash'.[21] Ironically, this defamation of Agrippa's character has more than likely contributed to his later popularity among would-be magicians seeking the darker side and secrets of Western magic. His *De Occulta Philosophia* has undergone several editions since its first publication in 1533 with one of the most recent republications by a new age book publisher appearing in the late twentieth century.[22]

Agrippa's legacy to the Western magical tradition lies both in the contents of his cabalistic and magical text book, *De Occulta Philosophia,* as a collection of Renaissance and medieval magic, and in his notoriety, which no doubt led to the continued allure and relevance of his work to future magicians. His treatment of cabalistic magic and the controversial reaction it garnered made it more socially accessible than the works of the Renaissance magi, which tended to be more theological and philosophical. This accessibility naturally lead to transmissibility assuring Agrippa his place as one of the most famous magicians in the history of Western magic and *De Occulta Philosophia* its prominence as a magical textbook.

Together with Ficino, Pico, Reuchlin and other Renaissance scholars, Agrippa helped to formulate a potent magical system, equipped with the appropriate components to enable it to survive for centuries. Even when faced with the intellectual trends established by secularization, empiricism and scientific naturalism, this magical tradition maintained its position, continuing to appeal to certain groups and individuals, and further assimilated and adapted the later esoteric traditions it encountered. The appeal of this tradition is found in the individual components of the system as much as it is found in the resulting synthesis. Hermeticism, Neoplatonism, natural magic, spiritual and demonic magic, and cabala all individually place emphasis upon having an ancient authority, an unknowable God, and the responsibility and potential power of the individual as an interconnected entity with the universe. Together, they strengthen these principles and the goal of Western magic, that is, the apprehension of the divine. In this way, magic satisfies the religious needs of those who seek such solace yet who also desire a more active role and more responsibility in their belief.

This Renaissance synthesis proved popular and durable and saw Western magic live on in this form of associations well into the nineteenth century. During the long years between Pico and MacGregor Mathers, magical practice and belief did not disappear but rather remained quite in fashion among certain circles throughout Europe. There was no drastic change in the fundamental components of this magical system nor in its interpretation, with the exception of French occultist Eliphas Lévi's inclusion of the tarot, which, as will be discussed later, while noteworthy, did not alter the basic structure of magic nor the nature of its transmission. This type of radical change would not come about until MacGregor Mathers exerted the influence of his immense imagination and creativity upon the magical tradition he inherited as one of the founding members of the Golden Dawn. Therefore, while the establishment of the Isis-Urania Temple marked the beginning of a magical revival, it was not a revival of magical practice or belief. It was, rather, a revival of the same process of synthesis with which Renaissance magic had enriched an already existent magical tradition.

The magic practised by members of the Order reflected that of their Renaissance predecessors, not only in this revived process of synthesis, but also in its fundamental structure. In Victorian magic, Hermeticism, Neoplatonism, natural magic, ceremonial magic, astrology and cabala, were brought together, along with other esoteric traditions, to form a complex underlying system. Much of the nature of Victorian occultism can be uncovered through reading the assorted writings and documents the Golden Dawn left behind. The available textual evidence shows the fundamental role played by Renaissance magical components and the overwhelming influence of other factors such as a renewed interest in Egyptian magic, the magical system of the Elizabethan magus, John Dee, and some rather obscure traditions of ceremonial magic.

The Golden Dawn has left behind four separate categories of textual evidence for the magic practised by its members. The first category consists of the official rituals of the Order. These are well documented, resulting in numerous versions, making it difficult to establish which ones are representative of the original texts. The second group is composed of writings concerning, for the most part, the necessary magical information members needed to learn in order to progress through the hierarchical grades of the Order. These writings are called the knowledge lectures and the Flying Rolls and also include other untitled general informatory papers prepared primarily by Westcott and MacGregor Mathers. These latter papers provide both historical knowledge of the different esoteric systems from which the Order drew its magical synthesis and administrative information. The material from these first two groups has been preserved in both private and public collections and some of this material has been published. The third group of textual evidence is found in MacGregor Mathers' creative work, both his translations of certain magical manuscripts discovered in libraries in London and Paris, and his assimilation of a certain magical system called Enochian magic. The three main systems of magic which he incorporated into Golden Dawn magic through these texts are this Enochian magic, a Solomonic tradition of magic, and Abramelin magic. The fourth and final category of textual evidence is found in the documentation of the extraneous activities of the Order's members. It was not uncommon for members to experiment by devising their own magical rituals and carry them out in groups or individually outside of the confines of the Order's ritual practice. It was also not uncommon for members to go on and pursue a specific path of magical exploration having been exposed to the many which compose the magic of the Golden Dawn. The material describing the extra-curricular magical activities of Golden Dawn members is preserved in private collections.

In all four of these categories there is a reliance on three main sources for magical composition. The first source can be referred to as a contemporary textual and practical corpus of the Western magical tradition. This source includes both written material and current ritual and esoteric practices that had been incorporated into the magical tradition by the late nineteenth century. The rituals carried out in contemporary secret societies such as the *Soc. Ros.* and the various orthodox and fringe Freemason lodges in existence at this time provided much of the initiatory material for many of the degrees in the Golden Dawn. The esoteric literature of supposed secret societies, namely the Rosicrucians, also contributed to the initiation rites of certain degrees, primarily in the Second Order. Such literature may also be labelled contemporaneous for, although it is difficult to provide historical accounts for the existence of societies practising the rituals described therein (apart from the Golden Dawn), Rosicrucianism and esoteric initiation remained a popular theme in much of the literature and popular culture of the nineteenth century, for example, Shelley's *St. Irvyne, or the Rosicrucian* and Edward Bulwer-Lytton's *Zanoni*.[23]

The second source for the magic and rituals of the Golden Dawn draws upon extraneous material, brought in from outside the mainstream Western magical tradition, and discovered, invented or assimilated by members of the Order, namely MacGregor Mathers. This extraneous material includes the Enochian magic of John Dee, which MacGregor Mathers developed into a comprehensive component of the Order's magical material, and Abramelin magic.

The third source is quite significant because it represents the direction in which members chose to pursue other kinds of magic after being introduced to the magical tradition through the canon of the Order. This source did not affect the literature used by the Order in its orthodox ritual or magical practice nor did it result in incorporation into the Order. It is, however, representative of the magic practised by members of the Golden Dawn, despite its practice being external to the precincts of the Order. The basis of this source is not found solely in texts, but also in the imaginations and creativity of the members themselves. The influence of this source can be found in the workings of the Sphere Group, an extra-curricular organization formed independently by some Golden Dawn members, and in the Rites of Isis, a revival of Egyptian magic initiated by MacGregor Mathers in Paris.

Within the Order, the influence of the first source will be apparent in the works of Westcott and in many of the Order's initiation rituals and knowledge lectures. The second source is most influential in MacGregor Mathers' work, particularly in his translations and in the rituals he devised for the Second Order. The third source, as has been stated, is represented by the extra-curricular activities of some of the Order's members.

The availability of Golden Dawn material has increased greatly over the past couple of decades as more and more researchers, scholarly and occult, have published the Order's original documents. A great deal, however, remains inaccessible to the public, hidden away in private collections. Were any of the original members alive today, most would undoubtedly be appalled at the breach of secrecy concerning the publication of the more accessible documents. The Order's members, following the instructional method of the Golden Dawn, made many copies of the original manuscripts. Each initiate was allowed to borrow the original manuscripts of the Order's rituals and lectures and make their own copies. It was strictly forbidden, however, for any member to make public the information contained therein to the uninitiated. This did not, however, prevent certain determined individuals from divulging all through publication of the rituals, be it for reasons of revenge or public acclaim. As we have already seen, one of the most notorious members of the Order, Aleister Crowley, published the rituals along with private letters from members in the occult journal, *The Equinox*, in 1909. Twenty-eight years later, in 1937, Israel Regardie began publishing a four-volume work, providing the full details of the rituals and teachings of the Order as he had learned them in the *Stella Matutina*, one of the offshoot groups of the Order of the Golden Dawn.[24] Regardie did so to offer the benefits he perceived to be associated with Golden Dawn magic, to a wider audience.[25] Other publications of Golden Dawn material include Francis King's *Ritual Magic of the Golden Dawn*, in which the Flying Rolls, the Order's official instructional documents, are presented, specifically those not already documented by Regardie.[26] In 1973, R.G. Torrens published the rituals of the First Order in *The Secret Rituals of the Golden Dawn*. Torrens claims that the manuscripts he used for his sources were in use prior to 1900 when the Order began to disintegrate owing to internal conflict and external scandal.[27] A comparison of the original manuscripts confirms that Torrens is likely to be correct in his claim.[28] Certainly the rituals found in Regardie, while essentially conveying the same content, are much more elaborate than the original manuscripts and use different terminology and symbolism, while Torrens appears to follow the original with the least elaboration. In Torrens, the version closest to the original rituals composed by MacGregor Mathers from the cipher manuscript, the candidate for initiation is frequently referred to as 'Child of the Earth' while in the Regardie version the candidate is also referred to as the 'Inheritor of a Dying World'. Another discrepancy found in Regardie is in the use of the term, 'Banner of the East', which he refers to as the 'Banner of the Morning Light'. These are slight deviations but they do serve to show that the rituals became more ornate and subtle in language over the years. The Torrens version also includes, within the ritual, a list of the requirements necessary for the subsequent ritual. The Regardie version simply states that certain subjects must be learned and tested in an examination prior to entering the next grade. One of the most recent additions to the published corpus of Golden Dawn texts is the actual cipher manuscript, the document upon which the entire foundation of the Order was based.[29]

The original sources for these publications, along with much unpublished material, are found primarily in private hands and also in institutional collections. Golden Dawn author R.A. Gilbert provides a detailed description of the nature and content of these collections.[30] There are seven sources in all; two of them are in libraries, and five are held in private collections. The library collections are the Gerald Yorke Collection at the Warburg Institute in London and the Yeats Collection at the National Library of Ireland.[31] Two of the five private collections can be named and they are that of the late Carr Collins of Dallas, Texas and the papers of another Golden Dawn member, Arthur Edward Waite, which are in Gilbert's possession. The remaining private collections are referred to as A, B and C. Collection A comprises the official records of the Golden Dawn and some of the Stella Matutina. Collection B is now in Gilbert's possession and contains papers originally held by a member of the esoteric society, the Independent and Rectified Order, which Waite went on to establish following the catastrophic events of the final days of the Golden Dawn. Collection C holds further documents of Waite's faction as well as the papers belonging to Westcott. The materials necessary for an examination of the magical rituals of the Order are the cipher manuscript, the early rituals of the First Order, the later rituals and Flying Rolls of the Second Order, and examples of independent workings of extraneous rituals by groups or individuals. The collections that provide all of these materials are A, C and the Yorke Collection. Unless stated otherwise, the manuscripts in the Yorke Collection at the Warburg Institute are those that have been consulted for the following examination of the Order's rituals. Private Collection C and the Yeats Collection are two of the other collections that have been used. The remaining collections are not vital for the scope of this examination as Private Collection A contains much of the same material found in C and the Yorke Collection. The same is true of Private Collection B which primarily contains documents pertaining specifically to A.E. Waite. The Collins Collection in Texas also holds much of the same material as found in C and the Yorke Collection.

The most significant documents in the first category of textual evidence are the initiation rituals of both the First Order and the Second Order. It is appropriate to begin with the document that began it all, the cipher manuscript, which contains the seeds of the original, First Order's initiation rituals. The long and complicated account of the origin of the cipher manuscript has already been thoroughly addressed by both Ellic Howe and R.A. Gilbert, and superficially so, by me in the first chapter.[32] It is enough to say here that the document was influenced by Rosicrucian myth and tradition even if it was not an authentic Rosicrucian text, and that it may or may not have been found by Westcott in a Masonic hall or in a bookstore; or it may have been given to Westcott by a fellow Mason, the Reverend A.F.A. Woodford. The manuscript has been dated as no earlier than 1870 and closer to 1880.[33]

More importantly, the curious manuscript provided the necessary legitimizing documentation required for the Order's formation. It contained the standard grade rituals, used by most esoteric societies of the time, a charter to commence the Order, an address of the Rosicrucian adept with the authority to inaugurate a new temple, and it provided the necessary shady, mysterious and slightly Rosicrucian lineage and authority most secret magical societies required.

The cipher in which the manuscript was written has been identified as one provided in *Polygraphiae*, a work that was readily available at the time, written by the monk and alchemist Abbot Johann Trithemius of Spanheim. A key has been provided in the collection of photostats of the cipher manuscript in the Yorke collection (originals in the Masonic Library in London) and, by all appearances, it is a fairly standard case of letter substitution with an artificial alphabet. The most important component in the cipher manuscript, for the purposes of this examination, is the brief and instructional description of the five unknown Rosicrucian rituals. These are the rituals that Westcott paid MacGregor Mathers to translate and elaborate upon in order to form the first five grade rituals of the Golden Dawn. These comprise the neophyte ritual, the zelator ritual, the theoricus ritual, the practicus ritual and the philosophus ritual. The original forms of these rituals, as found in the cipher manuscript, were quite stark in comparison to those described in Torrens and Regardie. As previously stated, the Torrens versions are likely to be those most similar to the rituals that MacGregor Mathers developed out of the skeletal material provided in the cipher manuscript. The material MacGregor Mathers used to flesh out these rituals is suggested by Ellic Howe in the following fragment from a letter to Gerald Yorke:

> the Cypher MS. contains the bare bones and Mathers thought up the rest. But not, as Regardie suggests, on the basis of his membership of the Soc. Ros. [*Societas Rosicruciana in Anglia*] or the AQC [*Ars Quatuor Coronati*] but, rather, on the basis of his wide reading at the B.M. [British Museum] between 1885–7. He simply had lots of imagination.[34]

These 'bare bones' introduce the general structure, necessary materials and participants in each of the five rituals. And these bare bones are indeed based upon nineteenth-century Masonic ritual and the structure of the *Soc. Ros.*, a society to which Westcott and MacGregor Mathers belonged and which admitted only Master Masons. It is largely only the framework of these rituals that borrow from Freemasonry and the *Soc. Ros.* The language and symbolism found in the actual content, however, is a synthesis of cabala, Egyptian mythology, astral magic, mystery religions and other mystical and esoteric systems. Therefore, it is probably correct that MacGregor Mathers developed the content of the rituals from his independent research at the British Museum.

The structure of the first five rituals is largely initiatory Masonic, complete with a hoodwinked candidate who must learn the appropriate knowledge for each grade prior to initiation. Some of this knowledge is learned before the ritual, some of it during. Other Masonic elements include the revelation of passwords, signs and handgrips during the ritual for each grade and the taking of an oath, swearing never to divulge the secrets of the Order to the uninitiated. The names of the grades themselves are borrowed from the *Soc. Ros.* which had adopted them from the late eighteenth-century German Masonic order, the Golden and Rosy Cross.[35] The officers of the rituals held titles of Greek origin: the *Hierophant*, the *Hiereus*, the *Hegemon*, the *Kerux*, the *Stolistes* and the *Dadouchos*. The *Hierophant* refers to the head of the Eleusinian cult, one of the Greek mystery religions, who was assisted by the torch-bearer or *Dadouchos*. The *Hiereus* is the priest, the *Hegemon* the leader or general, the *Kerux* the herald, and the *Stolistes* is the priest in charge of the sacred vestments.[36] These roles remain consistent throughout the five grade rituals. Each ritual began with an official opening ceremony and each ritual ended with an official closing ceremony. Throughout the entire ritual references are made to cabalistic, astrological, alchemical, Egyptian, Enochian and other esoteric symbolism. The symbolic path upon which the candidate travels during initiation corresponds with one of the paths of the sephiroth on the cabalistic Tree of Life. In such a fashion, each initiation also serves as an exercise in the acquisition of knowledge pertaining to the magical system of the Golden Dawn. As each individual act of the ritual is performed, its symbolism and correspondences with all the various systems that make up the Golden Dawn is explained.

The neophyte ritual is a mere introduction to the Golden Dawn, enabling the candidate to join the Order and to take a magical motto, symbolizing the new and magical life that has been commenced. Such mottos included Westcott's *Non Omnis Moriar* (I shall not wholly die), MacGregor Mathers' *Deo Duce Comite Ferro* (With God as my leader and the sword as my companion), Woodman's *Vincit Omnia Veritas* (Truth rules all), Moina Mathers' *Vestigia Nulla retrorsum* (No traces behind), Annie Horniman's *Fortiter et Recte* (Bravely and justly), Florence Farr's

Sapientia Sapienti Dono Data (Wisdom is given to the wise as a gift), Yeats's *Demon est Deus Inversus* (The devil is the converse of God), and Crowley's *Perdurabo* (I will endure). Such mottos could be quite indicative of the personalities of the various members and what they were seeking through their association with Golden Dawn magic and occultism in general. Having taken their new names, initiates could then go on to complete the rest of the grades of the First Order. The final four grade rituals correspond with the four elements, the four lower sephiroth, as well as with specific planets or stars through the incorporation of prayers to the spirits of each element and through the use of symbols pertaining to each element and planet. For example, the element of the zelator ritual is earth and its sephiroth is Malkuth. That of the theoricus ritual is Yesod, its element air and its planet is the moon. The practicus ritual employs symbolism of water, the sephiroth Hod and the planet Mercury; and the philosophus ritual uses fire, Netzach and Venus.[37]

Within the ritual one source includes a list of the requirements necessary for progression to the next grade. This information is quite useful in establishing what occult and esoteric learning was required and expected of members. For example, before admission to the zelator grade, the neophyte must learn the names and alchemical symbols of the four elements; the names, astrological symbols and elemental attributions of the 12 zodiacal signs; the names and astrological symbols of the seven planets; the names, characters, and numerical values of the 22 letters in the Hebrew alphabet; and finally the names and English meanings of the ten sephiroth.[38]

Overall, there is a notable lack of magical practice in these rituals. The initiation rituals of each grade are more educational and ceremonial. Each of these first four grade rituals (five if you include the neophyte ritual) is a rite of passage combined with an emphasis on the knowledge yet to come. There is an acknowledgement of achievement, even in the neophyte ritual in which the step from darkness into light is noted, yet there is also substantial reference to that which the candidate has yet to learn. It is partly the role of these rituals to pass on some of that knowledge. Explanation of occult symbolism abounds in these rituals. It is almost as if the ritual serves as an intense tutorial as well as a process of initiation. This dual role serves to emphasize the point that that despite the candidate having progressed to this grade, there is much yet to learn and accomplish. The overall themes of these rituals are progress and the dawning of the light of knowledge upon the darkness of ignorance.

The cipher manuscript provided the rough outline for these First Order rituals. MacGregor Mathers formulated them into more elaborate rituals and in 1891, claiming that he had established his own link with the secret chiefs of the Order, he developed rituals for the Second Order, the *Rosae Rubeae et Aureae Crucis*. MacGregor Mathers was the sole chief of this more secretive order and in it offered instruction in practical magic. In a letter dated 5 April 1912, Westcott wrote the following to a member of the Second Order, Frederick Leigh Gardner.

> About 1886 A.F.A. Woodford gave me Hermetic teaching & old MSS. information of GD 0=0 to 4=7 [the numerical symbols for the neophyte to philosophus grades]. Mathers helped me to work them up ... Then Mathers brought from Paris the 5=6 [the adeptus minor grade of the second order] and said it was the continuation of my GD 0=0 to 4=7 and I carried 5=6 on in England until M. became so eccentric that I resigned in 1897.[39]

The *R.R. et A.C.* was a more exclusive group, by invitation only, which catered specifically to those who wished to become accomplished magicians. Many progressed through the grades of the First Order without ever entering the second. By the end of 1896, of the 300 or so men and women who were members of the Golden Dawn, less than one-third progressed to this Second Order.[40] It was in this more exclusive order that the Flying Rolls were circulated and some were composed by the members of the *R.R. et A.C.* themselves. The Second Order carried out its rituals in a separate location and such were the requirements of the rituals that an elaborate vault was built, vividly and elaborately decorated with colourful images corresponding to a variety of occult symbolism. Before the initiation ritual, a candidate had to progress through the portal ritual, symbolizing the ascension from the First Order to the second. As part of this symbolism a temple veil called Paroketh symbolically separated both the two orders and the lower sephiroth from the higher ones on the cabalistic Tree of Life, and also served to physically hide the chief adept presiding over the ceremony throughout most of the ritual. The portal ritual comprised explanations of the cabalistic, alchemical and tarot symbolism to which the candidate was introduced in the First Order rituals. The candidate had to wait an appropriate gestation period of nine months before attempting the ensuing adeptus minor ritual.

The initiation rituals of the Second Order differ greatly from those of the First Order primarily because they are based upon the myth of Christian Rosenkreuz, the fifteenth-century legendary founder of Rosicrucianism, whose body was supposedly discovered by his followers after his death, preserved intact and entombed in an elaborate vault. This discovery is one of the central themes of the three-part adeptus minor initiation ritual in which the candidate similarly discovers the body of Christian Rosenkreuz, in the form of either MacGregor Mathers or Westcott, in the seven-sided vault of the Second Order. Another important part of the initiation is the symbolic death and resurrection of the candidate who is bound to a cross during one part of the ritual. The originality of this ritual was due to MacGregor Mathers' brilliant synthesis of occult and Hermetic symbolism and lore. While the First Order rituals closely resembled those of the Masons in structure and reflected the status of late nineteenth-century occultism as a synthesis of Renaissance magic, ritual magic and tarot, these Second Order rituals belonged to a category of their own. The years of research MacGregor Mathers had spent absorbing magical texts and systems found their culmination in these rituals. In particular, the *R.R. et A.C.* rituals incorporated the Enochian system of magic developed by John Dee and Edward Kelley. The non-initiatory rituals of the Second Order also demonstrate the importance of this Enochian system, which is based upon interaction with spiritual or angelic beings and shall be discussed in detail later in this chapter as part of the examination of MacGregor Mathers' introduction of new magical systems to the Order.

Other rituals practised by members of the Order were part of the overall learning required between each initiation. These rituals tended to be more magical in nature and there were not as many of them in the First Order as there were in the second. After completing the neophyte ritual, the successful candidate was taught the Qabalistic Cross and the Lesser Ritual of the Pentagram as part of the first knowledge lecture. This ritual required the use of a dagger in tracing occult symbols in four directions around the magician while pronouncing certain divine names. This ritual was used as a form of prayer, for banishing damaging thoughts, or as an exercise of concentration.[41] The Lesser Ritual of the Pentagram was really the only exposure that members of the First Order had to any sort of ritual magic. Most of the instruction of the First Order concerned teaching the basics of divination, elementals and the tarot.

It was not until a member was invited to join the ranks of the *R.R. et A.C.* that a full magical education began. In the Second Order, the adeptus minor had to learn a total of 17 rituals during a five-part education process.[42] These magical rituals included the full pentagram rituals and hexagram rituals, which were used for banishing and invoking spiritual beings; the rituals for consecrating the magical instruments used in the Order's rituals (the lotus wand, the Rose Cross Lamen, wand, cup, dagger and pentacle); and the ritual for consecrating the vault. All of these rituals required the magical techniques of talismanic magic, in which an object symbolizes a specific source of magical power, and evocation, in which the magician projects a magical force from an aspect of his own spiritual or psychological make-up.[43] Other non-ritual magical works that had to be learned included the Enochian system, and astral vision and projection. Most of the magical operations performed by the *adepti* of the Second Order ended after the consecration of their instruments. Howe suggests that the ceremonies were too elaborate and detailed to warrant repeat performances and also that the nervous strain on the individual might prove too much. 'One cannot decide to *do* some Ceremonial Magic with the same casualness with which one might propose, for example, a game of tennis or any other commonplace activity.'[44] There is evidence, however, that some members did make the effort and take the risk of practising magic after the consecration of their instruments. This is apparent in an analysis of the fourth category of textual evidence, the independent and extra-curricular magical workings of some members of the Golden Dawn.

While the obvious difference between First and Second Order rituals is the emphasis upon the more numerous magical rituals in the Second, there are many other striking differences. Namely, the purpose of initiation into each Order is quite different. After successfully completing the neophyte ritual, the new member undertakes a journey to accumulate occult knowledge not for selfish purposes or for the purpose of causing harm to another, as is plainly stated in the oath taken by the neophyte during the ceremony. The adeptus minor, on the other hand, enters the Second Order, taking an oath of dedication to the practice of magic and to the contribution to the 'Great Work', meaning that one will attempt to purify and exalt one's spiritual nature to attain to be more than human and to unite with one's higher genius.[45] The difference between the two goals is similar to that between being an apprentice and being master of a particular trade or profession.

The other ways in which the rituals of the two orders differ can be found in their structure, language and founding myths. The First Order was strongly influenced by Masonic structure and cabalistic mythology. While both the tradition of Freemasonry and of cabala feature prominently in Second Order rituals, the dominant theme there is the Rosicrucian legend of Christian Rosenkreuz. In the Second Order rituals, it is also evident that the Enochian system begins to gain more importance and, in fact, underpins all other traditions synthesized to form Golden Dawn magic. Some Enochian words did feature in the

First Order rituals but the magical system itself had yet to be assimilated into the overall synthesis. The reason for these differences between the rituals of the two orders, and also the reason for the similarities, can be clearly found in the origins of the rituals. Despite the controversy concerning where Westcott actually found the cipher manuscript, it has been dated as circa 1870–80 and is thus representative of the state of Victorian magic at that particular time. The nineteenth-century additions to the standard blend of Renaissance and ceremonial magic developed by Ficino, Pico, Reuchlin and Agrippa, are found in the form of references to the tarot, Masonic structure and the minimal use of Enochian language. To some degree the nineteenth-century interest in all things Egyptian is also partly responsible for the presence of Egyptian deities in the rituals; however, occultists had long looked to Egypt for the structure and content of Western magic. In a fashion, the cipher manuscript represents this original union of magical systems being developed and embraced in the nineteenth century. In comparison, the rituals of the *R.R. et A.C.* represent the result or development of this union. In the Second Order, the newer elements of the legend of Christian Rosenkreuz, Enochian magic and tarot are fully developed not only to complement, but in the case of Rosicrucian legend, to form the basis of the existent magical tradition with its elements of Hermeticism, Neoplatonism, cabala, astrology, alchemy, natural magic, and ritual magic. The First Order rituals are essentially documents with which MacGregor Mathers was confronted and asked to flesh out, while the Second Order rituals were his to compose from the very beginning. The information he acquired from his broad reading of magical manuscripts fuelled his imagination to bring all these strands of magic together in the rituals of the *R.R. et A.C.*

The next category of texts members would have encountered consists of the lectures that served to enlighten initiates in their progression from grade to grade. These lectures offered the theoretical component of Golden Dawn instruction whereas the rituals provided more of the practical. There are two types of lectures: those of the First Order are called knowledge lectures and those of the Second, Flying Rolls. The First Order knowledge lectures reflect the structure and content of the First Order rituals. They provide the standard knowledge required to make sense of the Western magical system inherited by the late nineteenth century. For example, the first knowledge lecture required the neophyte to learn the Hebrew alphabet, alchemical and astrological symbolism, the cabalistic Tree of Life and the significance and symbolism of the tarot. The lectures also included meditation exercises in which the initiate focused upon a particular series of symbolic associations drawn from the variety of systems that made up Golden Dawn magic. As already mentioned, the first knowledge lecture also included instructions for carrying out the Qabalistic Cross and the Lesser Ritual of the Pentagram, the one example of magical instruction in the First Order knowledge lectures. In this multi-purpose ritual, the influence of Christian ritual, ceremonial magic and cabalistic language is obvious.[46] The ritual includes the substitution of cabalistic words in a common Christian prayer; magical words such as *AGLA*; appeals to angels found in Christian mythology, the cabala, and in ceremonial magic; and the use of instruments and inscribed figures common to the practice of ceremonial magic such as a dagger and a pentagram.

The second knowledge lecture further expanded on the topics encountered in the first and also introduced new subjects including the four orders of the elementals, the presidents of the elementals (*kerubim*), the Tetragrammaton or the unpronounceable name of God, and the *qlippoth* or the evil demons of matter and the shells of the dead. In this knowledge lecture, the initiate is also introduced to the four different worlds or Neoplatonic realities of cabala and the divine names associated with the sephiroth. This second knowledge lecture taught its own meditation exercise which focused the mind on the figure of a square and upon the spirits of the earth.[47] The third and fourth knowledge lectures expanded yet again upon occult symbolism and introduced the astral and elemental spirits; a moon breath meditation, in which only the left nostril is used in breathing while the candidate repeats mentally the word 'Aum' and envisions symbols associated with the moon; the theory of geomancy; and a meditation on the rhomboid and mercury respectively.[48] The fourth knowledge lecture also included instruction on the general guidance and purification of the soul. The fifth, complete with further exposition of all that has been introduced in the earlier lectures and a meditation on fire and the triangle, was the most demanding as it required that the candidate write a thesis on the rituals, draw the crosses used as badges for each grade, draw the cabalistic Tree of Life and be able to control one's aura. In this fifth lecture, the candidate also learned the meaning and use of the colour scales which played an important role in the Second Order rituals.[49]

These lectures contain no revelations of magical wisdom and documented evidence shows that some members were quite disappointed once, having passed the necessary grade and being filled with the excitement over the sense of secrecy imparted by the ritual, they received these rather dull lectures. Quoting the text of the neophyte ritual, Aleister Crowley wrote in his *Confessions*:

> I had been most solemnly sworn to inviolable secrecy. The slightest breach of my oath meant that I should incur 'a deadly and hostile current of will, set in motion by the Greatly Honoured Chiefs of the Second Order, by the which I should fall slain or paralysed, as if blasted by the lightning flash'. And now I was entrusted with some of these devastating though priceless secrets. They consisted of the Hebrew alphabet, the names of the planets with their attribution to the days of the week, and the ten Sephiroth of the Cabbala. I had known it all for months; and, obviously, any schoolboy in the lower fourth could memorize the whole lecture in twenty-four hours.[50]

This sense of disappointment was also acknowledged by another Golden Dawn member, J.W. Brodie-Innes, who wrote in his 'Notes on the First Knowledge Lecture', in 1895:

> The newly initiated brother of our Order … experiences an involuntary feeling of disappointment – 'Is this all', he will say to himself, 'After all the promises, the elaborate ritual, the pledges of inviolable secrecy. A few symbols to be found in scores of books.[51]

Brodie-Innes goes on to comfort the disappointed initiate claiming that this knowledge is the alphabet of the sciences yet to be learned and explored. As for the authorship of these knowledge lectures, it is reasonable to assume that the authors were the same as those who had produced the First Order rituals, namely Westcott and MacGregor Mathers.

Once the knowledge lectures had been mastered and the eager candidate had undergone the five original initiation rituals of the First Order, as well as the bridging portal ritual, advancement as an adeptus minor was accompanied with the revelation of the theoretical lectures of the Second Order. These lectures, called the Flying Rolls, are a bizarre assortment. Written by various members of the Order including MacGregor Mathers, Westcott, Florence Farr, Dr E. Berridge, Percy Bullock and Moina Mathers, the lectures touch upon a variety of topics including astral projection, Rosicrucianism, clairvoyance, and the role of the imagination and will in occultism and alchemy. They range from the instructive to the administrative, with some of the former presented as personal accounts of experimentation. These lectures assume a knowledge of occult symbolism and the various magical systems employed by the Golden Dawn including tarot, astral vision, Hermeticism, Enochian magic and cabalism. This assumed knowledge would have been acquired, of course, during the earlier grades of the First Order through the knowledge lectures. In all, there are 36 of these Flying Rolls, all of which remain in some form or another for the historian, the would-be magician, or even the simply curious, to examine. These Flying Rolls were not learned all at once. The adeptus minor had to master ten of them in the first stage of the five-part degree. In the second and third stages, a further 24 were required reading. A notebook containing 27 of the Flying Rolls dating from 1892–5 in the Yorke Collection closely follows both those published in Francis King's *Ritual Magic of the Golden Dawn* and in Israel Regardie's four-volume compendium, *The Golden Dawn*.[52]

Some of the more interesting of the Flying Rolls recount the magical experimentation of individual members. Number 34, 'Notes of an Experiment in Exorcism' is a pre-1900 account by Second Order member J.W. Brodie-Innes of how he cured both his wife and himself of influenza. Brodie-Innes writes that he was suspicious that this influenza was caused by the obsession of 'some vampirizing elemental'. This suspicion was confirmed by a presence which gave him instructions to cast out this elemental by burning incense, performing the invoking ritual of the pentagram, and calling upon the power of the divine names. Once this was done, Brodie-Innes claims that 'A vague blot, like a scrap of London fog, arose before me' and then 'a most foul shape, between a bloated and big-bellied toad and a malicious ape' appeared before him. He then used more divine names to project a destructive force against this manifestation and the monstrous shape disappeared, as did the presence that had been so helpful. 'A slight shock like a "puff", a momentary foul smell, dimness for a second, and the thing was gone.'[53]

These kinds of Flying Rolls are valuable in that they reveal what members actually chose to do with the knowledge they acquired within the Order and how they interpreted it. They also serve to demonstrate how the magical mind works, interpreting mundane events in a different fashion from the non-magical mind. This Flying Roll demonstrates one of the fundamental basics of Victorian magic. That is, once the magician has learned the complicated interrelations of the different systems belonging to Golden Dawn magic, they can then use this knowledge combined with the power of their will to effect change in the physical world. This relies upon the Neoplatonic belief that the individual mirrors the world to such a degree that what occurs in one, affects that which occurs in the other. It is the power of the will that fuels this effect, however, and its importance is outlined and discussed in several of the Flying Rolls.

The Flying Rolls of the Second Order offer great insight into the kind of magic practised by the Golden Dawn. That is because members used the knowledge gained through the First Order rituals and knowledge lectures and through the unique Second Order rituals, to experiment with a more subtle form of magic, employing the will and the imagination to explore the non-physical. This is consistent with the mandate of the Second Order, which emphasized the esoteric goal of the magician rather than the magical means employed to reach this goal. This goal, referred to above, is stated in the oath taken by the candidate in the adeptus minor ritual:

> I will from this day forward apply myself to the Great Work, which is to purify and exalt my Spiritual nature, that with the Divine aid, I may at length attain to be more than human, and thus gradually raise and unite myself to my Higher and Divine Genius.[54]

This is also consistent with the shift in emphasis upon the nature and role of magic taking place at the end of the nineteenth century. Victorian magicians relied less upon intermediary beings to carry out the magical process than upon themselves and their own will and imagination to make use of their knowledge of magical correspondences and to become the active participant in the process. Rather than invoking demons to do their will, Golden Dawn members either invoked the power of another being or force to come forth within themselves or evoked a corresponding power originating from within.[55]

Also included in this second category of texts are the writings of one of the three founders, William Wynn Westcott. Westcott's work does not stand alone in a category, as does that of MacGregor Mathers, because of its similarity in content and sources to the knowledge lectures. Like these knowledge lectures, Westcott's work represents where the magical content of the Order came from, rather than in which new directions it was growing. While the Second Order Flying Rolls represent, to some degree, this magical growth, they are more suitably classified along with the knowledge lectures of the First Order as their equivalent instructional lessons.

Westcott was first and foremost a Freemason and this is very much reflected in his writing. His interest in secret societies, Rosicrucianism and Hermeticism are expressions of this basic characteristic. Westcott does not appear in historical accounts, or in his own writings, as much of a magician. His reliance upon MacGregor Mathers in formulating the Order's rituals demonstrates this fundamental lack in his magical make-up. Westcott provided the main link between nineteenth–century esotericism in its Masonic and cabalistic form and the Order. He gave the Order its Hermetic, Neoplatonic, Masonic and Rosicrucian roots, while it was MacGregor Mathers who gave the Order its magical direction of growth. Thus, what we find in Westcott's writing is the influence of contemporary nineteenth-century esotericism and Freemasonry and it is this influence that positions the creation of the Golden Dawn within a specific esoteric tradition. Westcott's main contribution to the Order was in giving it a history and establishing it within this specific esoteric context.

During Westcott's membership with the Theosophical Society, the *Soc. Ros.*, and his co-founding of the Golden Dawn, he produced numerous lectures that have been preserved in publications associated with these societies and in the private collections of some Golden Dawn members, including A.E. Waite and the Rev. W.A. Ayton. The most popular subjects upon which he wrote include Rosicrucianism, Freemasonry, cabala, mystery religions, and divination and how all of these shared a common history and tradition. Westcott also published several works on these particular topics. These include his version of the *Sepher Yetzirah, or Book of Formation*; *The Isiac Tablet or The Bembine Table of Isis*; *Numbers: Their Occult Powers and Mystic Virtue*; and a nine-volume series *Collecteana Hermetica*.[56] Westcott also penned most of the First Order knowledge lectures and many of the Second Order Flying Rolls. Those papers addressed to the members of the Golden Dawn shed the most light upon the magic believed and practised in the Order. Some of Westcott's other work will also warrant consideration in constructing an image of the esoteric and magical framework from which the Order emerged.

The influence of modern day traditional Freemasonry is never far beneath the surface of Westcott's writing. His pseudo-historical accounts of mystery religions, Rosicrucianism and even practical magic are all coloured by Christian references and interpretations. While never stating such a claim outright, it is obvious that Westcott wished to be, or at least is perceived to be, carrying on the tradition of the legendary society established by Christian Rosenkreuz. His definition of the original Rosicrucian order, given in an address to the Theosophical Society entitled, 'Christian Rosenkreuz and the Rosicrucians', seems to encompass his aspirations in founding the Golden Dawn:

the Order was essentially a brotherhood of philosophers living in a Christian country, and professing a nominal Christianity of Gnostic type, yet essentially a band of students of oriental lore and Eastern magical arts, professing and practising Kabalah divination and the knowledge of the ultra-natural planes of being.[57]

Here Westcott differs from the other members of the *Soc. Ros.*, in which he remained active long after the Golden Dawn's demise. For in the *Soc. Ros.*, there was no mandate to study magical arts and there was little emphasis upon the study of cabala. The society did give regular lectures on cabala and on Masonic symbolism but it was not a school for cabalistic or occult instruction.[58] His desire to resurrect true Rosicrucianism, complete with the study of occult arts resulted in the Golden Dawn. While it has been stated that Westcott's writing does not contain much of the practical magical instruction of the Order, it does outline the magical theory and doctrine embraced by its members. In a lecture entitled 'Man, Miracle, Magic' addressed to the Isis-Urania Temple membership at an unrecorded date, Westcott clearly expresses the Order's definition of magic as something that does not occur outside of the natural world and natural laws. Westcott claims that there is no such thing as a miracle in that no natural law is ever reversed or broken. He admits that 'supernormal' events may occur, but there is no such thing as a supernatural event.

If you find a teacher who can call down Rain from a cloudless sky, you do not see a Miracle, you see only that your master is possessed of more knowledge of nature's laws, and has more powerful faculties than you yet possess. It is a folly to think that any finality of science has been reached by modern Thought; it is equally a folly to think that no knowledge once common to the learned has ever lapsed.[59]

This is the view maintained throughout Victorian magic. Magic is not perceived as something extraneous to the natural world. Magic is achieved through an intimate knowledge of the correspondences within the natural world. And this knowledge is gained through concentration, will and effort by purity of mind and purity of body.[60]

This second category of Golden Dawn texts provides the content, theory and first-hand accounts of the magic practised within the Order. The First Order knowledge lectures contain the fundamental information describing the different systems at work within the overall magical structure of the Golden Dawn. They prepare the magician with the necessary language, symbolically and literally, with which to engage in the discourse of magic. The Second Order Flying Rolls offer advice and insight into the actual working of this magic. They demonstrate what the magician can do with the knowledge provided in the First Order lectures. Westcott's lectures, apart from those included in the knowledge lectures and Flying Rolls, are indicative of the already existent tradition upon which the Golden Dawn was founded. They also express the definition and understanding of magic as practised by the Order's members and, therefore, establish Victorian magic as an extension of Renaissance magic in that magic is part of the natural world and that its goal is knowledge of a higher power. All of these texts, with the exception of some of the Flying Rolls, represent where Golden Dawn magic came from. The next two categories of texts will demonstrate in which directions it developed.

MacGregor Mathers was the driving force behind the creation of rituals and doctrines of the Order. He was the one who took the structure presented by Westcott and developed it into the complex system of magic that characterizes the Golden Dawn. MacGregor Mathers did this by reintroducing systems of magic that were never properly assimilated into the Western magical tradition or had been marginalized over the years. He overcame the complexity of Enochian magic, uncovered the relatively unknown Abramelin text, and spent endless hours comparing the numerous editions of the Solomonic texts in the British Library – medieval *grimoires* which had once featured more prominently in the Western magical corpus. He then went on to produce his own versions of these texts. It is the introduction, and reintroduction in the case of the Solomonic *grimoires*, of these systems of magic that is the most telling feature of Golden Dawn magic and the most revolutionizing aspect of late Victorian magic. These systems of magic comprise the third category of Golden Dawn texts.

One of MacGregor Mathers' most important contributions to the Golden Dawn magical synthesis was Enochian magic. The Enochian system was developed by Dr John Dee and his seer, Edward Kelley, in the late sixteenth century. Dee was an Elizabethan philosopher, mathematician, and magician. Along with his magical interests, Dee was fascinated with enciphering, espionage, navigation and geography. He first became fascinated by cabala and cabalistic magic because of its usefulness in creating secret codes and ciphers.[61] A catalogue of his library has survived and can be found in the British Library. Among his collection of almost 2500 printed books and 170 manuscripts, this catalogue lists the works of Agrippa, Ficino, Pico, Trithemius, Albertus Magnus and

Paracelsus.[62] As a favourite of Queen Elizabeth, Dee was generally able to pursue his magical interests without condemnation or persecution save for a brief imprisonment in 1555 on charges of practising conjuring.

There is no need to go into the fascinating details of Dee's life; what is of most importance here is the system of magic he developed along with Edward Kelley between the years 1582 and 1588. In an attempt to discover the angelic and divine language of creation, which would lead to his dream of establishing a universal religion, Dee recorded conversations held with spirits through a process of scrying. In such a process, his seer, Kelley, would gaze into a crystal in which appeared various angels or spirits who conversed with the two men. These conversations are recorded in Dee's own diary and in Meric Casaubon's *A True and Faithful Relation of what passed for many years between Dr. John Dee and some Spirits*.[63] In his own words, what Dee was attempting to do was obtain 'some convenient portion of True Knowledge and Understanding of thy [God's] Lawes and Ordonnances, established in the Nature's and Properties of thy Creatures'.[64] Dee attempted to obtain this information through God's 'faithfull, and holy Spirituall Messagners ... (through the eye, and eare of E.K. [Edwarde Kelley])'.[65]

This process of scrying was quite traditional and has its precedents in ancient Egyptian magic whereby a child or young woman was used as a medium and would gaze into a bowl of water with a layer of oil floating on top in order to obtain visions.[66] By using Kelley as a scryer, Dee was trying to discover an Adamic language thought to exist since the creation of the world. Dee's library contained a copy of Guillaume Postel's *De originibus* (1553), which gave an account of the existence of such a language in a text called the *Book of Enoch*. This book supposedly contained the biblical figure Enoch's own record of the language God had taught Adam.[67] Dee was determined to discover this language and he was convinced that he may do so through magical means.

There has been much debate and disagreement over the intentions and honesty of Edward Kelley in his role in relating these visions to Dee. Some scholars believe that Kelley was just making things up to keep Dee content, while others argue that the reluctance and fear which Kelley frequently exhibited during these scrying sessions, is proof that he believed them to be real. One historian claims that while there were clear signs that Dee suspected Kelley at the beginning, he came to believe Kelley because his performance was so convincing.[68] Another suggestion is that while Dee was not always able to see and communicate with the angels and spirits, he was able to direct Kelley's mind in some fashion so that Kelley could. Another Dee scholar explains a process whereby the power of suggestion is employed by a magician to create 'extraordinary psychological effects' on a subject in magical work, thus implying such may have been the case with Dee and Kelley.[69] This interpretation coincides with one of the fundamental doctrines of Golden Dawn magic whereby one can control or affect another's imagination or visions through the power of one's mind. Golden Dawn member and poet W.B. Yeats relates such an occurrence while in the presence of MacGregor Mathers and his wife. In his essay 'Magic' written in 1901, he tells of a shared vision he experienced with the Matherses. Yeats describes testing the validity of this shared vision by withholding certain details as he described what he was seeing aloud. Without fail, Moina Mathers or her husband would eventually announce these omitted details, proving to Yeats that the vision was truly communal.[70] In Yeats's own words, the experience gave him:

> proof of the supremacy of imagination, of the power of many minds to become one, overpowering one another by spoken words and by unspoken thought till they have become a single intense, unhesitating energy. One mind was doubtless the master, I thought, but all the minds gave a little, creating or revealing for a moment what I must call a supernatural artist.[71]

In the case of Dee and Kelley, it has been suggested that Dee may have been such a master, controlling Kelley's visions yet unable to produce them on his own. The subsequent conversations Dee and Kelley held with these spiritual beings led to the revelation of 19 calls or keys, which were invocations in this angelic or Enochian language. These angelic messengers also divulged an entire alphabet in this strange language to Dee and Kelley. The following is an example of this language, taken from Dee's, *48 Claves Angelicae*, documented in Cracow, 13 April–13 July, 1584: 'O you heavens which dwell in the first ayre are Mightie in the partes of the Erth' The translation given for this passage is: 'Madriax dispraf LIL chrs Mi caolz saanir caosgo'.[72]

This language was dictated through the use of several grid-like tables consisting of 49 rows and 49 columns. Examples of these tables are provided in *The Book of Enoch revealed to Dr. John Dee by the Angels*, an original manuscript in Kelley's hand.[73] Dee's spirits also revealed to him an unusual hierarchy of angels and spirits governing various regions of the universe, based upon the number seven.[74] Such a hierarchy was by no means without precedent. Angelic and spiritual hierarchies were standard fare in most medieval *grimoires* and can be found in most of the Solomonic grimoires, the *Heptameron* and the *Fourth Book of Occult Philosophy*, all of which predate Dee. What was unique about Dee's system was the language itself. The method in which it was received was a fairly standard magical method of scrying. Most of the spirits or angels who appeared were predictable figures in magical experimentation with few exceptions. Salamian, Nalvage and Madimi were some of the more unusually named spirits or angels who visited Kelley and Dee, although Madimi can be found in Agrippa's *De Occulta Philosophia*. Dee's Enochian language has been identified as a completely unique and real language with its own syntax and grammar.[75] Part of the extraordinariness of Enochian magic and language is found in the unique goals of the magus who developed it. Dee desired to discover something that would, through its universality, enable one to achieve a higher and divine knowledge. Victorian magic was to embrace not only Dee's Enochian magic and its unique language but also Dee's understanding of language as a vehicle to knowledge.

The Enochian language and its accompanying system of magic were absorbed into Golden Dawn magic through the available texts. These were John Dee's diaries and writings held by the British Museum and the rather prejudiced version of Dee's later diaries, edited by Meric Casaubon: *A True & Faithful Relation of what passed for many Years Between Dr. John Dee and Some Spirits*.[76] MacGregor Mathers compiled the Golden Dawn's system of Enochian magic from these two sources for the benefit of the Second Order members, who had to learn this system as part of the fourth stage of the adeptus minor course of study.

> The Enochian system, bound up as it was with the concept of human interaction with superhuman beings, was central to the working of the Inner Order. It underlay all of the activities of the Order from the consecration of the lotus wand, magical sword and the four elemental implements (Fire Wand, Water Cup, Air Dagger and Earth Pentacle) to the construction of the Rose Cross Lamen, the vibration of divine names and the construction of telesmatic images: images of letters and elemental forces in the form of talismans – usually visualised as angels. In addition there were such rarified activities as Enochian Chess, in which the boards were multi-coloured 'Flashing Tablets' and the pieces symbols of Egyptian god-forms; astral traveling; and a wealth of divinatory practices.[77]

Dee's Enochian magic was also reflected in the construction and decoration of the inner order's vault. There are four Enochian Tablets called the Tablets of the Watch Towers and these were particularly important in Golden Dawn magic. They were depicted on the sides of the altar in the vault.[78]

Enochian magic was easily synthesized with the other magical elements of the Order because it was originally derived from those same elements. Dee developed his system after careful study of Renaissance magic including cabala, Hermeticism, astrology, alchemy, and natural magic. Once MacGregor Mathers had accomplished the difficult task of deciphering the structure behind Enochian magic, he simply brought it back to its source. Granted, the language itself was novel, however, its hierarchical nature, its goal of attaining divine knowledge and its method of interaction with nonhuman agents were not. The Enochian system provided a homegrown Renaissance magic the allure of which was made stronger by its obscure and exceptional language and its complex and detailed, yet readily assimilated, structure.

The next system of magic that MacGregor Mathers introduced to the Order is found in the manuscripts commonly referred to as belonging to a Solomonic tradition. This tradition owes its name to the biblical King Solomon and the legend that accounted for his wealth and power through magical commerce with spirits. MacGregor Mathers produced a version of *The Key of Solomon the King* in 1889, and two of the five books that make up the *Lemegeton*, or *The Lesser Key of Solomon*: the first book, the *Goetia*, in 1898 and the fourth book, the *Ars Almadel,* published in the journal, *Occult Review*, in 1915. *The Key of Solomon the King* is one of the most well-known and well-used texts in Western magic. The earliest date for the book is the fourteenth or fifteenth century. In compiling his edition of this compilation of rituals and invocations, MacGregor Mathers claimed to have used and translated seven manuscript versions in French, Italian and Latin, all of which he found in the collection of the British Museum.[79] In his edition, MacGregor Mathers attempts to steer the reader clear of black magic by advising against the use of blood, even where it is instructed in the text, and by having omitted certain sections of the original manuscripts which he decided were potentially too dangerous.[80] The complicated rituals, which require meticulous preparation of both the instruments to be used and of the magician, and even require certain climatic conditions, almost ensure the failure of the would-be magician. For example, before embarking on any of the rituals, the magician must fast for nine days while keeping a close eye on the weather; 'Note that the three last days should be calm weather, without wind, and without clouds rushing hither and thither over the face of the sky.'[81] The chances of stumbling upon three days of such fortunate weather after nine days of fasting are slim, especially in England.

The invocations themselves were typical of those found in medieval *grimoires* and provide detailed instructions on how potential magicians might obtain hidden treasure, detect a thief, become invisible and other useful activities, by raising certain spirits to do their will. As to what degree the magic of the Order was affected by this magical text, Golden Dawn scholar R.A. Gilbert remains doubtful. In his preface to the most recent edition of MacGregor Mathers' *Key*, Gilbert suggests that the greatest influence of this and other Solomonic texts on the Order's magic would have probably been found in the pictorial symbols, the pentacles and sigils, which would have been absorbed into the Order's complicated structure of symbolism. He also suggests that Golden Dawn members were not noted for any undue eagerness to perform the conjurations of low magic, and as respectable middle-class citizens, they would have balked at raising spirits to obtain either love or hidden treasure.[82] While Gilbert may be correct in suggesting that the members of the Golden Dawn were not sufficiently tempted by the promises of the *Key*, they no doubt valued the knowledge contained within its pages and heeded its closing promise and warning:

> Here endeth our Key, which if thou thoroughly instillest into thy memory, thou shalt be able, if it pleaseth thee, even to fly with the wings of the wind. But if thou takest little heed hereof, and despiseth this Book, never shalt thou attain unto the desired end in any Magical experiment or operation whatsoever.[83]

Only two of the five books that make up the *Lemegeton* or *Little Key of Solomon the King*, have appeared in published form under MacGregor Mathers' name. There is no reason to suspect, however, that he did not produce versions of all five books for the use and interest of the Order. The *Goetia* is the first book of the *Little Key of Solomon* and MacGregor Mathers produced his version for circulation among members by 1898. Six years later, Aleister Crowley published a copy without MacGregor Mathers' permission and with an insulting prefatory note referring to how MacGregor Mathers was so easily deceived by the Horoses.[84] The *Goetia* and the *Lemegeton* itself, as a compilation of five books of magic, date from the seventeenth century.[85] The *Goetia* is a catalogue of 72 spirits that provides descriptions of each of these, their functions, their invocations and the particular days of the week upon which these invocations should be performed. Some of these spirits appear quite benign in both appearance and in intention:

> The Twenty-second Spirit is Ipos. He is an Earl, and a Mighty Prince, and appeareth in the form of an Angel with a Lion's Head, and a Goose's Foot, and Hare's Tail. He knoweth all things Past, Present, and to Come. He maketh men witty and bold.[86]

While others appear slightly more malicious:

> The Twenty-ninth Spirit is Astaroth. He is a Mighty, Strong Duke, and appeareth in the form of an hurtful Angel riding on an Infernal Beast like a Dragon, and carrying in his right hand a Viper. Thou must in no wise let him approach too near unto thee, lest he do thee damage by his Noisome Breath.[87]

It has been suggested that the author of the *Goetia* was drawing upon three different sources in this spiritual catalogue: Johann Weyer's *De Praestigiis Daemonum* (1563), the first known English translation of Agrippa's *De Occulta Philosophia* (1651) and the version of the pseudonymous *Heptameron* attributed to Peter of Abano, which was published along with the pseudo-Agrippan *Fourth Book of Occult Philosophy*.[88]

The other four books of the *Lemegeton* are the *Theurgia Goetia*, *Ars Paulina*, *Ars Almadel* and the *Ars Notoria*. There is no reason not to suspect that Gilbert's conclusion concerning the practical employment of the invocations of *The Key of Solomon the King* by members of the Order also extended to the lack of use of the *Lemegeton*'s invocations. No doubt the Order found this *grimoire* useful for its images and language in expanding upon the Golden Dawn's own complex symbolism, colourful rituals and invocations. Overall, with two known exceptions, Golden Dawn members did not put these invocations into practice. These exceptions are Alan Bennett, who carried out considerable experimentation with the material found in the *Goetia* and passed on this interest and activity to Crowley, the second exception, who rarely shied away from the opportunity to practise any kind of magic no matter how questionable.[89]

The next *grimoire* MacGregor Mathers translated brought him outside of the Solomonic tradition and into a Faustian one. The *Grimoire of Armadel* is based upon a manuscript MacGregor Mathers discovered at the *Bibliothèque de l'Arsenal* and has been identified as belonging to a group of seventeenth-century German magical texts.[90] Its content does not stray far from that of the Solomonic texts, however, as it also provides a catalogue of spirits complete with their descriptions, invocations and seals. In his introduction to MacGregor Mathers' version, which was not published until 1980 although it was probably completed circa 1897–9, Golden Dawn author Francis King explains how members would have employed the magic found within the Armadel text. Members would not have believed in the world of spirits as an objective reality and thus would use neither the magic within the *Grimoire of Armadel* nor that within the Solomonic texts as it was straightforwardly prescribed. Spirits existed for these men and women as a 'reasonable working hypothesis'.[91] Thus, they employed the images provided by the sigils and seals of the spirits of Armadel, as talismans and as astral doorways. Golden Dawn talismans were imbued with a spiritual energy symbolized by the sigils found in texts such as the *Grimoire of Armadel* and meditation upon these symbols induced a self-hypnosis required for a type of astral projection practised by the Order.[92] Just as with the *Key of Solomon* and the *Goetia*, Golden Dawn magic adapted the magic of Armadel to complement its own curious and competent blend of magic. Unlike Enochian magic, however, these traditions did not become essential aspects of the structure and symbolism of the Golden Dawn.

The next magical text translated by MacGregor Mathers was also more complementary than fundamental to Golden Dawn magic. *The Book of the Sacred Magic of Abramelin the Mage*, published by John M. Watkins in London in 1898, provided an entire exercise in magical meditation that was a system and ritual unto itself. MacGregor Mathers also discovered this text at the *Bibliothèque de l'Arsenal*. The original French title is *La sacrée magie que Dieu donna à Moyse Aaron David Salomon et d'autres saints patriarches et prophètes, qui enseigne la vraye sapience divine, laissée par Abraham à son fils, traduite de l'hebreu*, 1458. Despite these claims, it is more likely that the manuscript was not of Jewish origin and was written towards the end of the seventeenth century.[93] MacGregor Mathers claims that the manuscript was first brought to his attention by a 'celebrated occultist', thought by some to be Kenneth Mackenzie, and then again by French author and friend, Jules Bois.[94] According to MacGregor Mathers, this occultist told him that the Abramelin manuscript was known to both the French magus Eliphas Lévi, and the nineteenth-century novelist Bulwer-Lytton, who incorporated his knowledge of the Abramelin system into his own occult works of fiction.[95]

The manuscript itself is written in a style of wisdom literature or 'instructions text' that is common in magical texts and dates back to early Egyptian magical literature.[96] In this style, the content is presented as if from a father to a son, passing on secret knowledge and wisdom. In his introduction, MacGregor Mathers indicates his belief in the claimed provenance and antiquity of the manuscript. He has praise for the originality of the magical ritual, which requires the magician to retire to six months of isolation and practise a rigorous yoga-like programme of ritual and meditation. The purpose of this time-consuming endeavour is to make contact with one's guardian angel, which will then enable the magician to make use of both good and evil spirits in magical ritual without fear of harm or negative repercussions. The Abramelin system differs greatly from the rituals described in most Western *grimoires* in its absence of ritual, consecration, magical instruments and protective circles. In the introduction MacGregor Mathers commends the method used to contact one's guardian angel in the Abramelin system for its lack of use of an intermediary. Traditionally, contacting the angelic or spiritual world made use of a third person. This practice dates back to ancient Egypt and continues right up to the time of the Golden Dawn and is exemplified by the magical work of John Dee and his scryer Edward Kelley and also by the nineteenth-century occultist Frederick Hockley who used a young girl to contact his spirits, as we shall see later. Usually, children or young women were employed as seers or mediums. MacGregor Mathers, however, supports the idea expressed in the Abramelin system whereby the magician eventually achieves the necessary purity to become the intermediary, thus nullifying the necessity of a third agent in the final stages of the process.

The Golden Dawn system pushes this idea even further, in the nullification of the necessity of a second agent. In this method the magician actually becomes the force that is invoked. MacGregor Mathers advises a system of magic whereby instead of working through and in the name of the deity of the invoked force, the magician calls the power of the deity into himself and actually becomes the deity.[97] This is exemplified in a ritual for knowledge of one's higher genius that MacGregor Mathers wrote based on a Greek magical papyrus he found in the British Museum. This ritual begins with the magician invoking a headless and 'bornless' deity and ends with the magician becoming that deity: 'Thee I invoke the Bornless One ... I am He, the Bornless Spirit.'[98] MacGregor Mathers does not completely endorse the teachings found in the Abramelin book, criticizing some of the advice given by the character Abraham to his son Lamech. He takes issue with the lack of tolerance expressed in the Abramelin manuscript for other occult systems and suspects that this is due to Abraham's fear of his 'son' becoming involved with black magic, and that unless one is to receive proper instruction in these other systems they are best left alone.

Owing to the extreme demands placed on the individual, most Victorian magicians had neither the time, nor perhaps the desire, to put the magic of Abramelin to the test. Though this is not to say that its effectiveness was doubted. MacGregor Mathers blamed many of the difficulties he encountered in publishing the text on the dangerous power of the Abramelin magic. Such difficulties included financial concerns and the actual loss of his manuscripts.[99] The one Golden Dawn member who actually attempted the demanding ritual supported these charges. Aleister Crowley wrote the following in his *Confessions*:

> Other misfortunes of every kind overwhelmed Mathers. He was an expert Magician and had become accustomed to use the Greater Key of Solomon with excellent effect. He did not realise that *Abra-melin* was an altogether bigger proposition. It was like a young man, accustomed to handle gunpowder, suddenly supplied with dynamite without being aware of the difference.[100]

Not surprisingly, Crowley naturally rose to meet the challenge offered by this powerful magic and set himself up in a secluded house in the fall of 1899 to begin preparations. He did not meet with complete success as he went on to a secondary stage of the magical process, consecrating certain talismans, before having achieved the first. This first was the most important stage and was to result in the magician experiencing the 'knowledge and conversation' of his guardian angel.[101] Crowley was the only member of the Golden Dawn known to have attempted this kind of magic, perceived by occultists to be so powerful and unique.

In his translations and incorporation of magical instructional texts and systems, MacGregor Mathers gave the magical structure of the Order two important things. First, the Solomonic *grimoires* established the Order more firmly within a tradition strengthened and supplemented by the Golden Dawn's rituals and by Westcott's writings. This is the Western magical tradition as shaped by the Renaissance magi, namely Agrippa because of his incorporation of the medieval *grimoires* into the cabalistic, Hermetic, and Neoplatonic magic that was Pico and Reuchlin's legacy. MacGregor Mathers performs an Agrippan task by assimilating the Solomonic literature to the already existent nineteenth-century magical corpus. This is a reassertion of the synthesis of the Western magical tradition. His original additions, and the second important thing he gave to the Order's structure, can be found in his reconstruction of John Dee's Enochian magic so that it formed the basis of Golden Dawn magic and in his introduction of the Abramelin magic, a magic that, in method, had more in common with the pseudo-Eastern spiritualism practised by the followers of Madame Blavatsky in the Order's theosophical counterpart.

This simultaneous renewal of the process of synthesis and re-establishment of the magical tradition is also found in the fourth category of magical evidence. The directions in which individual members chose to pursue magic, once introduced to the Golden Dawn system, demonstrate that, despite the attempt towards innovation, there is always a return to the past. Two members of the Golden Dawn, in particular, exemplify this desire to explore other methods of magical ritual and even attempt to invent their own. Florence Farr became a member of the Golden Dawn in 1890 and advanced to the Second Order the following year. She maintained a position of authority and respect throughout her 12-year membership, replacing Woodman in his administrative capacity in the Isis-Urania Temple after his death and writing three of the Second Order's Flying Rolls. Florence Farr was an actress and the performance aspects of ritual magic no doubt appealed to her thespian nature. She was at the centre of a group of 12 Golden Dawn members who formed their own independent magical offshoot that practised a form of astral projection under the name of the Sphere Group. The work carried out by this group focused on making contact with an astral plane in order to gain more magical knowledge. The 12 members represented particular sephiroth on the cabalistic Tree of Life and through the process of meditation the group would attempt to project a mental image of these sephiroth in a spherical scheme. A series of these spheres would be visualized as extending into the solar system, with each subsequent sphere expanding in size. One ritual of the Sphere Group describes this process with the first sphere being ten feet in diameter and projected over the headquarters of the Order where the group met. The next was nine miles in diameter taking St Paul's Cathedral as its centre. And so the ritual continued. It concluded with the retraction of this visualization accompanied with the repetition of the phrase: 'Let Ra live, let Apophis be destroyed.'[102] Members of the Sphere Group carried out this kind of astral travel ritual to achieve 'the transmutation of evil into good.'[103]

The Sphere Group met with great opposition from some of the Golden Dawn members, namely Annie Horniman and W.B. Yeats. Such offshoot groups were completely legal according to the rules and regulations of the Order however, and what the Sphere Group did was based on Golden Dawn symbolism. What was different about the practices of the group was that it ignored the procedure of proper astral travel or vision whereby any images appearing in the subconscious must be challenged with the appropriate signs and tokens of the Order in order to ascertain the allegiance or rank of that image. There was some concern that Farr and her group passively accepted whatever images appeared during their astral visions.[104]

Annie Horniman's greatest bone of contention, however, was with the Egyptian influence of the Sphere Group, namely with a certain Egyptian astral form central to the working of the group that she believed to be alien, hostile and ultimately damaging to the Order.[105] This use of Egyptian symbolism is just one example of Farr's growing interest in Egyptian magic. Certainly the Golden Dawn rituals were not bereft of any Egyptian symbolism or mythology, however, in general, this aspect was in balance with the many other systems of symbolism and myth that combined to form the Order's overall structure. This Egyptian element is evident in the establishment of the Golden Dawn and can be found permeating Westcott's works, the rituals of the First and Second Orders, and in the instructional manuscripts circulated to both orders. It was not until later in the history of the Golden Dawn that certain members developed and pursued this interest in Egyptian magic exclusively. Farr placed Egyptian symbolism at the centre of her Sphere Group; she wrote articles on Egyptology for a collection of occult papers edited by Westcott called *Collectanea Hermetica*; she gave public lectures on ancient Egypt and she wrote plays with Egyptian themes.[106] The name of one such play was *The Beloved of Hathor and the Shrine of the Golden Hawk*. In her *Egyptian Magic*, Farr relies primarily upon Egyptian and Gnostic mythology to outline and explain what she believes to be the doctrines of Egyptian magic.[107] Throughout this work she quotes the Neoplatonist Iamblichus, *The Egyptian Book of the Dead*, the Gnostic work *Pistis Sophia* and extracts from a Gnostic papyrus in the collection of the Bodleian Library. She shows her familiarity with C.W. Goodwin's commentary on a Graeco-Egyptian magical papyrus and with the work of other nineteenth-century scholars on Egyptian magic.[108]

Farr's fascination with Egyptian magic lead to the eventual establishment of at least one magical order. Rituals from an order called the S.O.S and from the Order of the G.O.T.S. can be found in Private Collection C. Gilbert suggests that the letters stand for Servants of Osiris the Saviour and the Order of Great Osiris the Saviour.[109] The four rituals of the Order of the G.O.T.S. are from 1914, well after Farr's initial involvement with the Golden Dawn. The rituals concern the Egyptian gods Osiris, Thoth, Horus and Hathor who represent North, West, South and East respectively. Each ritual involves a candidate being bound with four different coloured cords at different points of the body while the others chant 'Ra lives' and sing hymns to the Egyptian gods. As the final cord is cut these words were to be spoken:

> Oh Osiris, thou who art the Soul of the human race, grant that any error that we may have made in thus seeking to revive thine ancient ritual may be atoned for by the earnestness of those who have come thus far in their search for the wisdom that once lived in Egypt! Protect us in peace, now and in eternity. Shed light upon us here and forever.[110]

Following this last instruction, Florence Farr's handwriting appears in the text, asserting that that particular ritual was collected in 1899 or 1900 from Egyptian records dating from the fifth and twenty-fifth dynasties.

Another ritual from the S.O.S. involves a priestess playing the role of Isis as the virgin mother who frees the candidate, once again bound at four points, and commands the 'child of light' to come forth. Seven days following this initiation, the candidate is given the passwords to the order.[111]

In both rituals it is interesting to see that while there is a definite change in emphasis from the Golden Dawn rituals there remains the same hierarchy and structure, namely a progression of grades, in the case of the Order of the G.O.T.S., and an ordeal through which the candidate must pass. The focus upon Egyptian myth and magic is superimposed upon these familiar features.

It is obvious that Farr was well read in the Egyptology of her day and her work demonstrates her identification of Golden Dawn magic with the discoveries being made in Egyptian magic. For example, she writes of the contemporary scholarly stance that in Egyptian magic the 'most potent magical formula was the identification of the Ritualist with the God whose power he was invoking',[112] a practice exemplified in Abramelin magic and in another ritual composed by MacGregor Mathers, referred to above. Farr's discussion of Gnostic mythology demonstrates its affability with the synthesized Golden Dawn mythology, which brings together cabalistic myth, Neoplatonism and Hermeticism. Her fascination with all things Egyptian is a perfectly predictable outcome of her relationship with Golden Dawn magic.

Farr was not alone in her interest in Egyptian magic. The other member of the Golden Dawn who went on to embrace Egyptology and the rich reservoir of myth it provided was the founding magician of the Golden Dawn himself. MacGregor Mathers' Egyptian period came to its full development during his stay in Paris. It was there that he and his wife began theatrical performances of their Rites of Isis. As has been shown, Egyptian magic was not a foreign element to Golden Dawn magic. It was not until MacGregor Mathers and his wife moved to Paris however that Egyptian magic became central to his magical interests. In 1900, in a New York journal, *The Humanitarian*, Frederick Lees wrote about his 1899 encounter with the Matherses and the Rites of Isis.[113] Moina Mathers explained to Lees that their interest in exploring the revival of these Egyptian rites came about when the same Jules Bois who had told MacGregor Mathers about the Abramelin manuscript, asked the Matherses to give a public demonstration of an Isiac ceremony. They would have refused had it not been for the intervention of Isis herself, who appeared to Moina in a dream and encouraged her to revive these rites and to celebrate masses in Paris with MacGregor Mathers as the Hierophant Rameses and Moina as the High Priestess Anari. Lees attended two such masses and described the second one in this manner:

> In the centre of the stage was the figure of Isis, on each side of her were other figures of gods and goddesses, and in the front was the little altar, upon which was the ever-burning green stone lamp. The Hierophant Rameses, holding in one hand the sistrum, which every now and then he shook, and in the other a spray of lotus, said the prayers before this altar, after which the High Priestess Anari invoked the goddess in penetrating and passionate tones. Then followed the 'dance of the four elements' by a young Parisian lady, who, dressed in long white robes, had previously recited some verses in French in honour of Isis ... Most of the ladies present in the fashionable Parisian audience brought offerings of flowers, whilst the gentlemen threw wheat on to the altar. The ceremony was artistic in the extreme.[114]

In this same article, we learn that the Matherses claimed to have an increasing number of initiates into the Isis cult. They imparted sacred theological notions and a secret system of knowledge to these new members. Their following was increasing to such a degree, that the current chapel in which Lees witnessed the Isis ceremony was to be replaced by a temple which was in the process of being constructed. On the whole, Lees appeared quite impressed by his encounter with the Matherses and their revival of the Rites of Isis. In his testimony, he describes the universality of the reception that Parisian society gave to these ceremonies and masses.

> You will find people attending them of nearly every shade of opinion and of profession; Isis worshippers, Alchemists, Protestants, Catholics, scientists, doctors, lawyers, painters, and men and women of letters, besides persons of high rank.[115]

André Gaucher provides another account of these ceremonies in two articles called 'Isis à Montmartre' in *L'Echo de merveilleux,* Paris, 1 and 15 December 1900. Gaucher describes his meeting with MacGregor Mathers in which he expressed his desire to witness the rites, and his subsequent arranged 'abduction' in which he was blindfolded and taken to a place where the rites were to be performed. Once his blindfold was removed, Gaucher saw before him several men and women dressed in long robes all gazing at a statue veiled in white in a room filled with garlands of flowers. MacGregor Mathers and his wife appeared in priestly garb and performed what Gaucher calls a simple ceremony and then lit some incense in which they threw wheat and flowers. Gaucher goes on to describe an extraordinary and nightmarish experience as the ritual progressed. The statue of Isis came to life, as did an image of Osiris. Those in attendance either collapsed in ecstasy or catalepsy while others stood frozen, observing the fantastical scene before them. As for Gaucher, he lost consciousness and awoke in a car, on his way home.[116]

What Gaucher appears to have witnessed is that which MacGregor Mathers described to Lees:

> We believe as our predecessors did ... that divine force can be made to appear in statues. No we are not monotheists, and for that reason we have sometimes been called idolators. But is not the universe, God manifest in matter, a great eidolon? We are pantheists; we believe that each force of the universe is regulated by a god. Gods are, therefore, innumerable and infinite.[117]

This belief fits in with that of MacGregor Mathers and the Golden Dawn's belief that divine forces can be made to appear in people as well. The Isis movement in Paris is the direction in which MacGregor Mathers chose to pursue his magical and religious beliefs after having established the complex structure of the Golden Dawn. His interest in Egyptian magic and mystery religions continued throughout his entire occult career. His use of a particular Graeco-Egyptian magical papyri in composing a ritual to invoke one's higher genius in which the magician becomes that which is invoked (not to be confused with the Abramelin system which invoked one's guardian angel), demonstrates his earlier fascination with Egyptian magic. A large quantity of texts customarily described as the Greek Magical Papyri were produced between the first century BC and the fifth century AD. The original ritual used by MacGregor Mathers was Papyrus XLVI (Greek) as reproduced in *Fragment of a Graeco-Egyptian Work upon Magic from a Papyrus in the British Museum*, edited and translated by Charles Wycliffe Goodwin for the Cambridge Antiquarian Society. The ritual MacGregor Mathers developed from this original is 'The Bornless Ritual for the Invocation of the Higher Genius'.[118]

This development in the direction of Egyptian magic appears quite natural given its positioning by many occultists and by contemporary research as the fountainhead of Western magic. Once again, Victorian magic can be perceived as the classic modern occult system in its ability to marry the present with the past in rediscovering ancient or older magical systems and reinterpreting them within the present Western magical structure.

There is another example of the direction in which members of the Golden Dawn took the magical techniques they acquired within the Order. This example is found in a private ritual that is over 100 pages long and involves the invocation of good and evil spirits. This ritual is called the 'Ritual for the Formation, Building and Consecration of a Body, wherein to Travel, manifest & act in freedom from the Bonds & limitation of matter' and dates from 1899–1900. It is extraordinary in that it strays from Golden Dawn ritual by focusing on black magic or necromancy. It would appear to have more in common with the medieval *grimoires* that MacGregor Mathers translated, yet did not assimilate into the structure of Golden Dawn magic. This ritual calls upon:

> Creatures of the flashing Fire, & rushing Air – Spirits of water & Earth & Hell. Legions of Demons who manifest in the land of Twilight – Shades of the living who are Dead. Shades of the Dead who live – Dwellers in the howling wilderness – whose abodes are folded in the shadow of death – recognise in Me your master – turn ye – come & obey my will. Serve me & fear me.[119]

This ritual is curious in its uniqueness among Golden Dawn ritual and the rituals that members went on to compose and appropriate in their magical experimentation. It is not that unusual when compared with medieval necromancy. It would not have been difficult for a member of the Golden Dawn with an interest in a blacker sort of magic to obtain access to the necessary material with which to inspire the composition of such a ritual. MacGregor Mathers alone provided versions of the *Key of Solomon* and *The Lesser Key*. Certainly medieval *grimoires* and books of necromancy were easy enough to discover in the British Museum, a favourite haunt of many Victorian occultists.

In examining these four categories of magical texts or directions practised and taken by members of the Golden Dawn, we can begin to piece together the structure, doctrines and main themes of Victorian magic. Yeats summarizes these doctrines best in his *Ideas of Good and Evil* where he provides three principles he believes to have been handed down from early times and to be the foundations of all magical practice.

1. That the borders of our minds are ever shifting, and that many minds can flow into one another, as it were, and create or reveal a single mind, a single energy.
2. That the borders of our memories are as shifting, and that our memories are a part of one great memory, the memory of Nature herself.
3. That this great mind and great memory can be evoked by symbols.[120]

These three principles are drawn from a textual tradition, or rather, several textual traditions. The medieval *grimoires* translated by MacGregor Mathers, the diaries of John Dee, the Rosicrucian manifestos, the cabalistic and Neoplatonic works of the Renaissance magi and the Hermetic writings and Graeco-Egyptian magical papyri all influenced the magic and ritual of the Golden Dawn by providing it with the language and symbolism needed to support the magical principles above. These texts establish the antiquity of the magical tradition that the Order followed.

The innovation of the Golden Dawn is found in the texts it produced in drawing upon this older canon. The cipher manuscript, the knowledge lectures, the Flying Rolls, the rituals for the First Order, as well as those for the *R.R. et A.C.*, and the extra-curricular rituals all represent the culmination and synthesis of the magical knowledge gleaned from the older sources. It is in these texts that Egyptian deities meet Enochian language, Rosicrucian myth melds with cabalistic symbolism and ritual magic swords join with Egyptian magical words to form a new, cohesive, and incredibly complex, occult synthesis.

These textual sources reveal much about Victorian magic's origins and in which direction it was headed. They also point, however, to a dependency upon certain already established traditions. The Golden Dawn is also based on a structural ritual tradition, which would have been learned by the Order's founders through their participation in certain societies. These include the rituals of the Freemasons and of the *Soc. Ros.*, both of which influenced the rituals of the Golden Dawn in their language, structure and symbolism. The Egyptian element in these rituals is not something which was added by the Golden Dawn. Egyptian mystery religions, as understood in the nineteenth century, were very much a part of Masonic ritual. To uncover the origins of the ritual structure of Victorian magic, we must now examine the transmission of Masonic ritual, Rosicrucian ritual and the rituals associated with Egyptian magic and mystery religions.

3
Resurrecting the Past: Hiram, Isis and the Rosy Cross

Three dominant traditions rose to prominence in the nineteenth century and came to wield great influence on the shaping of Victorian occultism. Freemasonry, Rosicrucianism and Egyptian magic each entered the century already fused with other elements of a constantly evolving magical system. It was not until the emergence of Golden Dawn magic, however, that the three became so firmly wedded. Freemasonry provided the structure of the First Order rituals, while Rosicrucianism supplied the founding myth and dominant symbolism of the Second Order. Egyptian religion and mythology permeated much of the magical language and symbolism of both orders, and directed the future magical pursuits of at least two of the Golden Dawn's most prominent members. All three traditions have both a solid historical origin as well as nineteenth-century adaptations which were made in the spirit of the century, a spirit of invented traditions and appropriated histories. And, as we shall see, despite originating within specific historical frameworks, the role of these three traditions as fluid sets of ideas with continual potential for influence throughout history is of most interest and significance. Nonetheless, an understanding of the actual historical origins is vital in grasping the fundamental ideas these traditions embraced and how these doctrines changed and evolved into their nineteenth-century manifestations. In this way we can see to what degree Victorian occultism relied upon these contemporary forms, and to what degree it looked to the past for the original manifestations of Freemasonry, Rosicrucianism and Egyptian magic.

In the nineteenth century these three traditions became part of the process of synthesis so essential to Victorian magic. In fact, it is the work of the Golden Dawn, carried out primarily by MacGregor Mathers, which completes the synthesis of Freemasonry, Rosicrucianism and

Egyptian magic, not only with each other, but also with the other varieties of esoteric and occult thought embraced by the Order. Egyptian magic, as expressed through actual magical practices and mystery religions, is the most difficult tradition to isolate within this context, as its assimilation with almost every occult and esoteric system in Western culture complicates its extraction. The categorization of Egyptian magic with Freemasonry and Rosicrucianism in no way suggests exclusivity to these two traditions. Egyptian magic is grouped here for convenience, placing emphasis upon its influence on mystery religions and secret societies and it is in this form that its presence was most felt in esoteric circles in Victorian Britain.

Freemasonry was one of the more obvious influences on British magic. The building blocks of late nineteenth-century occultism were provided by the ritual and symbolism of the Masons. Freemasonry is largely associated, historically speaking, with the eighteenth and nineteenth centuries when lodges and orders, both orthodox and deviant, were springing up all over Europe. The proliferation of secret societies in the eighteenth century has often been associated with Freemasonry's popularity, although the influence of the continued quest for the invisible Rosicrucian brotherhood also played a part in this propagation. Freemasonry did not, however, emerge newly formed in the eighteenth century. Its historical origins and development are much earlier.

To speak of a history of Freemasonry some clarifications must be made. Two major misconceptions prevail. The first is the identification of England as the place where Freemasonry first emerged. The second is the idea that Freemasonry gradually evolved out of medieval Masons' guilds.[1] Another difficulty encountered when studying the history of Freemasonry is that, as with many societies dealing with esoteric traditions, Freemasonry has two accounts of its origins. The first is a strictly historical one, while the second is mythical, a fictitious or elaborated account created by those involved with Freemasonry for various purposes. These purposes include fulfilling the conventional desire of initiates of an esoteric society to belong to an ancient and established tradition, and providing an appropriate myth and symbolism analogous to the goals of the society. Both the historical and mythical account are important as the first reveals objective facts about the development of Freemasonry, and the second reveals how those involved chose to identify themselves and their societies. The two accounts could not be more different. Solomonic Jerusalem is the place where the mythical origins of Freemasonry are rooted, while late sixteenth-century Scotland holds the place of honour for its historical origins.[2]

Traditional Masonry differs from Freemasonry, or speculative Masonry, in its development, purpose and structure. Because of the transient nature of their business, medieval Masons established lodges in which they lived, near the building sites of their current employment. To identify themselves as proper Masons, they developed a system of secret signs and initiation so that one Mason could recognize another. These medieval Masons also had an elaborate mythology and stressed the practice of a certain moral and religious code. This mythical history asserts that the Masons descended from the following historical figures: Lamech, the great grandson of Noah; Hermes Trismegistus; Nimrod; Abraham; King Solomon and Euclid. The legend also equates Masonry with geometry and architecture, making it one of the seven liberal sciences. The features of medieval Masonry, a myth emphasizing the antiquity and importance of the trade, initiation, and secrecy, are not extraordinary. Most medieval trades had their own associations or guilds with similar features. Where medieval Masonry was unusual was in its surprisingly elaborate mythical history.[3] Otherwise there was no indication that the trade of masonry was to evolve into the definitive secret society of the eighteenth and nineteenth centuries.

Speculative Masonry, or Freemasonry, found its origins in a development of this medieval system that took place in Scotland in the late sixteenth century. This development however, was more creative than evolutionary.[4] Several characteristics mark this development as novel: the establishment of permanent lodges, as opposed to the transient ones of the medieval Masons; the earliest evidence of admission of non-practising Masons; the earliest evidence of initiation through a hierarchy of two degrees; and the earliest evidence of lodge Masonry connected with an ethical code dependent upon symbolic explanation.[5] The first lodges of speculative Masonry were established around Edinburgh and St Andrews eventually spreading to England and the creation of permanent lodges there by the 1680s. Not content to merely adopt the Scottish version, the English customized Scottish speculative Masonry by being the first to use the actual term 'Freemasonry', establishing the first Masonic lodge that was entirely non-operative, and providing for the first printing of the Old Charges, documents recounting the mythical history of Masonry. The English were also responsible for developing a third degree of initiation and for creating a national Grand Lodge in the early eighteenth century.[6]

The earliest record outlining the contents of the initiation rituals of this new form of speculative Masonry comes from the late seventeenth century. At this point, there were only the two initial grades. Admission to the first consisted of the candidate being shown the hidden signs and taught the mythical history of the masons. This included a description and explanation of the symbolism of the decorations of the lodge in relation to the original mythical lodge, Solomon's Temple. The initiate was also taught a secret handshake which involved the bodies of both Masons touching at five points during the exchange of a password. The initiation was invested with awe and mystery and an atmosphere of fear, emphasizing the necessity of secrecy and the dire consequences to be met should the candidate betray this secrecy. The ceremonies were intended to frighten the initiate and convince him that should he break the mason's oath, the others would murder him.[7] Like the first, admission to the second degree involved learning new signs and passwords. This second initiation, however, did not involve scaring the candidate.

When compared with modern Masonic ritual, this earliest record of initiation varies mainly in elaboration. The bare bones of the ritual are still there but with numerous ceremonial and symbolic additions. The modern initiation ritual for the first degree has developed in that the candidate is blindfolded and led by a knotted rope to the door of the lodge where he is admitted after being challenged. After attesting to his belief in a Supreme Being, the candidate is presented to the lodge and takes an oath of secrecy.[8] The symbolism of this ceremony is found in the tools of Masonry, kept on an altar in the middle of the lodge. The compass, the plumb line, and the level all symbolize specific attributes favourable to the character of the Freemason. By the time Freemasonry entered the nineteenth century, other important symbols had been added including the pentagram, the hexagram, the triangle and the square.[9] Initiation to the second degree differs from the first in that the candidate is not blindfolded and must demonstrate the knowledge learned in the first initiation concerning the symbolism of the tools. This difference is similar to the earliest records of Masonic ritual in which the candidate for the second degree was not frightened during the initiation.

The origins of these rituals and of the symbolism employed in these rituals cannot be found in Freemasonry's medieval predecessors. The esoteric and symbolic aspects belong to another era. Renaissance Hermeticism and the practice of the art of memory were influential in the formation of Masonic myth, ritual and symbolism.[10] Renaissance historian Frances Yates compares the Hermeticism embraced by Giordano Bruno to the underlying philosophy of Freemasonry:

> Where is there such a combination as this of religious toleration, emotional linkage with medieval past, emphasis on good works

for others, and imaginative attachment to the religion and the symbolism of the Egyptians? The only answer to this question that I can think of is – in Freemasonry.[11]

While it was the Age of Enlightenment that witnessed the popularity of Freemasonry, it was really a Renaissance creation characterized by mystery, ritual, secrecy and the quest for hidden truth. This Renaissance creation found part of its history in the medieval Masonic myth and its structure in the organizations and rituals of Scottish Renaissance Masonry.[12]

The mythical account of the origins of Masonry is equally as significant in assessing the influence of Freemasonry upon Victorian occultism for the tradition's mythological origins had achieved historical status in most esoteric circles by the nineteenth century, if not earlier. Medieval Masonic associations had a myth about the origins of their trade that dates back to King Solomon and the building of his temple. This fundamental myth persists throughout the development of medieval Masonry into speculative Masonry, or Freemasonry. This myth is taught to the initiate as he progresses through the ceremonies of the different grades. The candidate learns that there were three grand masters who presided over the two classes of Masons who were building the temple. These masters were Solomon, Hiram, King of Tyre, and Hiram Abiff. The three shared a number of secrets that were lost when Hiram Abiff was murdered after refusing to divulge them. Substituted secrets have since been put in place in anticipation of the restoration of these original secrets.[13] John Hamill, in his history of English Freemasonry, claims that this myth is not perceived by members to be literal; rather, it is understood to be an allegory through which the principles and tenets of Masonry are passed on to new initiates.[14] This foundation myth also functions in another way, by fulfilling a desire to lay claim to an ancient and continuous tradition. As Freemasonry developed in the eighteenth and nineteenth centuries, its mythological origins became embellished in reflection of contemporary developments in archaeology and cultural tastes.[15] The most significant of these new developments and discoveries were in the areas of Greek and Roman mystery religions and Egyptology. Freemasonry was eager to add this new information about antiquity to its own invented history as part of an attempt at authentication through age and tradition. This was done carefully and in such a manner that these new additions did not seem either new or additional and therefore did not jeopardize the prerequisite of an ancient and continuous tradition. In eighteenth- and nineteenth-century books on Freemasonry, this embellishment and re-creation of the society's foundation myth is easily observed. In a late eighteenth-century text, *The Philosophy of Masons in Several Epistles from Egypt, to a Nobleman,* the narrator speaks of meeting Masons in Egypt who had records of their history extending back to ancient Egypt. These same Masons claimed that the Greek philosophers had learned all their secrets from Egyptian Masons who later regretted having shared this knowledge as the Greeks went on to expose them to the world.[16] The late nineteenth-century text, *The Obelisk and Freemasonry,* by John A. Weisse, claims to provide proof that an institution, similar to Freemasonry, existed in Egypt long before the pyramids and the obelisks. This apparent proof was that Masonic tools would have been needed for their construction. This same text goes so far as to make the claim that Freemasonry commenced from creation, and was established by the family of Seth.[17]

Together with a proliferation in secret societies in general, the eighteenth and nineteenth centuries saw the formation of many off-shoots of Freemasonry throughout Europe. These offshoots strove to preserve this same image of their society as a continuation of an ancient order by identifying with a supposedly more genuine version of Masonry or by reverting to an alleged purer form. A Masonic order with no claim to an ancient authority and tradition would, by the very definition of Masonry, not be Masonic. In their assertions of a more genuine or purer ancestry, these offshoots frequently developed their own degrees and rituals.

Apart from the importance of the allegorical and authenticating purposes of the Masonic myth, there are two major features of Freemasonry that are significant for this study. The first is the religious toleration expressed in the language and symbolism of the rituals, and the second is the fraternal nature of the lodge. The changes made in the eighteenth century by the English in their adoption of speculative Masonry included the introduction of the title 'Supreme Architect of the Universe'. 'Supreme Being' was another title used in reference to this deity in which a candidate must believe for admission to a lodge. Freemasonry may have been a monotheistic organization but there was no particular Christian emphasis in its rituals and symbolism and, in fact, there was no particular religious emphasis of any kind. This is exemplified in *The Philosophy of Masons in Several Epistles from Egypt, to a Nobleman.* The writer of these epistles is a Mason who meets two Jewish brothers, also Masons, in Egypt, the traditional meeting place for such encounters. They teach the writer all they know about the ancient history of Masons that originated in Egypt and debate with the writer over divine revelation and Christianity. The brothers maintain that the discovery and acknowledgement of truth, a goal central to the Masonic fraternity, is incompatible with the existence of established religion.[18] This late eighteenth-century sentiment concerning the compatibility of Christianity, or any organized religion, with Masonry extends to the present day. In *Darkness Visible, A Christian Appraisal of Freemasonry*, Walton Hannah examines Masonic rituals in order to decide whether dual allegiance to Christianity and Freemasonry is possible for a devout Christian.[19] His conclusion is that the workings of Freemasonry are predominantly non-Christian in several ways, namely in their portrayal of all gods as equal in their use of pagan, pre-Christian mysticism and in their incorporation of aspects of non-Christian contemporary religions.[20]

> Freemasonry is frankly humanist in tone, and yet at the same time includes a great deal of mystical and symbolic nonsense about geometry and astronomy which no educated Mason in this enlightened age would dream of taking seriously.[21]

While the religious toleration expressed in the lodges of the Freemasons may not be appreciated by all, it did provide a social organization based upon an ethical code, steeped in ritual, symbolism and myth, that was open to all, or at least, to all men.

This introduces another mythical aspect of the history of Masonry. It has been suggested in some of the eighteenth- and nineteenth-century texts referred to above that Masonry could be best compared to Mithraism in its structure and purpose. Mithraism, in practice as early as 100 CE, was a mystery religion centred around Mithras, a Bronze Age Indo-Iranian deity identified with the sun. The followers of Mithras were men who met in caves in complete secrecy where they held initiations and other rituals. Much iconography remains of the practices of these men including pictorial accounts of the slaying of a bull and sacrificial meals. There is, however, no accompanying literal myth with which to interpret this iconography so we cannot know what the followers of Mithras did at their secret meetings.[22] What little is known about Mithraism tells us that it is similar to Masonry in its strictly male membership, its hierarchy of initiation grades (Mithraism had seven grades), its secretive nature, its patriarchal monotheism and its lack of emphasis on the role of religion or faith. Mithraism is more philosophically than religiously oriented, and offers initiates hope and a 'safe anchor' in life.[23] Masonry parallels this with the comfort offered through belonging to such an ancient and established organization. So far these comparisons have been made without any allegations that Mithraism was the original form of Masonry. It certainly predates Masonry and shares many of the same characteristics. There is, however, no historical evidence that Mithraism was the predecessor of Masonry in the sense of a developing continuous tradition. Its similarities with Masonry can be used as evidence to argue for a predisposition of people, particularly men, to form secret societies that provide them with an ancient and established philosophical and moral code. It does not provide evidence that Masonry is a direct descendant of Mithraism.

Interestingly, one Mason, William Wynn Westcott, one of the founders of the Golden Dawn, a magical society founded almost entirely upon a mythical history, invested much research and study on the subject in an effort to dispute such a claim.[24] In fact, Westcott exerted the same effort to discredit the apparent belief that the Essenes were an original source for the creeds and customs of the Freemasons.[25] It would seem that Westcott was on a mission to free Freemasonry from its mythical history, or at least from the components being added to this mythical history through the influence of recent archaeological discoveries in the eighteenth and nineteenth centuries. He systematically went through his sources, discrediting claims that Mithraism was the predecessor of Freemasonry. Westcott was able to see the similarities in the initiation process, the secrecy, rituals and ceremonials, and the devotion and hope of advancement that such a hierarchical society could provide. He concluded, however, that there is no basis for the suggestion that the origins of Freemasonry have any direct relationship with Mithraism.[26] Nonetheless, Mithraism was one of the many components which Freemasonry added to its own elaborate and mythical history over the years as developments in the fields of comparative religion and comparative mythology in the nineteenth century provided new information ready to be assimilated to the ever-growing myth. It is interesting to see how at least one of the more prominent members of the Golden Dawn, indeed the founding member most frequently accused of forging the Order's own origins, was so meticulous in discrediting the mythical origins of a contemporary esoteric society, and one to which he belonged.

Secret societies enjoyed immense popularity in Britain and, indeed, in the rest of Europe in the eighteenth and nineteenth centuries. With Freemasonry as one of the more popular societies at this time with its numerous offshoots, it is not surprising that as other societies were established, they based their structure and rituals upon this most common form. Historian Ronald Hutton estimates that by the beginning of the twentieth century, just 12 years after the formation of the Golden Dawn, millions of men and hundreds of women in Britain were familiar with the Masonic-style secret society that involved blindfolding initiates, challenging and testing the initiate, taking an oath and passing through an ordeal as part of initiation. Another common feature of these societies was the incorporation of historical figures and events into their mythological pasts.[27] In this fashion, the Golden Dawn was just another nineteenth-century secret society, part of a trend. The Order was also influenced, however, by direct contact with Freemasonry. Its three founding members, Westcott, MacGregor Mathers and Woodman, were Master Masons and a good many of the male members of the Order had also been initiated into Masonic lodges. Westcott joined a lodge in Somerset shortly after completing his medical degree in 1871. MacGregor Mathers was initiated in 1877 and became a Master Mason in 1878. Woodman would also have achieved the status of Master Mason, as did Westcott, for both held membership in the *Soc. Ros.*, which only admitted Master Masons. Westcott wrote several papers on Freemasonry, many, as we have seen, with the purpose of discrediting claims associated with the eighteenth and nineteenth-century elaboration of Freemasonry's origins. In one such paper, Westcott reveals his understanding of the main characteristics of Freemasonry:

> the culture of brotherly love, relief [belief?] and truth, that is to say, charity and benevolence with universal tolerance; the performance of ceremonials, which include most solemn oaths to keep secret the *modes* of recognition; and an extensive ritual use of builders' terms and material things as symbols of moral and spiritual truths.[28]

Victorian occultism was directly and culturally influenced by Freemasonry. The ways in which this influence was felt was in the structure and symbolism of the Golden Dawn's First Order rituals. In fact, the names of the five degrees of the First Order are based on those of a German Masonic order, the *Gold-und Rosenkreuz Order*. The *Soc. Ros.* had adopted these names initially and they were subsequently appropriated by the Golden Dawn. It was not only the names of the degrees, however, that the Golden Dawn borrowed from Masonic, and arguably Rosicrucian sources, but also the initiation rituals as described in the mysterious document, the original cipher manuscript, which lays out the basic structure, tenets and learning of the Order. The contents of this manuscript reveal that the similarities between Golden Dawn and Masonic ritual include a hoodwinked candidate who is challenged, tested and then taught some of the elementary symbolism and history of the Order. The initiate takes an oath of secrecy that parallels that of the Masonic oath in the frightful consequences to be met should the oath be broken. In the original cipher manuscript, this is described as the neophyte grade initiate taking an 'obligation to secrecy under threats of expulsion and death or palsy from a hostile current of will'.[29] Another influence of Freemasonry can be found in the symbolic instruments of the Golden Dawn.[30] Instead of compass and level, however, the Golden Dawn member has a cup, dagger, pentacle, wand, sword and a Rose-Cross Lamen, the latter a result of Rosicrucian influence.

Freemasonry thus had a strong influence on the structure, ritual, language and symbolism of the First Order of the Golden Dawn. There are, however, important areas in which the Golden Dawn deviated from conventional Freemasonry and these deviations are part of what made the Order unique. First, and most importantly, the Golden Dawn admitted women. This was largely due to the influence of Madame Blavatsky's Theosophical Society and Anna Kingsford's Hermetic Society, both late nineteenth-century esoteric societies open to men and women alike. The Order was also following in the footsteps of some unorthodox Masonic developments which saw the admission of women beginning in eighteenth-century France with the Rite of Adoption. Another example of how the Order departed from Freemasonry was in the Golden Dawn's emphasis upon Christian symbolism, an emphasis that was in part due to Rosicrucian influences. While the Freemasons were content with a Supreme Architect and the symbolic tools of their trade, the Golden Dawn made great use of the symbol of the cross and borrowed from Christian prayer in the wording of its rituals.

It is obvious that many of the ways in which the Golden Dawn deviated from Freemasonry were largely due to the influence of other societies or traditions. Rosicrucianism in particular directed the Golden Dawn away from Freemasonry, especially in the Second Order's ritual and symbolism. Rosicrucianism as an esoteric tradition began with the publication of three manifestos in the early seventeenth century. The first text *Fama Fraternitatis, dess Löblichen Ordens des Rosenkreutzes* (the Declaration of the Worthy Order of the Rosy Cross) was published in Kassel, Germany in 1614. The document had been in circulation prior to its publication for at least two years, as a 1612 reply to the document exists, supposedly in response to a 1610 manuscript of the same manifesto.[31] The *Fama* reveals the existence of a secret society established in the fourteenth century. It tells the story of how the society came to be founded and how the tomb of its founder had recently been discovered, thus heralding the dawn of a new age. The founder of the secret fraternity is a mysterious man named Christian Rosenkreuz who had journeyed to the East in search of wisdom. There he learned magic and cabala and continued his travels spreading his newly acquired knowledge and healing the sick. He returned to Germany and established the Fraternity of the Rose Cross which was originally made up of four members.[32] The fraternity eventually grew and members were dispersed around the globe to do good works and to share and learn knowledge. They observed six rules: first, they were to have no other profession other than healing the sick for free; second, they were to wear the clothes of the country they were in and not clothe themselves in any particular or extraordinary fashion; third, they must all reunite annually upon a certain day; fourth, each member must find a successor; fifth, the initials C.R. (Christian Rosenkreuz) must be their seal, mark, and character; and sixth, the fraternity must remain a secret for 100 years. The original members and their eventual successors carried on in secrecy according to the regulations of the fraternity until the occasion for the manifesto's publication took place. This occasion was the discovery of Christian Rosenkreuz's tomb in which his corpse was found to be whole and without any signs of decay. This tomb was in a vault, the description of which features prominently in the manifesto. The vault was decorated with geometrical signs on its seven sides and was divided into three parts. While no sunlight entered the vault, it was lit by an interior source referred to as 'another sun'. Along with the tomb of Rosenkreuz, the vault contained numerous mysterious treasures including bells, lamps and 'artificial songs'. The tomb's discovery signalled the call for reformation and a new age.

> Howbeit we know after a time there will now be a general reformation, both of divine and human things, according to our desire, and the expectation of others. For it is fitting, that before the rising of the sun, there should appear and break forth Aurora, or some clearness, or divine light in the sky. And so in the mean time some few, who shall give their names, may join together, thereby to increase the number and respect of our Fraternity ...[33]

The *Fama* then ends with a mysterious call for recruitment – mysterious in that there are no contact details – and a promise of material, physical and spiritual benefits to new recruits. The *Fama* was followed the next year by the second Rosicrucian manifesto, the *Confessio Fraternitatis*, published in Latin in 1615. The *Confessio* was a continuation of the *Fama* and restated its message, expanding upon the philosophy of the secret brotherhood and further explaining the allegories contained in the first. It concludes with a prophecy of reformation, a condemnation of the pope, and a reassertion of the fraternity's intention to do good under the cloak of secrecy:

> although we might enrich the whole world, and endue them with learning, and might release it from innumerable miseries, yet shall we never be manifested and made known unto any man, without the especial pleasure of God; yea, it shall be so far from him whosoever thinks to get the benefit and be partaker of our riches and knowledge, without and against the will of God, that he shall sooner lose his life in seeking and searching for us, than to find us, and attain to come to the wished happiness of the Fraternity of the Rosy Cross.[34]

This second manifesto was published at a time when the excitement and frenzy produced by the first was reaching its height. It served to sustain this interest and to produce numerous printed works in response as people wrote to enquire as to how to join either in the work of the fraternity, or the fraternity itself.[35] Several people were also encouraged by the publication of these first two manifestos to publish their own denunciations of the religious, political and philosophical ideas expressed in the Rosicrucian works.[36] It is not necessary to go into the details of these arguments here; it is enough to note that the manifestos provoked opposing responses, enthusiasm from those wondering where they could sign up and outrage from those whose own politics, religious beliefs or social positions were threatened by the teachings of this secret fraternity. Interestingly, there was a further differentiation in the way in which the manifestos were received. Among both those enthused and outraged, there were those who took the manifestos literally, and there were also those in both camps who understood the manifestos allegorically.

The third Rosicrucian work was published the following year, in 1616, and was much different in style and content from the first two. It was published in German under the title *Die Chymische Hochzeit Christiani Rosenkreutz* or *The Chemical Wedding of Christian Rosenkreutz*. Unlike the first two manifestos, the *Wedding* was a romance about the marriage of a king and queen at a fantastical castle which housed a mysterious vault, not lit by the sun. The wedding guests went through ordeals to weigh their worth. Some were initiated into a chivalric order while others were beheaded and subsequently resurrected. The hero of the first two manifestos, Christian Rosenkreuz, founder of the secret fraternity, is invited to this wedding and narrates the story. The wedding is an alchemical allegory for the mystical marriage of the soul that the narrator undergoes during his experiences as a guest at the castle. The fantastical and allegorical nature of this third Rosicrucian work suggests an emphasis upon the mythical aspect of the Rosicrucian manifestos in order, perhaps, to redirect those who had mistaken the first two as literal. If such is the case, then the Rosicrucian writings were meant as an intellectual catalyst and this third publication was written to show that the physical notion of a secret fraternity was a myth. Therefore, whoever wrote the manifestos was attempting to present the notion of a brotherhood of mind and spirit, rather than of flesh.[37] Historian Frances Yates agrees with this interpretation of the Rosicrucian manifestos. She claims that her own extensive research has failed to uncover the existence of any real Rosicrucian society associated with these publications. What it did uncover, however, was plenty of evidence of a real and impassioned search for such a society, as well as much condemnation from those opposed to the political and philosophical tone of the manifestos. Given the invisible nature of this supposed fraternity, the publications were intended to be allegorical and the ensuing assumption that there was an actual secret society was a popular misunderstanding.[38]

This misunderstanding was responsible for turning the myth of the Rosicrucian brotherhood into a reality. The manifestos themselves were not responsible for the creation of secret societies, but certainly for their ensuing proliferation and popularity. It has been argued that the mythical Rosicrucian fraternity described in the manifestos was modelled on a sixteenth-century German society, *Orden den Unzertrennlichen*, or, *Indissolubilisten*, the Order of the Inseparables, an order concerned with the techniques of alchemy. The Rosicrucian manifestos condemn popular alchemy while containing many alchemical references and symbolism. The Rosicrucian philosophy was opposed to the common alchemical pursuit for gold while supporting the more spiritual and esoteric form of alchemy, which was concerned with the purification of the soul and with divine union. This Order of the Inseparables used alchemical symbolism and a secret alphabet and was structured upon a system of grades.[39] While this claim is difficult both to support or disclaim, research certainly shows that the Rosicrucians, as an esoteric society with its own secretive language or alphabet, were not a novelty in seventeenth-century Germany. What was unusual was the open publication of their existence paired with their complete invisibility. To those already engaged in esoteric and alchemical pursuits, whether in already established societies or not, the Rosicrucians must have appeared as the genuine article and were likely to have encouraged the formation of further brotherhoods in search of hidden knowledge.

Owing to the popularity of alchemy at the time the manifestos were published. Rosicrucianism, despite its condemnation of the alchemical search for gold, became closely associated with this form of alchemy. Another addition to the Rosicrucian myth was its development as an ancient secret doctrine dating back to biblical times. One seventeenth-century German source traces the wisdom of the Rosicrucians back to Adam, who supposedly retained some divine wisdom after the Fall. This wisdom was passed on through Noah, Zoroaster, the Chaldeans and the Egyptians and was preserved in the Jewish kabbalah. The few men who managed to recover this wisdom include Agrippa, Reuchlin, Ficino, Pico della Mirandola and of course, Christian Rosenkreuz.[40] In this way, it is apparent that the Rosicrucian myth, emerging at approximately the same time as that of Freemasonry, was subject to the same kind of elaboration, placing it within both biblical and Neoplatonic Renaissance traditions.

In the seventeenth century, currents of thought flowed freely throughout England and continental Europe. The excitement created by the manifestos in intellectual circles in Germany and France soon spread to England. Links have been established between Rosicrucian philosophy and English esotericism through the works of Francis Bacon, John Dee and Robert Fludd, thus establishing the framework for Rosicrucianism to come into contact with Freemasonry. One of the earliest records of a Masonic initiation at an English lodge was that of Elias Ashmole in 1646. Ashmole was more than familiar with the philosophy of the Rosicrucian brotherhood, having copied out the manifestos himself in a letter requesting permission to join the fraternity. Sir Robert Moray's initiation into a lodge in Edinburgh in 1641 however, predates Ashmole's, thus supporting the argument that Scotland was the place where it all began. Both Moray and Ashmole shared an interest in alchemy and chemistry as well as memberships in both the Royal Society and speculative Masonic lodges.

The earliest written reference to both Freemasonry and Rosicrucianism, and to the Masonic word, is found in a poem published in Edinburgh in 1638.

> For what we do presage is not in grosse,
> For we be brethren of the Rosie Crosse:

> We have the Mason's word and second sight,
> Things for to come we can fortell aright![41]

This demonstrates that at this early date there was an association of Freemasonry with Rosicrucianism and the inference that members of both societies had some sort of unusual abilities as suggested by their having the 'second sight'. While this may be a satirical comment linking different kinds of contemporary superstition, it does provide evidence for this early association of Freemasons with Rosicrucians.

Rosicrucianism played a role in the increasing popularity of Freemasonry in the seventeenth and eighteenth centuries. The proliferation of lodges and growth in membership was influenced by the driving desire to uncover the invisible brotherhood of the Rosicrucians. While the Rosicrucians remained undetectable, the Masons offered a more substantial fraternity and may have been the society for which Rosicrucian-hopefuls settled.[42] Rosicrucianism may also have influenced the early development of Freemasonry, contributing its myth of a secret brotherhood to the 'already mixed bag of Masonic lore'.[43] Certainly, the influence of Rosicrucianism upon Freemasonry was soon to be felt within the very organization of the grades. In the eighteenth century a new grade was developed called the Rose Croix grade with an emphasis upon Christian mysticism and chivalry. The details of this grade are provided in the anonymously authored *Text Book of Advanced Freemasonry* of 1873. The grade's emblems include the eagle, the pelican, the cross and the rose, and its initiation tools consist of three crosses and a crown of thorns.[44] In his *Royal Masonic Cyclopaedia* published in 1877, Mason and occultist Kenneth Mackenzie writes that a large number of Rose Croix chapters existed at the time of the publication of his book and that the number was constantly growing. The obligatory meeting days of this grade, Maundy Thursday, Easter Sunday and Shrove Tuesday, further suggest the Christian nature of the Rose Croix grade.[45]

This brings us to an important difference between Freemasonry and Rosicrucianism. Both may have shared the goal of creating an ideal society and used allegory and symbolism to communicate this goal to members, however, the myths and symbolism of Freemasonry and Rosicrucianism are quite distinct. The latter was definitely a Christian esoteric movement with no initial claims to an exotic Hermetic past such as those held by Freemasonry. Thus the blending of Rosicrucianism with Freemasonry often resulted in Christian forms of Freemasonry such as in the case of this Masonic Rose Croix grade.

Another mix of Freemasonry and Rosicrucianism emerged in the eighteenth century, this time in the form of a Masonic–Rosicrucian order, the *Gold-und Rosenkreuz* or the Order of the Golden and Rosy Cross. This was an alchemical brotherhood based on the structure of a Masonic lodge and its purpose was to:

> make effective the hidden forces of nature, to release nature's light which has become deeply buried beneath the dross resulting from the curse, and thereby to light within every brother a torch by whose light he will be able better to recognize the hidden God ... and thereby become more closely united with the original source of light.[46]

This aristocratic German pseudo-Masonic order developed elaborate rituals and was predominantly interested in practical and spiritual alchemy.[47] The fraternity had nine grades. The higher grades were closed to average members and reserved for near-superhuman secret chiefs. This concept of an esoteric society being headed and guided by extraordinary and unknown superiors appears to date from this period and its enduring appeal into the nineteenth century is exemplified by the Mahatmas of the Theosophical Society and the secret chiefs of the Golden Dawn.[48] It was also from the Golden and Rosy Cross that the *Soc. Ros.* and subsequently the Golden Dawn borrowed the names for their grades.

As Rosicrucianism spread its influence, its original message became more and more marginalized as the characteristics of the traditions with which it associated were assumed. The depiction of the secret wisdom at the basis of the Rosicrucian message was confused with the secret wisdom behind alchemy leading to the transmutation of gold or the elixir of life. The interpretation of Rosicrucianism as a component in the transmission of ancient knowledge dating back to biblical times became even more deeply entrenched. The call for change and reform that was central to the original Rosicrucian message was easily adopted by many causes and traditions. Those traditions that depended upon ritual and initiatory rites, such as Freemasonry and fringe occult societies, found Rosicrucianism ripe with symbolism and myth, features with which they could expand their own systems. As a result, 1888 saw the establishment of two Rosicrucian-style occult societies. In France, *l'Ordre Kabbalistique de la Rose Croix*, the Qabalistic Order of the Rosy Cross, was formed and of course, across the channel, Britain produced the Hermetic Order of the Golden Dawn. To appreciate the Rosicrucian influences on the Golden Dawn we must go back a few decades to 1865 and the establishment of the English Masonic–Rosicrucian order, the *Soc. Ros.* The society was founded by Freemason Robert Wentworth Little who adapted the grade structure used by the Order of the Golden and Rosy Cross from old rites he claimed to have discovered in the storerooms of Freemason's Hall.[49] Despite being only open to Master Masons, the society was not strictly a Masonic lodge. It focused on the study of esoteric subjects such as occultism, cabala and comparative symbolism and no oath was taken upon admission, 'it being contrary to the genius of a philosophical society', according to Kenneth Mackenzie in his entry on Rosicrucianism in his mammoth work *The Royal Masonic Cyclopaedia.*[50] Most scholars who have researched the *Soc. Ros.* agree that the society was Rosicrucian only in name. The activities of the small Masonic fraternity included quarterly meetings at which members worked some brief rituals, presented occasional lectures on a variety of esoteric topics, and held an annual dinner.[51] King claims that 'on the whole the early members of the Societas Rosicruciana were a second-rate lot, and with a few exceptions they seem to have had little knowledge of the inner nature and teachings of traditional Rosicrucianism'.[52] In his paper 'Christian Rosenkreuz and the Rosicrucians', Westcott writes that the *Soc. Ros.* was a Masonic body:

> composed of Freemasons who have gathered themselves together to study the old Rosicrucianism and the origins of Freemasonry, a connection which has been alleged to exist by many historians belonging to the outer world. The members of this Order, as such, make no claim to be in possession of the secret wisdom of the pupils of Christian Rosenkreuz ...[53]

While it is likely that the three founding chiefs of the Golden Dawn learned little of Rosicrucianism through their association with the *Soc. Ros.*, they no doubt acquired their knowledge of Rosicrucian myth and symbolism from other sources. The influence of Rosicrucianism on the writings of Westcott and in the entire basis of the Second Order rituals attests to this knowledge. Through the name of the *Soc. Ros.* itself, it is obvious that the Rosicrucian myth had survived into late nineteenth-century culture, as is demonstrated by some of the occult literature of the time. One book in particular was immensely influential on Westcott and MacGregor Mathers, both of whom make reference to it in their own work. This is the 1842 novel *Zanoni* by politician and novelist Edward Bulwer-Lytton who was falsely rumoured to have served as the Grand Patron of the *Soc. Ros.* in 1871. *Zanoni* features a Rosicrucian-type hero, from whom the title takes its name, who belongs to a secret and ancient society. Zanoni gives up his eternal life, obtained through the elixir of life, when he falls in love and abandons his immortality. The pretext of the novel is that a deciphered manuscript falls into the hands of the author after a discussion about Rosicrucians at an occult bookstore. The content of the novel was sufficiently Rosicrucian to convince both Westcott and MacGregor Mathers that Bulwer-Lytton possessed a wealth of occult knowledge and held some sort of connection with the real Rosicrucians. In 'Data of the History of the Rosicrucians', a paper published for the *Soc. Ros.* in 1916, Westcott claims that Bulwer-Lytton was initiated into a German Rosicrucian lodge at Frankfurt-on-the-Main, which fell into abeyance in 1850. Westcott surmised that Bulwer-Lytton drew from this experience in composing the Rosicrucian elements in *Zanoni* and in his other works.[54] This lodge was called *Zur aufgehenden Morgenröthe* (The Rising Dawn) and attracted young, progressive, wealthy, Jewish initiates who were attracted to the more social goals of the order.[55] In another article, 'The Rosicrucians, Past and Present, at Home and Abroad', Westcott reasserts Bulwer-Lytton's Rosicrucian adeptship despite Bulwer-Lytton's apparent dismissal of such a claim. Westcott states Bulwer-Lytton refused to admit his adeptship for 'public reasons'.[56] MacGregor Mathers, in the introduction to his book on Abramelin magic, claimed he was told that Bulwer-Lytton knew of the manuscript from which MacGregor Mathers made this translation and that Bulwer-Lytton had based his description of one of the Rosicrucian adepts in *Zanoni* on Abramelin.[57] Through *Zanoni* we see how the myth of an invisible brotherhood with the goal of doing good for mankind persisted from its seventeenth-century German origins into Victorian literary culture and myth. And regardless of the contradictory claims concerning the author's membership in various Rosicrucian societies, Bulwer-Lytton's involvement in occult circles in the mid-century is undeniable. His presence at a magical ritual in 1861 in which the French occultist Eliphas Lévi made an appearance, as apparently did the Pythagorean teacher and miracle worker from the first century CE, Apollonius of Tyana, is undisputed. We will look more closely at this evocation and the magical group responsible for it in the following chapter.

Despite the immense significance of *Zanoni* upon Victorian occultism, it did not stand alone as an influential literary work. Other books dealing with occult and esoteric subjects also carried great weight with members of the Golden Dawn, most of these however, were works of non-fiction.

It is possible to identify which books in particular by looking at the contents of the Golden Dawn's library. The William Wynn Westcott library was founded in 1891 and by 1897 was located in West Kensington, London. Golden Dawn initiate, Frederick Leigh Gardner, was the librarian at this time and produced a catalogue of the books contained in the library.[58] One of these books is very useful in its description and examination of Rosicrucianism and the role it played in Freemasonry. It is likely that many of the members of the Golden Dawn shared similar views of these two movements, as expressed in this book. *In the Pronaos of the Temple of Wisdom, Containing the History of the True and False Rosicrucians* was written by Franz Hartmann, who, in support of the theory earlier expressed, depicts the original Rosicrucians as a spiritual fraternity and not as a material or external organization of people. Interestingly, Hartmann deviates slightly from this belief that the original manifestos were meant to be allegorical. Hartmann sees the manifestos as works of sarcasm produced in response to a wave of superstition that was embracing seventeenth-century Germany with its pseudo-alchemists, astrologers and diviners. Yet Hartmann maintains that the manifestos appear to have been composed by a true Rosicrucian as they contain Rosicrucian principles.

> The whole object of these pamphlets seems to have been to present great truths to the ignorant, but to dish them up in a fictitious form, appealing to the curiosity of the people, and to the prevailing craving for a knowledge of the mysteries of Nature, which the majority of the people of these times wanted to know for the purpose of obtaining selfish and personal benefits.[59]

Hartmann then goes on to explain that those who wished to believe in a material and real society, managed in a fashion to bring such a society into existence. A renewed excitement about Rosicrucianism occurred with the establishment of the Rose Croix grade in French Masonry but Hartmann insists that those searching for true adepts among the members of this grade, would do so in vain as modern Masons had 'long ago lost the Word and will not find it again unless they dive below the surface of external ceremonies and seek for it in their own hearts'.[60] Hartmann condemns the subsequent Rosicrucian mania that erupted for its attraction of those wishing to learn forbidden secrets, including vagabonds and charlatans, to the very real Masonic fraternities. Here, Hartmann echoes eighteenth-century critiques of Freemasonry and Rosicrucianism. In 1797, John Robison, Professor of Natural Philosophy and secretary of the Royal Society of Edinburgh wrote that it was in

France and Italy that Masonic lodges first became the 'haunts of many projectors and fanatics'. He argues that Rosicrucians, not real ones, but rather a group of alchemists, took advantage of the existing Masonic structure and society:

> the Rosycrucian Lodges have always been considered by other Free Masons as bad Societies, and as gross schismatics. This did not hinder, however, their alchemical and medical secrets from being frequently introduced into the Lodges of simple Free Masonry; and in like manner, exorcism, or ghost-raising, magic, and other gross superstitions, were often held out in their meetings as attainable mysteries, which would be immense acquisitions to the Fraternity, without any necessity of admitting along with them the religious deliriums of the Rosicrucians.[61]

These examples demonstrate that the ability of Rosicrucianism to be readily assimilated into the structure of Freemasonry was clearly established and recognized.

As opposed to Bulwer-Lytton's fictional *Zanoni*, which offers a traditional, romanticized image of the Rosicrucian, Hartmann's non-fictional account offers an objective and reasonable nineteenth-century representation of the opinions held by those schooled and interested in occult subjects. The more sceptical and logical view that Hartmann offers of Masonic and Rosicrucian fraternities and how they have strayed from their original purposes is likely to be representative of the views held by Golden Dawn members. That these views were offered in a readily available library founded and run by the Golden Dawn makes it all the more likely that members were exposed to these notions, if they did not share them themselves. Both the ideals embodied by Rosicrucianism and Freemasonry, and the material realities as represented by nineteenth-century societies were no doubt obvious to Golden Dawn members. Indeed, so obvious that the reason for the establishment of the Order and the reason that many members joined was to lessen this gap between the ideal and the actual.

The influence of Rosicrucianism, both in its ideal and actual form, on Victorian occultism is evident in Westcott's writing and in the rituals of the Second Order. As we have seen, Westcott presented several papers to the *Soc. Ros.*, the Theosophical Society and to members of the Golden Dawn. Many of these papers dealt with Rosicrucianism, primarily the myth of Rosicrucianism as found in the original manifestos, and a Rosicrucian lineage through which contemporary Rosicrucian societies traced their origins to Christian Rosenkreuz, or even further to the source of the wisdom he acquired. In the original myth, Rosenkreuz acquired this knowledge in the East, and, as has been previously mentioned, Rosicrucianism differed from Freemasonry in that it did not claim its origins lay in the occult lore of ancient Egypt. Westcott's writings indicate that the original Rosicrucian myth had since expanded to include Egypt as its point of origin. He writes that Christian Rosenkreuz learned the esoteric doctrines of religion, philosophy and occult science from Arabian sages who inherited the culture of Alexandria.[62] Elsewhere, Westcott refers to Rosicrucianism as descending from Egyptian priests, Neoplatonists, Alexandrian Hermeticists, and Jewish and Christian cabalists.[63] Through these references, it is obvious that the late nineteenth-century occult interpretation of Rosicrucianism included an Egyptian and Hermetic heritage, something that was missing in the original manifestos. The Christian motif of Rosicrucianism also undergoes a transformation in Westcott's writing. He argues that what may appear as a Christian theme running through the Rosicrucian myth, is really a Gnostic one, a point upon which McIntosh elaborates in his modern study on Rosicrucianism.[64] McIntosh claims that Rosicrucian teaching is a late revival of Gnostic thought, the belief that the human spirit is trapped, living a half-life and made aware of this through the accumulation of knowledge which enables the trapped spirit to reunite with its real divine element.[65] As for the existence of Rosicrucian adepts, Westcott claims to have met one through the Theosophical Society, a society whose leader, Madame Blavatsky, he compares to Christian Rosenkreuz. Westcott's understanding of the underlying philosophy of Rosicrucianism is interesting, for while it may differ from that expressed in the original manifestos, it is indicative of his hopes in establishing the Golden Dawn.

> The Fraternity has, however, instructed its pledged members in the doctrine of human Reincarnation, has declared that the law of cause and effect acts in the spiritual, as well as in the physical world, that man has around him unseen beings related to elemental forces, that man is influenced by the Sun, Moon and Planets, and that special training and the use of certain personal Processes will in some students lead to supra-normal spiritual functions and a high form of clairvoyant faculty in the present life; provided that the body be duly cared for, the mind well cultured, and the highest morality preserved.[66]

Westcott is writing about a Rosicrucian fraternity here, but the description is easily applied to the Golden Dawn. This indicates that his aspirations for the Order were, in part, Rosicrucian in nature. Another interesting insight garnered from a reading of Westcott's writings on

Rosicrucianism, is the view held by the Golden Dawn on the Victorian phenomenon of spiritualism. The Order's view distinctly sets itself apart from spiritualism. One of the earlier documents made available for the information of candidates included the following claim:

> The Chiefs of the Order do not care to accept as Candidates any persons accustomed to submit themselves as Mediums to the Experiments of Hypnotism, Mesmerism; or who habitually allow themselves to fall into a complete Passive Condition of Will; also they disapprove of the methods made use of as a rule in such experiments.[67]

This negative view of spiritualism is echoed in Westcott's 'Man, Miracle and Magic', a lecture read to the members of the Isis-Urania Temple. In this paper he positions the spiritualistic medium in opposition to the Rosicrucian:

> He (the Rosicrucian) is living trained vital energy illumined by the Spiritual above; the Medium is a negative being, the prey of every evil influence, and of anyone with malign passion: he is deceiving and self deceived, the catspaw of every elemental force, and baneful misdirected energy.[68]

This contrast of the Rosicrucian with the medium points to the kind of occultist or student the Golden Dawn wished to attract. Clearly, the perceived image of the Rosicrucian was the character with which the Order chose to identify itself and its students.

This identification with Rosicrucianism extended to the rituals of both the First and Second Orders of the Golden Dawn. The names of the ten grades of the Order corresponded almost exactly with those of the *Soc. Ros.*, the exception being that the Golden Dawn had an extra first grade (neophyte) while the *Soc. Ros.* began its grades with zelator. While it has been shown that the *Soc. Ros.* was not very Rosicrucian, it is still significant that the founders of the Golden Dawn chose to associate, through the naming of its degrees, with an esoteric society that perceived itself to be somewhat Rosicrucian. The rituals of the Second Order are where the Golden Dawn relies upon original Rosicrucianism as revealed in the seventeenth-century manifestos. This intended association with Rosicrucianism is evident in the very name of the Second Order, the *Rosae Rubeae et Aureae Crucis*, or the Rose of Ruby and the Cross of Gold. The Second Order rituals were based around the myth of the finding of the tomb of Christian Rosenkreuz.

The vault is the primary feature of the adeptus minor ritual where the initiate comes face to face with the corpse of Rosenkreuz in the form of either MacGregor Mathers or Westcott. As in the *Fama*, the vault was seven-sided and was elaborately decorated with various occult symbols and colours. The ceiling decoration continued the Rosicrucian theme with a depiction of a rose with 22 petals (esoterically significant as the number of letters in the Hebrew alphabet, the number of tarot trumps, and the number of paths on the tree of life).[69] On the floor was another rose, this one red, placed in the centre of a gold cross. The final rose was to be found on the altar, set upon a black cross. This rose and cross theme was continued throughout the decoration of the vault.[70] Another way in which Rosicrucian symbolism was appropriated by the Golden Dawn, was in the form of the magical instrument, the Rose Cross Lamen. All members had to make their own, based upon this Rosicrucian image of a rose placed upon a cross.

The Order used both Rosicrucian mythology and symbolism in its rituals, teaching, and physical surroundings. The founders were responsible for incorporating these influences and they learned this myth and symbolism through the form of Rosicrucianism that had emerged in the nineteenth century. This form consisted of Masonic and other occult appropriations of the original Rosicrucian myth and it was characterized by certain Masonic additions, a newly acquired Egyptian past and a Gnostic interpretation. Another important contribution to nineteenth-century Rosicrucianism came from a variety of literary depictions such as that found in *Zanoni*. This Rosicrucianism, which the Golden Dawn went on to add to its magical system had already been synthesized to some degree through its acceptance and use by the esoteric and occult world since its arrival in intellectual history in the early seventeenth century.

This earlier synthesis can also be seen in the actual beginnings of the occult revival of late Victorian Britain and the seemingly inconsequential *Soc. Ros.* While this society has already been dismissed to some degree as an Old Boys' club characterized by ineffective Rosicrucian pretensions and an annual roast dinner, it was from this innocuous group that a smaller faction developed, focused more on the occultism we eventually see practised in the Golden Dawn. This group is likely to have emerged in the mid-1840s and included prominent mid-century occultists such as Kenneth Mackenzie, Richard James Morrison, Francis Irwin and his son Herbert.[71] Morrison was heavily involved in the British revival of astrology in the nineteenth century and was responsible for beginning an astrological almanac under his pen name Zadkiel. It was in his 1870 edition of *Zadkiel's Almanac* that the goals of this new occult society were announced. The group hoped to 'resuscitate in England, and spread through Europe, India and America – The Most Ancient Order of the Suastica; or The Brotherhood of the Mystic Cross'.[72] The order appeared to have little success until in 1873 Francis Irwin developed its principles and created a more influential occult society, the Brotherhood of Light or the *Fratres Lucis*. Irwin received the rituals for this organization through the process of crystal gazing, or scrying. He was contacted through the crystal by the spirit of the legendary Count Cagliostro who assured Irwin that the original *Fratres Lucis* was established in fourteenth-century Florence and over the years had included such illustrious members as Ficino, Emmanuel Swedenborg, Franz Anton Mesmer and Cagliostro himself. The goal of this society was the study and practice of cabala, natural magic, mesmerism, astrology, alchemy and several other occult interests. Irwin attracted initiates including Mackenzie and some of his other esoteric colleagues, namely Frederick Hockley and Benjamin Cox.[73]

From the *Fratres Lucis* descends one more branch on the tree of historical development of British occultism. In 1883, another seemingly inconsequential secret order, the Society of Eight, was established. This order was focused primarily on the study of alchemy and was made up of members of the *Fratres Lucis,* including Irwin, Hockley, Mackenzie and Cox. The others were chemist and founder of the society, Frederick Holland, John Yarker, Westcott and perhaps the Reverend W.A. Ayton.[74] With these latter two we start to see the obvious connection between these earlier occult societies and the Golden Dawn. We also see how the interests of fringe Masonic and pseudo-Rosicrucian societies were refined, propagated and further synthesized through these various manifestations. This relationship is made even more obvious when MacGregor Mathers takes Hockley's place in the Society of Eight upon the latter's death. It is not until 1884 and the establishment of yet another occult society, the Hermetic Brotherhood of Luxor, however, that we see the direct relationship between an earlier society's curriculum and that of the Golden Dawn.

The Hermetic Brotherhood of Luxor was founded in 1884 by Peter Davidson and officially announced to the British public on the last page of a Hermetic text published by Robert Fryar of Bath:

Students of the Occult Science, searchers after truth and Theosophists who may have been disappointed in their expectations of Sublime Wisdom being freely dispensed by Hindoo Mahatmas, are cordially invited to send in their names to the Editor of this Work, when, if found suitable, can be admitted, after a short probationary term, as members of an Occult Brotherhood, who do not boast of their knowledge or attainments, but teach freely and without reserve all they find worthy to receive.[75]

The Brotherhood seems to have set a suitable precedent for Golden Dawn study in that it offered instruction in practical occultism according to a set canon of texts and manuscripts available to initiates. The Hermetic Brotherhood of Luxor differed from the Golden Dawn, however, in that initiates could go it alone, carrying out their own initiations and instruction through mail order. As for the fraternity's initiations, they very possibly involved drugs, either hashish or opium, contained in a pill and conveniently provided through one's mail order request.

Another significant deviation from Golden Dawn initiation and instruction involved the content of the esoteric teachings. While the actual readings were nothing extraordinary, there was an emphasis within the Brotherhood's instruction upon sexual matters and the cultivation of spiritual and physical benefits through the medium of sex. The society proved to be hugely influential and its practices were adopted throughout occult circles in Britain and France. When scandal struck the Brotherhood, many of the more respectable British members left, including Ayton and probably Westcott, providing the perfect opportunity for the Golden Dawn to fill an obvious esoteric need.[76] As we will see, this coincided with the demise of charismatic esoteric leader Anna Kingsford and her British Hermetic organization, making the Golden Dawn's arrival even more opportune.

In examining the influences of Freemasonry and Rosicrucianism on Victorian magic, the topic of Egyptian religion, ritual and magic has surfaced several times either in the names of many of the orders or in the rituals of these societies. What are known as the Egyptian mystery religions (technically Greek and Roman mystery religions that appropriated Egyptian deities, ritual and symbolism) had an enormous effect on the myths and structures of both Rosicrucianism and Freemasonry and thus upon Victorian occultism itself.

The Egyptian influence upon nineteenth-century occultism comes in two forms that may be discussed independently, but should be understood as closely related. Both Egyptian magic and Egyptian mystery religions have different histories of development and different collections of literature arising from such development. Both have also played a significant role in shaping Western magic. Traditionally, those interested in ancient and hidden knowledge have long looked to Egypt, its ancient and glorious culture and civilization being the inspiration for its exalted status. This interest in and reverence for Egyptian culture dates back to the ancient Greeks and their perception of Egypt as the source of all learning. In the third century CE, Clement of Alexandria wrote that Egypt was the 'mother of magicians'. In the sixteenth century, Giordano Bruno held the theory that the oldest and truest religion was the magic of ancient Egypt.

The practice of magic in ancient Egypt is most notable for its complete lack of marginalization, a process from which it seems magic has been unable to escape ever since. An established political and cultural institution, ritual magic in ancient Egypt was endorsed by the state for at least three thousand years.[77] Textual evidence exists for the practice of magic in ancient Egypt spanning four and a half thousand years.[78] Part of the reason for magic's established and enduring position in Egyptian culture was its close relationship with Egyptian religion. The Egyptian deities themselves were believed to practise magic. Isis was the goddess most commonly associated with it, one of the epithets commonly used in reference to her being 'Great of Magic'.[79] Thoth was the deity credited with the invention of magic as well as that of writing and he went on to become associated with Hermes Trismegistus, the supposed author of many of the esoteric Greek texts composed in Egypt between the first and fourth centuries CE that make up the Hermetic corpus. As for the nature of the magic practised by the ancient Egyptians, this was demonic, involving the invocation of all kinds of spirits including those of the underworld. Any distinction between demonic and natural magic may not be applicable in ancient Egypt, however, as commerce with spirits of the underworld and raising the dead, a practice that was also apparently quite legal, were not associated with any form of moral corruption. Necromancy and the conjuring of spirits from the Egyptian hell may have been perceived as dangerous, but not wrong.[80]

The most prominent features of Egyptian magic were its emphasis upon language and image. As previously stated, most of the sources for Egyptian magic were textual, a form that encapsulates both of these aspects, making the language of magic visual, a process which in itself must have appeared as magical, as would the ability to interpret these visual images as spoken words. Other significant aspects of Egyptian magic include a belief in the creative power of words and images to summon gods and other spirits. This is an important aspect in examining the influence of Egyptian magic on Victorian occultism. The power of the spoken word and of symbolism is central in nineteenth-century magic. Colour also held an important place in Egyptian magic, as did names. Part of the goal of the Egyptian magician was to reveal the true nature of beings and objects and the connections that they may or may not share through their colour and through the sound of their names.[81]

References to the magical power of words and names proliferate throughout nineteenth-century books on Egypt. A survey of the literature from this era, namely texts and authors familiar to Golden Dawn initiates, shows that the power of the spoken word was the recognized key feature of Egyptian magic. In the Hibbert Lectures, P. Le Page Renouf, a scholar whose work influenced Florence Farr, claims that belief in the magical power of words was the source of 'a frightful amount of superstition' in ancient Egyptian religion.[82] Another author referred to by Farr, Lewis Spence, in his *Myths and Legends of Ancient Egypt*, discusses 'right speaking', which, in Egyptian magic, is a process whereby once a magician had successfully carried out a spell, he was careful to repeat it exactly in similar tone and circumstances when he wished to execute the same spell again.[83] In these spells, words of power were often names of gods and other supernatural beings. They were not merely the common names, but special names that gave those who knew them power over that particular god. The renowned Victorian Egyptologist E.A. Wallis Budge, whose works were in the Westcott library and are referred to in Farr's manuscripts, wrote about the power channelled through language as fundamental to both Egyptian magic and religion.[84] The power lay not merely in specific names and words, but also in nonsensical sounds strung together in invocations. Another late nineteenth-century text addresses this form of magical utterance. Alfred Wiedemann, in his *Religion of the Ancient Egyptians*, claims that some of these nonsensical sounds were originally names and titles of foreign gods. Wiedemann goes on to state, however, that generally the invocation was 'a string of syllables apparently utterly destitute of meaning, but which sounded mysterious and incomprehensible and was on that account credited with all the greater significance.'[85] The goal of this string of nonsense was to express the secret name of a god who would then be bound to do the will of the magician.

The main texts through which Egyptian magic was transmitted in the nineteenth century are the *Book of the Dead* and the Graeco-Egyptian magical papyri. The former is a group of funerary spells collected from three different periods of Egypt's history, spanning the years 1540 to 332 BCE. The book contains practical advice and magical assistance for surviving in the afterlife. For example, some spells concern how to prevent one from forgetting one's name, how to protect oneself from crocodiles and snakes in the hereafter, how to transform the deceased into various forms, and what names should be used to pass through the gates of the afterlife.[86] The *Book of the Dead* has remained one of the most popular esoteric texts since the time of its first publication in English by Budge, the Keeper of Egyptian Antiquities at the British Museum in 1901. This work has since been continually reprinted.

The Graeco-Egyptian magical papyri had more of an impact on the mid- to late decades of the nineteenth century and were more influential upon Victorian occultism. These texts, dating from the first century BCE to the fifth century CE, represent more of an 'international school of magic' owing to their late emergence and use of Greek, Egyptian, Jewish, Persian, Babylonian, Gnostic and Christian language and symbolism. They are, however, based upon precedents established in earlier Egyptian magic such as identification with gods, invocation of the dead, protective amulets, and the invocation of gods through the use of secret names. One of these spells has already been examined in the previous chapter, concerning the invocation of one's higher genius in which the magician actually becomes the invoked deity. The magical spells contained within the Graeco-Egyptian papyri differ from earlier Egyptian magic in that they are concerned with material and personal gain for the magician, such as sexual pleasure, increase in finances and social success, whereas the earlier Egyptian spells were more concerned with protection or healing.[87] This presents a comparison of the magic of the Graeco-Egyptian papyri with that found in many medieval *grimoires*. This comparison is furthered by the introduction in these papyri, of the earliest explicit instruction in necromancy, or the exploitation of the dead for private magic.

Some of the spells documented in the Graeco-Egyptian papyri outline divination techniques that are similar to those used in a form of magic for which Egyptian priests were renowned, theurgy. Theurgy is one of the murkiest areas of magic, of which much remains unknown. It is generally agreed, however, that theurgy involves personal union with the divine achieved through ritual and through the summoning of divine visions or manifestations. The theurgic technique to induce a trance-like state described in the Graeco-Egyptian papyri, but not for the purpose of summoning the divine, rather for the more mundane purpose of material and personal gain, is consistent with the nature of the magical goals of the papyri.[88]

The Neoplatonists provide some of the most important textual sources on theurgy. Iamblichus, writing in the fourth century CE, presents much of the little information available on theurgy. Iamblichus is also significant because of the influence that his work continued to wield in the nineteenth century. Westcott's library contained the major works of both Iamblichus and Porphyry, along with several other texts containing commentaries on the Neoplatonists.[89] In her later Egyptian work, Florence Farr frequently refers to Iamblichus. Earlier on, in the middle of the nineteenth century, Charles Wycliffe Goodwin compares Iamblichus' conclusions on theurgy with the contents of the Graeco-Egyptian papyrus, which he translated and published in 1852 and with which both MacGregor Mathers and Farr were so familiar. In *On the Mysteries of Egypt* or *De mysteriis Aegyptiorum*, Iamblichus describes the art of theurgy in a defence of the magical art. Iamblichus believed that theurgy, the process of divine inspiration or manifestation, involves the actual possession of the human individual by a divine spirit. This possession is often a visible phenomenon.

> The principal thing in the evoking of a spirit is that the spirit is seen coming down and entering into an individual ... and he is mystically persuaded and governed by it. The form of fire is seen by the recipient before the receiving of the spirit, and sometimes, either when the god is descending or when he is withdrawing himself, it becomes visible to all the Beholders.[90]

Iamblichus describes this possession as being manipulated by the divinity and the inspired individual as merely a passive recipient whose imagination is made use of by the divinity through the imposition of visions.[91] All of this was part of Iamblichus's belief that the human soul was essentially corrupted through its descent into the physical world. The soul's only opportunity to return to its pure state through ascension and unite with the divine was through theurgy and, therefore, this divine experience was not exclusive to the elite but rather something attainable for anyone who carried out the appropriate ritual.[92] In remembering that Iamblichus was defending theurgy, his emphasis upon the complete domination of the divinity is a logical position in clearing the individual against any charges of magic. Theurgy becomes a divine art and not a magical art in this Neoplatonic garb. Because of the paucity of information available on theurgy prior to the Neoplatonists, it is difficult to discern how much this Neoplatonic spin changes any original definition or practice of theurgy as it existed in ancient Egypt. However, this basic understanding of theurgy as a process through which the summoning of a divinity or spirit involves the possession of the magician by that divinity or spirit is one that persists in Victorian occultism. The primary differences being that the Victorian magician is allotted much more control in this process and that the occultist's imagination, far from being passive, is the controlling factor.

Neoplatonism did not only influence the future perception of Egyptian magic in the form of theurgy, but it also played an important role in the transmission and interpretation of mystery religions. This is the second form of Egyptian influence upon Victorian magic. Egyptian mystery religions are really Hellenistic appropriations of Egyptian myth superimposed upon the framework of the Greek and Roman mystery religions. From the fourth century BCE, when the Greeks came into contact with Egyptian culture, they gave special prominence to two Egyptian deities, Isis and Osiris. Isis became the most popular of the Egyptian gods. Initially she was worshipped in Athens unofficially and by foreigners in the form of a cult.[93] By the end of the third century BCE, the cult of Isis achieved official public status and grew steadily until the middle of the first century BCE, attracting worshippers from the wealthier classes in Athens.[94] By the Hellenistic period, the worship of Isis and Osiris was well established in one form or another among both the Greeks and Romans. In Roman times the most frequent form of this worship was expressed not in the original cults of these gods, but in the Graeco-Roman mysteries based on them.[95] These mysteries opened up the earlier cults by admitting both men and women, regardless of social rank.[96] The resulting cults and rituals to arise from this are important in this examination, as it is in the rites of Isis and in the orders dedicated to Osiris the Saviour that we see expressed the Egyptian interests of certain Victorian occultists.

Mystery religions are rituals of initiation into a cult. They tend to have three main components: an ordeal, revelation of the secrets of the mystery, and an oath to keep this newly acquired knowledge secret. The ordeal frequently includes some sort of symbolic death of the initiate and subsequent rebirth. The symbols used in association with the death aspect could involve the setting for initiation. It could either take place in a dark environment, such as in a cave or in a forest, or at night. The ordeal may involve physically harming or humiliating the initiate. This was done to prepare the initiate for the revelations to follow. According to Walter Burkert in his *Ancient Mystery Cults*, this 'unsettling experience has the effect of shaking the foundations of personality and making it ready to accept new identities'.[97] Most ancient mystery cults, however, chose to prepare the initiate in another, less harmful way, through ritual purification. The revelation imparted to the initiate was generally of a divine nature and intended to produce a spiritual change in the initiate as he, or she, was admitted to a privileged elite whose members all share in this secret. The final component of initiation into the mystery was the taking of an oath to keep its secrets from the uninitiated.

Mystery religions were a form of personal religion embarked upon through personal choice at the instigation of the individual. Initiation, however, did not mean adherence to a specific religious tradition. There was no demarcation of one religion against another; the various forms of worship were not exclusive but rather appeared as variations on one form of ancient religion.[98]

Owing to the necessarily secretive nature of mystery religions, it is difficult to know what actually went on during initiation ceremonies, apart from the vague understanding that there was an ordeal, a revelation and an oath. One thing we do know about the cult of Isis is that its rituals required a house or temple because of the tradition in Egyptian cults in which the divinity was believed to reside within statues.[99] This is interesting when speculating that the ritual may have involved the animation of these statues by the divinity, or even, in a theurgic spirit, the animation of those taking part in the ritual. This speculation was one held by MacGregor Mathers and his wife in their re-enactment of the rites of Isis in Paris, and the account we have of one observer attests to this animation.

The earliest account of what took place during mystery religion rituals is provided in the second-century Roman novel, *The Golden Ass*, by Apuleius. The main character, a young man named Lucius, is initiated into both the mysteries of Isis and Osiris at the end of his trying travels in the form of an ass, into which he had been magically transformed. He has a visit from the goddess herself in a dream and she informs him that she will help him transform back into a man and in return, he must dedicate himself to her through initiation into her mysteries. While Lucius is waiting for his initiation, this is what he has to say about the approaching ceremony:

> For the keys of hell and the guarantee of salvation were in the hands of the goddess, and the initiation ceremony itself took the form of a kind of voluntary death and salvation through divine grace. Such as might be safely entrusted with the great secrets of our religion, when they had passed through life and stood on the threshold of darkness, these the power of the goddess was wont to select and when they had been as it were reborn return to them a new lifespan.[100]

Other aspects revealed are that the ceremony was an expensive one for which the initiate was responsible; a priest read to the initiate from books written in unknown characters, telling him what the initiate needed to purchase for the ceremony; the initiate had to abstain from 'pleasures of the table' and animal flesh and wine for ten days; the initiate was bathed and purified by the attending priest; and finally, on the day of initiation, people came with gifts when the initiate, dressed in a linen robe, was conducted into the innermost part of the temple's sanctuary by the priest.[101] As for what follows, Lucius, would only reveal so much to the uninitiated reader.

> I dare say, attentive reader, that you are all agog to know what was then said and done. I should tell you if it were lawful to tell it... But since it may be that your anxious yearning is piously motivated, I will not torment you by prolonging your anguish. Listen then, but believe; for what I tell you is the truth. I came to the boundary of death and after treading Proserpine's threshold I returned having traversed all the elements; at midnight I saw the sun shining with brilliant light; I approached the gods below and the gods above face to face and worshipped them in their actual presence. Now I have told you what, though you have heard it, you cannot know. So all that can without sin be revealed to the understanding of the uninitiated, that and no more I shall relate.[102]

After being initiated into the mysteries of Isis, Lucius appeared the following morning in 12 richly decorated robes, and a three-day celebration commenced.

This was not the end of Lucius' experience with mystery religions. He was informed by Isis that he was to be initiated again, this time into the mysteries of Osiris. The author here offers a humorous glimpse at the predicament in which this favour of the gods places Lucius. He has to sell his wardrobe in order to afford this second initiation. The preparations were similar to those for Isis but the ceremony, however, was different. 'Though the nature and cult of the two deities were closely connected, indeed one and the same, yet the process of initiation was quite different.'[103]

A third and final initiation comes a little later. It would appear that Lucius is determined that this be his last call for initiation as he goes well over the advised ten days for fasting and splurges on the lavishness of provisions for the ceremony. This third initiation is indeed the last, and Lucius credits the rest of his life's success to the favour he has received from the gods.

All of the elements of an initiation ceremony are found here. The element of purification is present in the fasting and cleansing prior to initiation. Another aspect representative of the ordeal component is

Lucius' having come face to face with the gods above and below, an event that was no doubt glorious yet terrible. The element of a symbolic death is referred to specifically by Lucius, as quoted above, as a voluntary death and salvation, and in his claim that he came to the threshold of Proserpine, a Greek goddess associated with the underworld. The element of revelation is implied by his account of seeing the sun at midnight; undoubtedly a metaphor for the light of knowledge or of the divine, piercing the darkness of ignorance and of the uninitiated. The final component of an oath to secrecy is also present here, with Lucius describing at great length how he is forbidden to reveal anything of the mysteries themselves.

This is all we can glean from the description of the mysteries of Isis and Osiris provided by Apuleius in *The Golden Ass*. As a work of fiction, it may be questioned what merit this description holds as historical evidence. Fritz Graf, in his study of Theocritus' *Pharmakeutriai*, a third-century BCE narrative involving the use of magical ritual, offers this answer. He concludes that while the *Pharmakeutriai* offers no authority on the history of magical rites, 'it testifies to the imaginary world of magic'.[104] Graf also justifies the importance of the text in that it demonstrates what magic represented to Theocritus and his contemporaries.[105] *The Golden Ass* offers the same opportunity. At the very least, this story offers a second-century perspective of the common perception of mystery religions. It provides insight into what was understood to take place during initiation into the mysteries of Isis and Osiris: purification, lavish preparations, a secret ritual involving union with the divine, and a symbolic death and rebirth. Apuleius' fictional account reflects the curiosity of the uninitiated and describes the appropriate atmosphere of mystery that shrouded these ceremonies. Through the silliness of the situation in which Lucius finds himself, due to the numerous initiations that Isis and Osiris command him to go through, and through the many references to the cost of preparations, this account also suggests that there may have existed suspicion that these mysteries had some sort of profit-making agenda, or that the mysteries were perceived as expensive assurances to those lacking conviction that they had the blessing of the gods. This is the earliest account of a mystery religion initiation and its discernible components are those to which later initiatory esoteric societies, such as the Freemasons, the pseudo-Rosicrucians and their offshoots, remain true.

As mentioned before, Neoplatonism had a role to play in the transmission and shaping of mystery religions. The Neoplatonists took the format of the mystery religion and assimilated it to Gnostic myth to produce an understanding of mystery religions as a ritually guided experience of the reunion of the soul with the divine. This interpretation spread throughout Europe, surviving through the Middle Ages, until it was reinterpreted yet again in the Renaissance revival of Neoplatonism.[106] Thus there is yet another similarity between mystery religions and the Rosicrucian movement, both in the manifestos and in the ensuing popular reaction they created. For, as discussed earlier, the Rosicrucian myth has been interpreted as based upon Gnostic mythology. Both Rosicrucianism and mystery religions provide adequate structures for the imposition of Gnostic symbolism.

The transmission of Egyptian ritual and magic was facilitated during the early modern period by the assimilation of certain aspects of mystery religions by the growing number of secret societies devoted to uncovering the mysteries of Rosicrucianism and Freemasonry. The same aspects of initiation are all present in many of these fraternities and there is an obvious effort made by such societies to make a connection with the mother country of magic, Egypt. It was not until the late eighteenth century however that Freemasonry and Egypt were so firmly wedded through the legendary Count Cagliostro's Egyptian Rite of Freemasonry. Claiming to have discovered the pure form of Freemasonry, Cagliostro sought to spread its true message which was reunification with the divine.[107] Cagliostro's Egyptian Rite served to highlight the Egyptian ingredients in the already extraordinary concoction of fringe Masonic activities.

It remains to be shown how Egyptian magic and the mystery religions of Isis and Osiris compare to the 'Egyptian' rites developed by Victorian occultists. In compiling their rituals MacGregor Mathers and Farr drew from different sources. The rituals of Osiris the Saviour and those of the Order of Great Osiris the Saviour, are still very much in the vein of Masonic ritual structure as found in the First Order rituals of the Golden Dawn. The Egyptian influence is found primarily in the language of the rituals, specifically in the use of the names of Egyptian gods and in the basic employment of Egyptian mythology. Where the rituals resemble mystery religion initiations, it is arguable, and much more logical, that these resemblances occur because the Masonic rituals on which they are based resemble mystery religions.

The Rites of Isis devised by MacGregor Mathers are a different matter. It is possible that his extensive research resulted in his having left behind almost entirely the Masonic framework upon which the Golden Dawn was based in these new Egyptian rites. In the description of MacGregor Mathers' rites provided by André Gaucher (see Chapter 2),

MacGregor Mathers told the narrator that there were two types of rites, one open to the uninitiated and one closed.[108] Gaucher convinced MacGregor Mathers to let him attend the rites for the initiated. What he witnessed was a meeting of men and women in long, multi-coloured robes in a room decorated with flowers and featuring a veiled statue of Isis. MacGregor Mathers and his wife played the roles of priest and priestess and lit incense at the feet of the statue while scattering wheat and flour. The statue of Isis came to life followed by the animation of a statue of Osiris. In the nightmarish and frightening moments that ensued, Gaucher claimed to have seen the faces of several gods including those of Horus and Anubis in the statue of Osiris.[109] Gaucher was quite frightened by all of this and apparently passed out. MacGregor Mathers was evidently aware that ancient Egyptian magic involved the animation of statues of the gods. This may even be what was perceived as happening during mystery religions when the initiate supposedly came face to face with the gods and goddesses.

Farr, on the other hand, merely imposed what little she garnered from reading the *Book of the Dead*, several other nineteenth-century texts on Egyptian civilization and some Graeco-Egyptian papyri, upon an already existent framework, established through her membership in the Golden Dawn.[110] So we see that the influence of Egyptian magic and mystery religions upon the Golden Dawn was most obvious in the rituals that members went on to create after their association with the Order. This influence was felt in varying degrees and was the result of different factors. Farr was much more influenced by the popular nineteenth-century trend favouring Egyptology and the archaeological discoveries that were happening at the time she was setting up her Egyptian orders. MacGregor Mathers, on the other hand, while no doubt encouraged in his interest in Egyptian ritual by the popularity it was enjoying culturally and academically, strove to establish his rites in authenticity, seeking not merely to impose Egyptian myth upon the current ritual structure, but to rediscover Egyptian ritual itself. In doing so he radically altered the structure and format of the rituals to which he had become accustomed in the Golden Dawn.

Egyptian magic and ritual, Rosicrucianism, and Freemasonry all helped to shape the development of Victorian occultism. Freemasonry, arguably, had the most direct influence in that the original notion of Freemasonry can be seen to progress historically from its sixteenth-century origins into the late nineteenth century. MacGregor Mathers, Westcott and Woodman were all Freemasons and the rituals in which they took part would no doubt be recognizable to Freemasons of the late sixteenth and early seventeenth centuries. In the composition of the Golden Dawn's First Order, and to a lesser degree, the Second Order rituals, MacGregor Mathers and Westcott were firmly establishing their society within a Masonic tradition of ritual.

Rosicrucianism has a less tangible connection, but was not less influential because of this. There was no direct historical progression from the publication of the first manifestos in the seventeenth century to the founding of the Golden Dawn. This is primarily because the manifestos themselves were ideas in suspension, grounded only in their published format with no society or individuals to whom they could be attached. The resulting creation of Rosicrucian fraternities out of the manifestos is where we must look for tangible evidence of a Rosicrucian influence upon the Golden Dawn. Freemasonry was the ideal receptacle for Rosicrucian myth and symbolism and the outcome of that absorption can be found, to some degree, in the *Soc. Ros.* Unlike its seemingly passive assimilation of Masonic ritual, the Golden Dawn intentionally implemented Rosicrucian elements into its magic and ritual, primarily in its use of the Rosicrucian myth and symbolism in the Second Order, the *Rosae Rubeae et Aureae Crucis*. The Rosicrucian influence upon Victorian occultism is one which was sought out and encouraged by the magicians themselves, namely MacGregor Mathers. There is a similar case with Egyptian magic and ritual.

Egyptian magic and ritual have been continually assimilated throughout history from their fourth-century BCE Greek appropriation, through their Hellenistic interpretation as mystery religions, and their Renaissance revival through Hermeticism, right up to their nineteenth-century re-appropriation. Throughout those various assimilations and interpretations much has been lost and gained. What has remained constant has been the geographical placement of Egypt as the source of esoteric wisdom. In the form of mystery religions, Egyptian magic survived to influence the structure and function of later esoteric societies. As we have seen, Mithraism was not an actual predecessor of Freemasonry in any direct historical sense. It was, however, an earlier expression of the same ideas of fraternity, initiation, revelation and secrecy that are found within Freemasonry. The same holds true for the Egyptian mystery religions. The elements of initiation, ordeal, the acquisition of secret knowledge and an oath of secrecy were all part of most nineteenth-century esoteric societies. The mystery religions are the earliest examples of rituals involving the revelation of secret knowledge. They set a precedent to which future ritual-makers referred and, thus, we have Egyptian elements in the symbolism, myth and ritual of the

Freemasons and subsequently, of Victorian occultists. The influence of and interest in Egyptian magic increased in the late nineteenth and early twentieth centuries and this growth was associated with contemporaneous archaeological and textual advances in the field of Egyptology. Therefore, there are two sources of influence of Egyptian magic and ritual, one through the historical transmission fraught with reinterpretation and assimilation as part of Western magical and esoteric traditions, and the other through more recent scholarship with a direct link to the past.

Victorian magic was dependent on these three traditions of ritual and myth. The founders of the Golden Dawn were all members of societies that embraced and employed the myths and symbolism of all three. In the case of Freemasonry, its structure and ritual were direct ancestors to those of the Golden Dawn while, in the case of Rosicrucianism and Egyptian ritual, the founders looked to the nineteenth-century ideas of these traditions as they had been formulated throughout history. These three traditions, however, were not exclusive of each other and Freemasonry assimilated the myth and symbolism of the other two in its expansion into Hermeticism, Neoplatonism and other esoteric traditions. This passive reception of Rosicrucianism and Egyptian magic through the vehicle of Freemasonry has also been shown to be just one of the ways in which these traditions influenced Victorian magic. Members of occult societies also actively sought out the details of these traditions in their creation of new rituals both at home and abroad.

The Renaissance provided Victorian magic with the first wave of occult syncretism through the literary work of Ficino, Pico, Reuchlin and Agrippa. The second wave came in the form of Freemasonry as it carried on the work that began in the Renaissance, introducing Rosicrucianism and re-introducing other elements such as Egyptian myth and symbolism. If we are to use the metaphor of waves for these first two, then what Victorian occultists went on to produce was a deluge. They took what was provided from these first two, added some components of their own, and created something entirely daring and new, a school for practising magicians.

This chapter has dealt primarily with traditions and institutions. We must now put a face to these influences and take a close look at the men and women responsible for the creation of Victorian magic.

4
Preservation and Improvisation: Nineteenth-Century Magicians

The hierarchical and ritual nature of secret societies and the supernatural setting of the spiritualists provided the perfect ingredients for the development and nurturing of Victorian occultism. The formulation of its doctrines was deeply entwined with a reliance and reinterpretation of other esoteric and marginal traditions. As a product of its time, *fin-de-siècle* magic was subject to the literary, philosophical, political and religious influences of the era. Nineteenth-century thought was fundamentally affected by the rising popularity of secularization and science and Victorian occultism was no exception. Nineteenth-century people were necessarily having to deal with an understanding of themselves both as individuals independent of the determinism implicit in the Christian understanding of creation, and as individuals who were progressively becoming superior to all that came before.

Two seemingly opposed systems of thought rose to prominence in the second half of the nineteenth century. Victorian Britain witnessed the curious blend of scientific naturalism and the belief in magic. The doctrine of the former maintained that belief in any non-physical agencies was superstitious and indicative of a culturally dysfunctional society. Naturalist thinkers wished to establish a scientifically directed culture and to eradicate religious belief entirely. The doctrine of the latter sought to establish, within the natural world and governed by natural laws, the mystery and spirituality traditionally associated with religious and magical thinking. Both arose from a growing disillusionment with Christianity and from advancement in scientific methodology.[1] The result of this disillusionment was exemplified in the scientific naturalism popularized by leading scientific figures such as Thomas Huxley and John Tyndall. These naturalist thinkers opposed the authoritarianism of organized Christianity and objected to clerical involvement in the scientific world. Tyndall and his colleagues were quite vocal in condemning the seemingly supernatural pursuits of spiritualism and occultism. Their outright rejection of religion and spirituality was but one response to the growing tension between religion and science. This response was not only characteristic of scientific naturalists but also proved to be that of a radical segment of the working-class. Another response, embraced by a more moderate majority, sought a reconciliation of the new scientific methodology with religious ideals and aspirations. While traditional Christianity had proved to be too limited for the changing Victorian intellect, this new science was proving to be too restrictive in its exclusion of subjective experience. While many scientists incorporated developments in their field with their religious beliefs, adopting a non-literal interpretation of certain biblical texts questioned by these scientific developments, others opposed scientific naturalism for the very reasons they rejected religion. Both proved to be too narrow for the ongoing redefinition of the role of the individual.

Belonging to this more moderate majority was also a growing number of individuals, primarily of the middle class, who were involved in spiritualism and occultism. Those who belonged to the growing number of spiritualist and esoteric societies in the late nineteenth century understood magic as the interaction of the human will with visible and invisible correspondences within the natural world in order to effect change. And they understood magic to be scientifically valid. Some of these individuals attempted to reconcile science with religion by striving to restore the Christian faith through the development of an esoteric and spiritual Christianity based upon intellectual and popular movements such as Hermeticism, Theosophy, spiritualism, and magic.

One of the most prominent doctrines that held this anti-establishment thought together was the concept of a 'one origin' theory. With the growing professionalization of the study of religion, the theory of a universal mythology or religion as the source of all religions had been rejected. In its accumulation of cast-off scientific and religious theories, anti-establishment thought appropriated this theory and took on the challenge of trying to create a system in which ritual magic, astrology, alchemy, Hermeticism, cabala and everything else, all played a role in a universal 'one origin' theory.[2]

Although it acted primarily as a receptacle for all kinds of rejected knowledge, this opposing intellectual movement could not help but be affected by the scientific mentality of the era. Evolutionism, rationalism and scientific methodology all worked their way into this occult system of thought, creating a new kind of occultism. This new occultism was

expressed in the individual work of certain people who played influential roles, both intellectually and practically, in the creation of Victorian
magic.

Despite the dominance of science and materialism in mainstream
thought, forms of magical belief still persisted in the late eighteenth
and early nineteenth centuries, expressed in the practice of popular
magic such as astrology, magical cures and divination.[3] On a smaller
scale there is also evidence supporting the existence of serious scholars
of magic who collected and studied the works of Agrippa and the other
Renaissance magi, in search of higher magical knowledge. The cabalistic
magic and the brilliant synthesis of esoteric traditions that was carried
out in the Renaissance by Ficino and Pico della Mirandola had not
disappeared. As we have seen, many of its philosophical tenets were
preserved and assimilated into Rosicrucianism in the seventeenth century. It was, however, not exclusive to the Rosicrucians. The texts of the
Christian cabalists fell into the hands of many individual scholars and
potential adepts. There are accounts of astrologers and 'cunning men' in
England from the beginning of the seventeenth century who practised
astrological and talismanic magic similar to that described in Agrippa's
famous magical textbook, *De Occulta Philosophia*.[4] Evidence of occult
interest and activity prior to the nineteenth century can be found in the
activities and publications of certain seemingly eccentric individuals.
One such person was the magician, alchemist and patron of the arts,
Thomas Britton, whose library boasted a large collection of grimoires
and occult tools including a seven-foot magical circle, a seven-foot
magical staff, and a scrying glass. Britton was completely equipped to
work the angelic magic of John Dee.[5] Presumably he was not alone.

The practice of ceremonial magic throughout the eighteenth century
is also verified by the existence of occasional publications such as those
of the well-known astrologer and magician, Ebenezer Sibly. Despite his
death in 1799, Sibly embodied the true spirit of Victorian occultism in
his attempts to integrate progressive scientific developments with traditional Hermeticism.[6] The results of these attempts can be found in his
principal publications, *Celestial Sciences*, 1784 and *A Key to Physic, and
the Occult Sciences*, 1794. Sibly has been characterized as an extraordinary old man who plagiarized seventeenth-century works in his compilations, having nothing new himself to contribute to astrology or the
occult sciences.[7] In *The Theosophical Enlightenment*, Joscelyn Godwin
argues that even the presence of such contemporary complaints indicates the existence of a knowledgeable group of occultists who were
able to critique Sibly's work as unauthentic.[8] Sibly was not alone in his

magical interests and others most certainly had access to the appropriate literature to cultivate both an appreciation of and expertise in ceremonial and cabalistic magic. During Sibly's day, however, this kind of magic tended to be classified alongside astrology, alchemy, witchcraft, and other supposed superstitious practices and beliefs. England's intellectual circles had yet to embrace this type of magic as a singular and popular pursuit.

It was not until the publication of Francis Barrett's compilation, *The Magus or Celestial Intelligencer* in 1801 that the comprehensiveness characteristic of the Renaissance cabalists was once again evident in Western magic. By presenting in a single book a large portion of occult literature available in English translation, Barrett's compendium acts as historical evidence for the state of magical knowledge and practice in England at the beginning of the nineteenth century. That the book was written and published at all testifies to an interest in occult studies in certain intellectual circles of the time. Many critics accuse Barrett of plagiarism and recognition of *The Magus*'s contribution to the corpus of occult literature has been little acknowledged.[9] *The Magus* does, however, hold quite a significant place in the history of Victorian magic by offering proof of the continuation of a cabalistic tradition developed in the Renaissance and by providing the vehicle for the evolution of this tradition into a more accessible and practical one; one that was to exert immense influence on the magical corpus of the Golden Dawn.

Barrett emerges from a relatively quiet period in the history of magic. It is unlikely, however, that he was alone in his occult interests. In his biography of Barrett, Francis King claims that the occultist studied with Ebenezer Sibly, learning the technique of crystal gazing or scrying.[10] In *The Magus*, Barrett attests to the presence of other observers and participants at certain magical experiments. According to his testimony, there were several others of his acquaintance who were interested in magic and who were engaging in magical activity.

Little is known of Barrett's history. King pieces together a life that presents him first as an apothecary's apprentice, then following a profession related to the sea, and finally as a daring, and generally unsuccessful, hot-air balloon adventurer.[11] Barrett's physical attempts at ascension by balloon are mirrored in his spiritual attempts through magic. Interestingly, a century later, another important figure in Western magic, and an inheritor of Golden Dawn magic, Aleister Crowley, also matched his desire for magical ascension with physical ascension in his passion for mountain climbing.

The purpose of *The Magus*, as set out by its author, is to provide a remedy for the inconvenience and expense of obtaining the sources Barrett himself has used in creating this compilation.[12] This remedy comes in the form of three books, which cover the standard divisions of magic established by Agrippa in his *De Occulta Philosophia*. These divisions are natural magic, talismanic or constellatory magic, and cabalistic and ceremonial magic. Barrett ends the compendium with a magical biography of those individuals whom he believes to have contributed significantly to Western magic. This list of magicians is the typical magical canon and includes many of the usual suspects including Agrippa and John Dee.

In providing an authoritative source for occult studies, Barrett relies heavily upon Renaissance sources, especially Agrippa and the Christian cabalist tradition. Barrett also provides a link between the cabalistic magic of the Renaissance and nineteenth-century magic by incorporating sixteenth- and seventeenth-century sources and their interpretations of magic and various occult interests. Barrett claims to draw upon the work of Jean Baptiste van Helmont, a famous Belgian alchemist and mystic physician of the late sixteenth and early seventeenth century. Barrett also makes direct reference to two seventeenth-century books in his section on magnetism: *The Sympathetical Powder of Edricus Mohymus of Eburo* published in 1639,[13] and a book concerning various magnetical cures published in 1611 by a certain Uldericus Balk. The most obvious sources for Barrett are the translations of Robert Turner, a seventeenth-century astrologer and botanist. Barrett draws much of his material for his sections on natural magic, ceremonial magic, talismanic magic, and cabalistic magic from Turner's translations of Agrippa's *De Occulta Philosophia*, the pseudo-Agrippan *Fourth Book of Occult Philosophy* and *The Heptameron*, falsely attributed to Peter of Abano. That these Renaissance texts were available in English translations from the middle of the seventeenth century on is proof of their continuous dissemination and availability. A further connection, providing evidence for a continual transmission and tradition of British occultism can be found in Barrett's source for his seventeenth-century material. He made use of texts from Sibly's library which had fallen into the hands of *The Magus*'s publisher, Lackington. The occult bookseller John Denley went on to purchase some of the library's contents.[14]

Barrett's *Magus* did more than simply provide a vehicle for the transmission of Renaissance magical texts. He deviated from the traditional conception of Christian cabalistic magic by incorporating passages from necromantic texts such as *The Fourth Book of Occult Philosophy* and *The Heptameron*. Necromancy, or the raising of the dead, is demonic magic and is a different kind from that developed by the Renaissance magi and that found in most of Barrett's book. Throughout his compendium, Barrett clearly presents exhortations for piety and emphasizes the role of Christian-like morality in magical experimentation. This union of piety and necromancy, however, is not uncommon in black magical texts from the Middle Ages and the Renaissance. This blend was frequently deliberate in order to render a text and its owner more orthodox. Many of the owners of such black magic texts were members of the clergy, hence the necessity to endow the books with a religious and orthodox nature.[15] Barrett discusses two different methods of necromancy. One involved the use of blood to raise a corpse while the other involved conjuring the shade of the dead.[16] As for raising the dead body, complete with its soul, Barrett asserts that God alone has the power to safely employ that kind of magic.

Barrett's sources for necromancy are *The Fourth Book of Occult Philosophy* and *The Heptameron*. Both pseudonymous works date from roughly the same time, the late sixteenth and early seventeenth century. *The Fourth Book of Occult Philosophy* ties itself to that of Agrippa's through both its title, implying that it is a continuation of Agrippa's first three books, and through its content. Almost all of the material contained within this book is borrowed directly from the third book of Agrippa's *De Occulta Philosophia,* which deals primarily with ceremonial magic. The originality of this supposed 'fourth' book is found in descriptions of the spirits of planets and in the instructions for constructing and using a *Liber Spirituum*. A *Liber Spirituum,* or Book of Spirits, is a magical book containing the names of various spirits and demons. It is an essential tool in the invocation of demons.[17]

The Heptameron is falsely attributed to Peter of Abano, an Italian physician and astrologer accused of heresy, who died in 1316. It was rumoured that Abano's heresy ranged from denying the existence of demons and evil spirits, to seeking counsel from seven imps that he kept locked up in a bottle.[18] The book itself provides practical procedures for the invocation of spirits and for conjurations specific to each day of the week.

The sections of *The Magus* which rely primarily upon these sources are much more practical and instructive than those concerned solely with Christian cabalistic, natural and talismanic magic. The book, and indirectly its author, reflects the existing curiosity in the occult at the beginning of the nineteenth century, as well as the willingness of some to cross the line of the cleaner Christian cabalistic rituals and venture into the darker realms of necromancy. In this way, *The Magus* exemplifies both the assimilation that has taken place between the works of the Christian cabalists and the black magical *grimoires* of the Middle Ages, and the original state of ancient Egyptian magic in which black magic was accepted alongside its cleaner forms. The one difference being that the characterization of black magic as immoral that was missing from Egyptian magic would not have been absent in this nineteenth-century context. This fusion created a new kind of cabalistic magic, more ambitious in its pursuits than its Renaissance predecessor. Cabalistic magic is not only used here for attaining self-knowledge leading to union with the divine, but also for getting whatever the magician desires materially, as well as spiritually. This kind of fusion has been seen before in the Graeco-Egyptian magical papyri, but this is the first time it appears in conjunction with cabalistic magic.

The Magus is also quite significant because it presents a person, in the form of the author, who practises the magic he preaches, frequently in cooperation with other magicians. Throughout the text Barrett describes his own personal experimentation with magic. In one example he claims that a man can kill a toad merely by looking at it with intense fury for 15 minutes. Barrett claims to have successfully carried out this experiment with other reptiles as well. He records other successes with magic including conjuring a thunderstorm and using a form of oral telepathy to speak with others at a distance.[19] In another section, Barrett describes having witnessed the wounds of a dead man bleeding anew when touched by the man who had committed the murder.[20] These passages from *The Magus* provide proof that magical experimentation of some sort was going on in Barrett's day and that he was not alone in these experiments.

The Magus also heralds a new way of learning and transmitting magical knowledge. At the end of his book Barrett takes the opportunity to drum up business, advertising his availability to provide private instruction in the occult sciences, and encouraging people to call at 99 Norton Street, Mary-le-Bonne between eleven and two o'clock.[21] Barrett was not the first to try to attract students of the occult. An earlier announcement of such ambitions came from a William Gilbert in London in 1792. Gilbert specialized in making magical talismans. He announced his intentions in May of that year to start an occult college at his house.[22] It is not clear if Gilbert found any takers and this is not important in establishing that a new format and forum of learning magic was beginning to take shape. Barrett had at least one student, a Dr Parkins, who went on to teach the occult arts he acquired from his teacher ins Lincolnshire. An 1802 manuscript on invoking spirits, currently held in the library of the Wellcome Institute, ends with the following statement: 'This most noble Science of Divine Magic which is the highest Branches of Learning is regularly taught in all its parts by Dr. Parkins. Pupil to the later Mr. F. Barrett.'[23] There is also a tradition that Barrett's magical system lived on in a small group of students from which arose a Cambridge group of adepts. There is rumour that this group still existed in 1945, and that this group was at Oxford rather than Cambridge.[24] It is probable that Barrett had students and that a later occult society surrounding the novelist Bulwer-Lytton owed its origins to Barrett.[25] In all likelihood, Barrett's advertisement drew in curious students other than Dr Parkins. That members of his circle would go on to found new occult groups is also possible. Barrett's work and his students would have provided the appropriate literature and manpower to feed the growing interest in occultism and secret societies. By creating a magical textbook and establishing the notion of a magical school, Barrett had introduced a new accessibility to magical studies. Cabalistic magic need be no longer the domain of an academic elite or the philosophically inclined. Through his compilation of *The Magus*, Barrett helped to set in motion a process resulting in the institutionalization of magic by the end of the century. In assessing the merits of Barrett's work, his critics have not been so kind. Occult scholar E.M. Butler, for example, claims that none of the content of *The Magus* was new, and that it failed to 'advance the art of ceremonial magic by one iota'.[26]

Another critic, Donald Tyson, in his introduction to a recent publication of the 1651 English translation of Agrippa's *Three Books of Occult Philosophy*, claims that Barrett deserves nothing but contempt for his lack of originality and for having plagiarized Agrippa.[27] Such criticism ignores the value of Barrett's compilation and his role in reformatting the way in which magical knowledge could be transmitted. This resulted in magic being taught in magical schools, with the first, the Hermetic Order of the Golden Dawn, appearing at the end of the century. Before that happened, however, the study and practice of magic had to proceed through the nineteenth century.

Uncovering the status of the study and practice of magic in the middle of the century is a difficult task. Decades later pseudo-Masonic and esoteric societies were to leave behind enough documentary evidence of their practices and beliefs to keep any historian content and as a result, this middle period has remained largely unexamined.[28] The institutionalization of magic had yet to occur in the mid-nineteenth century and with no solid evidence of the supposed magical circle following Barrett's teaching, any proof of the practice of magic must be sought among individual scholars and would-be adepts. Another problem in tracing a continuous tradition of magic through this particular era is the emergence of a new trend in occultism, that of spiritualism. Most mid-century occultists were involved in some capacity in spiritualism and its associated practices of mediumship and crystal gazing. Other occult pursuits, including cabalistic magic, while still studied and practised by these individuals, became secondary to this more popular form. While spiritualism initially overshadowed its occult counterparts, it was partly responsible for enabling cabalistic magic to be practised and studied in a more social setting. Typically, those with such interests pursued them alone. The more social atmosphere of spiritualism lured would-be magicians out into the open and provided a venue for people of similar interests to make contact. One of the leading occultists of the mid-century, Frederick Hockley, was one of these individuals whose magical interests were nurtured in this spiritualist environment.

Hockley aptly represents the type of individual interested in occultism and spiritualism in the nineteenth century. The demarcation between science and religion, as understood today, was still blurred and scientific explanations of supernatural phenomenon were not yet of the completely dismissive nature. Because of this, intelligent, curious, normal people pursued magical and spiritual interests with little fear of intellectual condemnation. Frederick Hockley was one such person. An accountant by profession, Hockley was one of the most notable occultists of the Victorian period, known for his immense collection of esoteric and occult literature. Through the contents of his library, Hockley can be identified as following the same magical tradition represented by Francis Barrett. Hockley's collection included the works of Ebenezer Sibly, John Dee, several manuscripts belonging to the *Key of Solomon* and an original copy of *The Magus*. His library will be subject to closer scrutiny in the following chapter.

It has been suggested that Hockley was a student of the magical school supposedly established by Barrett and that Hockley was at the centre of a magical group in the 1850s and 1860s that experimented with the magic proscribed in *The Magus*.[29] There is no historical evidence to confirm this. Hockley was, however, a member of Morrison's Order of the Swastika which probably started around 1844. It is not known whether this group specifically practised the magic outlined in Barrett's text. Hockley's library, however, certainly confirms his interest in the magical tradition described within the pages of Barrett's compendium.

His acquisition of *The Magus* alone testifies to this. There is also further evidence of Hockley's familiarity with Barrett's work. Hockley did some work for John Denley, the occult bookseller who had acquired books from Sibly's collection. Hockley obtained the rights and the manuscript plates of *The Magus* from Denley who had purchased them from Barrett's publisher. Hockley's opinion of Barrett, however, was not flattering. He called Barrett a 'mere book-maker', claiming that he had borrowed all the material used in compiling his book from Agrippa and the *Key of Solomon*.[30] Such an unfavourable assessment proves, however, that not only was Hockley familiar with the magic of Barrett's compilation, he was also familiar with Barrett's sources.

Hockley's esoteric interests were many and varied. As with most occultists of the era he dabbled in spiritualism. His preferred method for communicating with spirits was scrying. This process involved the use of a crystal or a mirror to contact spirits. This form of occultism was one of the most popular in the nineteenth century and the most enduring, finding precedents in English history in individuals such as Roger Bacon, John Dee, William Lilly and John Aubrey.[31] Hockley's purpose for communicating with these spirits was to gain knowledge of the divine, leading to union with this divinity and spiritual perfection. In both method and goal, Hockley reflected the earlier work of his predecessor, John Dee. Like Dee, Hockley could not see or communicate with the spirits himself. Rather, in the fashion of ancient Egyptian magic, he relied upon a 'speculatrix', usually a young girl. He worked with one young woman in particular, his landlord's daughter, Emma Louise Leigh, who functioned as Hockley's crystal medium from the time she was 13 until her death seven years later.[32] Hockley worked with Leigh to obtain the spiritual answers to more than 12 000 questions over numerous years of magical experimentation. Hockley discusses Dee's use of the crystal in a letter to *The Zoist* in which he argues against the theory that what the seer apprehends is the result of thought transmission from the caller (Dee would be the caller and Kelley the seer, or more pertinently, Hockley the caller and Leigh the seer).[33] Hockley recorded the results of his own experiments with the crystal and some of these were published in pseudo-scientific journals including *The Zoist* and *The New Existence of Man upon Earth*.[34]

A true occultist of his era, Hockley was both a Freemason and a member of the *Soc. Ros.* He was initiated into the former in 1864 and the latter almost 11 years later. One possible reason for joining the *Soc. Ros.* so late is that he leaned towards a more allegorical and spiritualistic interpretation of Rosicrucianism and he preferred the hands-on approach to occultism offered by scrying. The *Soc. Ros.*, on the other hand, was predominantly theory-based despite the extra-curricular activities of many of its members. Another reason for his having held off on joining the society had to do with his personal feelings for another prominent occultist and member of the *Soc. Ros.*, Kenneth Mackenzie. This relationship will be addressed later when we meet Mackenzie and discuss his influence on nineteenth-century magic.

As we have seen, Hockley was a member of the pseudo-Rosicrucian groups, the *Fratres Lucis*, the Society of Eight and the earlier Order of the Swastika.[35] Apart from having membership in many of the same occult organizations as MacGregor Mathers, Westcott and Woodman, Hockley was directly named in Westcott's Golden Dawn's official history lecture, as one of the Order's adepts who was 'possessed of the power of vision in crystal', and whose M.S.S. are highly esteemed'.[36] This is untrue. Hockley was never a member of the Golden Dawn, dying three years before its establishment. What such a claim points to, however, is the desire of the founders of the Order to associate its tradition of magic with Hockley. That Golden Dawn members made use of Hockley's magical manuscripts further supports this claim. A.E. Waite had access to three manuscripts: *The Journal of a Rosicrucian Philosopher*, *Crystallomancy*, and *Collectanea Chemica*. Florence Farr and W.A. Ayton made transcripts from Hockley's manuscripts and Percy Bullock had in his possession, at one point, *The Journal of a Rosicrucian Philosopher*.[37] So while Hockley did not participate in or consciously influence the Golden Dawn, his work and writings were claimed by the Order in its formulation of its own history and system of magic. Given his work for the occult bookseller John Denley, it is even suggested that Hockley may have had a hand in transcribing or even inspiring the Golden Dawn's founding document, the cipher manuscript.[38]

Another key mid-century figure who played an influential role in the development of Victorian magic is Kenneth Mackenzie. Mackenzie claimed to have received Rosicrucian initiation in Austria where he spent much of his childhood. In 1851, he returned to England and began a career writing articles and translating texts on a variety of topics. His publications ranged in genre from romance novels and translations of fairy tales to scientific articles and publications on foreign cultures and cities.[39] The work for which Mackenzie became best known, however, is his *Royal Masonic Cyclopaedia*, published in 1877. As a Masonic reference, this book was initially a flop because, despite its title, the contents drifted from a pure Masonic theme and concentrated on dubious descriptions of even more dubious degrees. The book did eventually become a primary sourcebook for occultists once its merit as a hodge-podge of esotericism and a catalogue of almost every secret society that ever existed, as well as several that had not, was established.

Mackenzie's varied interests and his proficiency in German, Latin, Greek and Hebrew made him a prime candidate for membership in many of the esoteric societies taking shape in the middle of the century, as well as other more conservative organizations. He was a member of the Royal Asiatic Society from 1855–61 and a fellow of the Society of Antiquaries in 1854. Through a family connection, Mackenzie was initiated as a Freemason but resigned within the same year, finding the fringe Masonic societies in operation at the time more tantalizing. He became a member of the *Soc. Ros.* in 1872, and gave several papers on esoteric subjects prior to his resignation in 1875. That same year he joined an obscure society called the Royal Order of Sikha and an even more obscure one, the Sat B'hai. The latter is described in his *Royal Masonic Cyclopaedia* as originating in India and was structured along a hierarchy of seven degrees.[40] R.A. Gilbert claims that this quasi-Masonic order also admitted women; an important detail to note in assessing Mackenzie's influence on the Golden Dawn.[41] Another interesting society with whose members Mackenzie claimed familiarity was the Hermetic Brothers of Egypt. Mackenzie claims that this occult fraternity originated in ancient times and had mastered the art of invisibility. Mackenzie describes another dubious order which he himself founded, the Order of Ishmael, as an ancient Eastern order headed by three chiefs and with a hierarchy of 36 degrees.[42]

Mackenzie's membership and interest in both obscure and more conventional esoteric societies brought him into contact with the men behind the Golden Dawn. His familiarity with Westcott is obvious enough in a private letter announcing the establishment of the Society of Eight in 1883. In this letter Mackenzie insists to F.G. Irwin, fellow Mason and occultist, that Westcott not be admitted.[43] Upon Mackenzie's death in 1886 Westcott assumed his position as Grand Secretary of the Swedenborgian Rite of Freemasonry and collected Mackenzie's papers from his widow. These papers may have included the controversial cipher manuscript which may have been originally intended for use in the Sat B'hai in order to spice up the rituals of that order.[44] Just as with the speculation of Hockley's involvement with the cipher manuscript, this suspicion has been impossible to verify given the historical evidence available. Certainly, what is known about both Hockley and Mackenzie easily confirms their influence on the founders of the Golden Dawn and their direct involvement with the cipher manuscript is not a necessary piece of the puzzle from which to draw this conclusion.

Mackenzie also played a significant role as a link between the developing occultism taking place in France and in Britain. In December 1861 Mackenzie went to Paris to visit the leading French magician of the nineteenth century, Eliphas Lévi. Lévi was born Alphonse Louis Constant and, early in life, followed a calling to the priesthood. Disillusioned with that path, he turned to occultism and developed the tarot system that was eventually adopted by the Golden Dawn and synthesized into Victorian magic. Lévi was the first to incorporate the tarot with cabala and his integration of this blend into the existing occult tradition was so thorough that it became impossible to isolate and examine the tarot as an individual component of Western magic. Lévi's status as the founder of Western occultism is due to this incorporation of the tarot with other aspects of magical imagery.[45] By using the tarot in conjunction with cabala and other occult symbols, Lévi believed he could uncover hidden truths and gain access to divine esoteric knowledge. He presented his occult synthesis in his influential and popular works *Dogme et rituel de la haute magie*, 1854–56, *Histoire de la magie*, 1860, and *La Clef des grands mystères*, 1861. The main doctrine behind all of these books was the antiquity, efficacy and ubiquity of magic. Lévi believed that the symbolism of all religions answered to the one universal faith based upon the doctrines of magic and that, through magic, humanity could repossess the divine powers it once held.[46] This famous French magus is also claimed by the Golden Dawn as one of its own in Westcott's official history lecture, another false claim.[47] Just as with Hockley and Mackenzie, there is also a story linking Lévi with the cipher manuscript, suggesting that it was once in his possession. Howe dismisses this rumour and notes that even if it were true, the manuscript would have meant little to Lévi, as he was not very proficient in English.[48] However, Lévi did maintain that the only serious magical texts were those written in manuscript and codes created by Trithemius, as is so with the cipher manuscript.[49]

Mackenzie made Lévi's acquaintance at a time when the French magus was enjoying immense popularity. An account of their meeting appeared in the journal *The Rosicrucian and the Red Cross* in May 1873. Lévi reportedly found Mackenzie to be 'very intelligent, but excessively involved with magic and spiritualism'.[50] According to some accounts, Lévi thought Mackenzie was quite gullible and indulged in 'a good deal of leg-pulling'. There is a story of Mackenzie mistaking a tobacco jar in Lévi's house for a statue of the goddess Isis, to the amusement of his host.[51] Mackenzie returned from Paris full of enthusiasm and ideas for occult societies and rituals. He took great delight in introducing the British occult world to the significance of tarot symbolism.

Not surprisingly, Mackenzie is also named as one of the Golden Dawn's adepts in its official history lecture.[52] And not surprisingly this claim is also doubtful. It is certain, however, that Mackenzie knew the Order's three founders. He shared membership in many societies with Westcott, MacGregor Mathers, and Woodman, and as mentioned above specifically named Westcott in one of his private letters. Mackenzie was also acquainted with Hockley. Their acquaintance began on friendly terms. Mackenzie's interest in crystal scrying began after meeting a man, most certainly Hockley, in a bookbinder's shop who introduced Mackenzie to the technique.[53] Mackenzie admired Hockley's skill as a spiritualist and occultist and dictated the details of his visit with Lévi to Hockley upon his return from Paris. Apparently Hockley became tired of Mackenzie's fondness for the bottle of which he complained to another member of the *Soc. Ros.* in 1873, and ended the friendship.[54] This failed friendship may account for Hockley's late admission to the *Soc. Ros.* He did not join until after Mackenzie resigned.

Mackenzie died in 1886 and did not live to see the establishment of the Golden Dawn. His wife, Alexandrina Aydon Mackenzie, joined the Golden Dawn after his death but did not play any active role and resigned in 1896.[55] While Mackenzie had no direct hand in the Order's establishment, the addition he made to the century's synthesis of occult knowledge was considerable. His contribution to nineteenth-century magic is reflected in the magic practised by Golden Dawn occultists. Without Mackenzie's transmission of Lévi's tarot synthesis, the Golden Dawn's magic would not have been as comprehensive as it was, ensuring it a lasting and enduring status in Western magic.

The immense influence that Hockley, Mackenzie and Lévi had upon the development of Victorian occultism, is evident in that members of the Golden Dawn perceived these men to be their predecessors. The Golden Dawn intentionally associated its history and teachings with the work of these earlier occultists. Some of the Order's members met Mackenzie and Hockley through shared membership in some of the same Masonic and esoteric societies. Others read the literature produced by these three. Hockley, in accumulating such a rich and impressive occult library and in his associations with like-minded individuals, preserved and passed on the magical tradition expressed in this collection. He also placed emphasis upon the practice of crystal gazing and communication with spirits that had been part of John Dee's contribution to Western magic. Lévi began anew the process of synthesis so vital to the development of magic and its process of invented tradition, by introducing the symbolic relevance of the tarot. As an admirer of both Hockley and Lévi, Mackenzie bridged the gap between French and British occultism, introducing Lévi's occult synthesis to the numerous esoteric societies to which he belonged. In understanding Victorian magic as following a continuous tradition of synthesis, the role of these three is further emphasized. They preserved the magical synthesis first established in the Renaissance, enabled the acquisition of Rosicrucian, Masonic and French *occultisme* elements, and then passed this new creation on to their magical successors, the Golden Dawn. The process of synthesis, however, was not yet complete. Two women in the late nineteenth century added the final ingredients of Christian esotericism and Theosophy to this legacy.

One of the most influential and the most overlooked individuals in the history of Victorian occultism is Anna Bonus Kingsford. Her unique experimentation and interest in practical magic is where her influence on British occultism was most felt. Kingsford was an extraordinary Christian mystic and doctor with a passion for social reform. Her varied interests ranged from antivivisectionism to occultism. She frequently experienced visions, both while sleeping and awake, which may have been the result of an alleged addiction to chloroform which she used to ease a chronic pulmonary condition.[56] Another interesting side effect of this chloroform use was her ability to act as a vessel of spiritual communication. Throughout his biography of Kingsford, Edward Maitland, her partner in spiritual experimentation, attests to having held several conversations with Kingsford in which spirits spoke through her voice.[57] It was Kingsford and Maitland's belief that these visions and voices were divinely sent in order to guide them in recovering an ancient theological system that would mend the growing rift between science and religion. This system was a universal religion and its basic doctrines encompassed dualism, pantheism, Gnosticism, Hermeticism and evolutionism. Kingsford and Maitland recorded this system in *The Perfect Way, or, The Finding of Christ*, published in 1882. This book offered a reasonable intellectual and spiritually hermeneutical approach, at a time when science was threatening to bring about the demise of religion and the spiritual. The authors offered a balance between the two opposing ways of thinking, scientific and religious, by reining in the dogmatism of both. *The Perfect Way* advocates a return to a perceived pure state of religion in which both matter and spirit are placed in a necessary and harmonious balance. Modern religion is criticized for straying from its role as the 'culture of the soul' and modern science 'falsely so-called' is condemned for having surrendered credibility in its acceptance of materialism as its primary doctrine.[58]

Kingsford and Maitland argued for the rationality of religion once its true nature and purpose is revealed and *The Perfect Way* offered the path to this discovery.[59] Thus the authors concur with the naturalists that the current state of the Christian faith is irrational, confounding and erroneous. Unlike their naturalist contemporaries, however, Kingsford and Maitland do not subsequently reject religion. Instead, they seek its cure through the re-establishment of a supposed original state of religion and a reinterpretation of it through recently discovered scientific theories.

Kingsford authored many other books, with Maitland and on her own, on the subject of this esoteric Christianity.[60] She also wrote numerous articles and papers on another of her passions, antivivisection. Kingsford gained first hand knowledge of scientists experimenting with vivisection during the completion of her medical degree in Paris which she began in 1874. At the time, vivisection was an accepted and valid form of medical experimentation. The success of scientists such as Louis Pasteur and Claude Bernard in using vivisection to carry out medical research further glamorized the method. In her writing Kingsford compares vivisectors to black magicians and monsters and their methods to blood sacrifice in ritual magic. Calling vivisection a 'resuscitation of the old and hideous cultus of the Black Art',[61] she compares the laboratory of the scientist to the chambers of the medieval sorcerer.

Kingsford's hatred of this type of experimentation was such that she attempted to murder several scientists using magical means. These means consisted of using her will to project an invisible and magical force of destruction against her target. She claimed to be responsible for the deaths of two scientists, Bernard and Paul Bert, who died while she was in Paris, but her primary target, Pasteur, remained elusive.

> The will *can* and *does* kill but not always with the same rapidity. Claude Bernard died *foudroyé*; Paul Bert has wasted to death. Now the only one remains on hand – Pasteur, who is certainly doomed, and must, I should think, succumb in a few months at the utmost … *I* have killed Paul Bert, as I killed Claude Bernard; as I will kill Louis Pasteur and after him the whole tribe of vivisectors, if I live long enough.[62]

Kingsford's conflation of science with magic is represented in some of her works against vivisection. In *Violationism: or sorcery in science*, a paper presented to the members of the British National Association of Spiritualists, she proposed to show that 'sorcery has indeed been revived in modern times to a considerable extent, but that its revival has taken place, not in the domain of Spiritualism, but in that of "Science" itself'.[63] Kingsford depicts vivisectors as sorcerers who have revived the black arts to poison science. She goes so far as to demonize Pasteur in another paper.

> Born of unbelief and agent of the Pit, the demon of Vivisection will work havoc with many a soul before the time of his rage is spent. Of all the workers on this side of atheism there is none so potent as this particular Beelzebub.[64]

Kingsford did not consider her own experimentation with magic as black magic, despite the intention to take another's life, because of her opinion of the vivisectors as evil and demonic. She clearly saw herself on the side of good in her attempts to rid the world of such evil. During her final bout with the chronic illness that eventually took her life, Kingsford differentiated between good and bad magic in a diary entry. She understood bad, or black, magic as involving the lower aspects of the personality and the individual will, whereas she understood good, or white, magic as involving a divine will, transcending any personal principle.[65] This conception of magic is similar to the principles involved in Neoplatonic theurgy. Kingsford's understanding of magic can be seen as a continuation of the Neoplatonic theurgy revived in the Renaissance. Her use of esoteric, occult, and Hermetic myth and symbolism, in support of the religious system expressed in *The Perfect Way*, places her even more firmly in the tradition of the Renaissance magic of Pico and Ficino, in the strengthening of Christianity through other religious and esoteric systems.

Kingsford's views and writings were quite accessible and well received. Rave reviews came from all quarters. Medical journals commended her work on vegetarianism, esoteric journals from all corners heaped praise on her work, and her fellow occultists admired the wisdom they found in her writing.

> Ably and clearly written: marked by great lucidity and thorough knowledge of the topic. We have a high opinion of its merits. – *Health*.[66]

> A fountain of light, interpretative and reconciliatory ... No student of divine things can dispense with it. – *Light* (London)

> We regard its authors as having produced one of the most – perhaps the most – important and spirit stirring of appeals to the highest

instincts of mankind which modern European literature has evoked. – *Theosophist* (India)

> We regard 'The Perfect Way' as the most illumined and useful book published in the nineteenth century. Amid all the stars that have recently shone forth in the new heaven of spiritual literature, this seems to us to shine the brightest. – *Gnostic* (USA)[67]

In this last advertisement, glowing recommendations from private individuals are also included. 'Your book has had the most extraordinary effect on my mind, removing not one veil but many veils which shut out happiness in various directions.' 'The moment my mind touched this book I drank it in as does the ground rain after a long drought.' 'It is a perfect mine of occult wealth, – so harmoniously consistent, and so logically true.' Sir Francis Boyle, Professor of Poetry at Oxford University added this: 'It is like listening to the utterances of God or archangel. I know of nothing in literature equal to it.'[68]

Perhaps the most important review of Kingsford's work, in asserting her influence on Victorian occultism, comes from the Golden Dawn's chief magician. MacGregor Mathers dedicates his book, *The Kabbalah Unveiled*, to the authors of *The Perfect Way*.

> I have much pleasure in dedicating this work to the authors of 'The Perfect Way.' As they have in that excellent and wonderful book touched so much on the doctrine of the kabbala and set such value on its teachings. 'The Perfect Way' is one of the most deeply occult works that has been written for centuries.[69]

It was not only through her written works, however, that Kingsford influenced British occultism. The popularity of her work resulted in her being a sought after speaker at many esoteric and social reform organizations. She was also an active member of several of these societies. Both Kingsford and Maitland gave lectures on their brand of esoteric Christianity to private audiences in London in the spring and summer of 1881. It was in this setting that they first encountered members of the Theosophical Society, a group that was to play an important role in British occultism and a society whose flamboyant founder was to have great influence on Victorian magic.

Helena Petrovna Blavatsky founded the Theosophical Society in 1875 in the United States along with others interested in the growing spiritualist phenomenon that was taking the US and England by storm.

Born in the Ukraine, Blavatsky had been a medium in New York City prior to founding the society. Seven years after its American beginnings, Blavatsky opened the society's Indian headquarters. An English branch was established in London in 1878; however, Blavatsky did not arrive in London until six years later. Her arrival heralded the beginning of the popularity that Theosophy was to enjoy for several decades, and continues to enjoy, to a lesser degree, to this day. Blavatsky believed that it was her mission, to reveal through the Theosophical Society, an ancient knowledge that had been communicated to her by hidden masters she called 'Mahatmas'. She claimed that she had studied under one of these Mahatmas in Tibet, where she had learned the ancient truths that she went on to present to the world in her *Isis Unveiled*, a two-volume work published in 1877, and *The Secret Doctrine*, published in 1888.

Blavatsky's theosophy was based on a system of religious and mystical thought that she drew from Western Hermeticism, Buddhism and Hinduism. She initially placed equal emphasis upon Eastern and Western spirituality and mysticism, as is evident in her first work, *Isis Unveiled*, but later developed a preference for Eastern doctrines. This shift is demonstrated in her second work, *The Secret Doctrine*, in which the Western elements of her mystical synthesis are diminished in favour of elaboration of the Eastern aspects. Blavatsky followed in the early nineteenth-century tradition of universal theories and tried to prove the fundamental unity of all religions while attempting to bolster the weakening status of religion and spirituality in the face of materialism and science.

Blavatsky offered instruction to both men and women in a school-like setting. The structure of the society reflects the influence and fashionableness of Freemasonry. Based upon an examination of Blavatsky's letters and articles, Daniël van Egmond argues that there were three distinct sections or grades in the Theosophical school. The first was exoteric in which students learned basic Theosophical teachings. The second required a pledge from members that they would devote their lives to the cause of humanity. The third belonged to advanced individuals, the masters of the Theosophical movement.[70]

Many doubted Blavatsky's claims of having exclusive access to these Mahatmas and the wisdom they revealed, some believing her to be a fraud. There were easily as many, however, who, finding no satisfaction with conventional religious beliefs, welcomed Blavatsky and her teachings with open arms as the bearer of the wisdom and truth which they sought. Thus when Anna Kingsford entered the arena of the

Theosophists, her teachings were also readily embraced. Her *Perfect Way* had much in common with Theosophy in offering a universal religion and access to the divine. The fundamental difference between the two was that Theosophy valued Eastern thought above Western, whereas Kingsford's emphasis was quite Christian. This difference eventually led to conflict and a parting of ways. Prior to any such conflict, however, Kingsford and Maitland were welcomed into the Theosophical fold and were even voted president and vice-president of the British Theosophical Society in 1883. The society's name was changed soon after to the London Lodge of the Theosophical Society. Despite her absence, Blavatsky was well aware of Kingsford and Maitland and was eager to have them involved in her society, realizing no doubt that the popularity of *The Perfect Way* would increase membership if its authors were on side. This beneficial arrangement was not to last long, however, as Kingsford had little toleration for Blavatsky's Mahatmas and disagreed with the society's preference for Eastern beliefs. The conflict reached its peak after the prominent Theosophist A.P. Sinnett published his *Esoteric Buddhism* in 1883. Sinnett's earlier publication, *Occult World*, 1881, served as an introduction of Blavatsky and her theosophy to the London public. This second publication, *Esoteric Buddhism,* was not well received by Kingsford and Maitland, and even Blavatsky had criticism for the book. In it Sinnett claims to reveal the Theosophical teachings he personally received from the Mahatmas. Blavatsky, in *The Secret Doctrine* corrects some of Sinnett's claims concerning the exclusivity of his knowledge.[71] Kingsford and Maitland published their opposition and criticism of Sinnett's work in a pamphlet entitled 'A letter addressed to the fellows of the London Lodge of the Theosophical Society, by the president and a vice-president of the Lodge'. In it they proposed that two sections be created within the lodge, one headed by Sinnett to study the teachings of the Mahatmas, and the other to study esoteric Christianity and Western Theosophy. This proposal was never realized, however, and the conflict between East and West was finally resolved with Kingsford's and Maitland's resignations in 1884, despite pressure from Blavatsky to stay.[72] Kingsford remained on good terms with Blavatsky, although her opinion of the Theosophist's intellect and abilities was not very high. In a letter concerning the use of certain Masonic symbolism, Kingsford writes, 'Do not talk about this to Madame B; she cannot know it; she is an occultist, not a mystic; and she is incapable of comprehending this Upper Triangle.'[73]

Kingsford and Maitland promptly set up their own society, dedicated to the study of Western esotericism. The objectives of the Hermetic Society, founded in May 1884, were published in the occult journal, *Light*.

Its chief aim is to promote the comparative study of the philosophical and religious systems of the East and of the West; especially of
the Greek Mysteries and the Hermetic Gnosis, and its allied schools,
the Kabalistic, Pythagorean, Platonic, and Alexandrian, – these being
inclusive of Christianity, – with a view to the elucidation of their
original esoteric and real doctrine, and the adaptation of its expression to modern requirements.[74]

Over the next two years, Kingsford gave lectures at well-attended society meetings on everything from animals and their souls to extraneous spirits and obsession.[75] MacGregor Mathers and Westcott not only
attended these meetings but also presented their own lectures on the
subjects of cabala and alchemy. MacGregor Mathers gave two in 1886:
'The Kabala' and 'The Physical or Lower Alchemy'. Westcott's lecture
from the same year was titled 'Sepher Jetsirah'.[76] In 1887, Kingsford's
health, which was not robust to begin with, began to decline drastically.
She had long suffered from asthma attacks and delicate nerves. She died
of tuberculosis in 1888 and the Hermetic Society died with her. It is
tempting to conclude, given the dates, that the Golden Dawn was established as a continuation of the Hermetic Society. Some suggest that the
foundation of the Isis-Urania Temple of the Golden Dawn, eight days
after Kingsford's death, indicates the intention of MacGregor Mathers
and Westcott to continue her work and to fill the void in Hermetic
studies left by her death.[77] The Golden Dawn's agenda, however, was
rather different from that of the Hermetic Society. Despite Kingsford's
own personal involvement with magic, there is no indication that her
organization was ever anything but an esoteric study group. The Golden
Dawn's Masonic structure, combined with its admission of both men
and women and its emphasis upon practical magic, makes it a unique
society in the history of nineteenth-century occultism. The Order's
other emphasis upon the study of Hermeticism and cabalism is similar
to the goals of the Hermetic Society, as is its admission of men and
women. While the Golden Dawn does not necessarily pick up where the
Hermetic Society left off, it is reasonable to conclude that Westcott saw
Kingsford's death as an opportunity to begin his own magical society,
having observed that there was adequate interest in Western occultism
and esotericism through his association with the Hermetic Society and
also with Blavatsky's Theosophical Society. It has also been suggested
that the abandonment of many British occultists from the Hermetic
Brotherhood of Luxor at this same time provided the impetus for the
establishment of the Golden Dawn.[78] Certainly the Brotherhood's

emphasis on practical magic is more in keeping with the Golden Dawn focus. I would argue that the demise of both the Hermetic Society and the Hermetic Brotherhood contributed to creating the conditions for the nascence of the Golden Dawn.

Through their common interests, MacGregor Mathers and Westcott were familiar with Kingsford and her society. They both gave lectures to her Hermetic Society and both make reference to Kingsford in their writing. In the official history lecture of the Order, Westcott calls Kingsford a great Hermeticist saying 'she was indeed illuminated by the Sun of Light and no one who ever heard her lectures and discuss Hermetic Doctrines will ever forget her learning or her eloquence, her beauty or her grace'.[79] As previously mentioned, MacGregor Mathers dedicated his *Kabalah Unveiled*, to both Kingsford and Maitland. Moina Mathers wrote a preface to the 1926 edition of the *Kabbalah Unveiled* in which she claims Kingsford introduced MacGregor Mathers to Blavatsky. She also claims that her husband preferred Kingsford's ideals of esoteric Christianity and the advancement of women to Blavatsky's Eastern focus. 'Moreover he was profoundly interested in her [Kingsford's] campaign against vivisection in which he vigorously aided her.'[80] This brings us back to Kingsford's magical attacks on the scientists she met in Paris, who were experimenting with vivisection.

Maitland records in his biography of Kingsford that in the summer of 1886, 'a notable expert, who, being well versed in Hermetic and Kabalistic science, had attained his proficiency in the best schools' encouraged Kingsford to experiment with practical magic. Maitland claims that this expert proposed that Kingsford use the power of elemental forces against the scientists, particularly Pasteur, in order to cause physical suffering through magical means.[81] This notable expert could well have been MacGregor Mathers, and Moina's comments in the preface to *The Kabbalah Unveiled* could support such a conclusion. At this point Kingsford would have made the acquaintance of MacGregor Mathers as his name appears on a programme for the Hermetic Society's lecture series that same year. Whatever the true identity of this notable expert, Kingsford took his advice and launched a magical attack on Pasteur that involved such effort she collapsed with exhaustion and fell ill shortly thereafter. Kingsford suspected that this particular bout with illness, from which she never recovered, was either the result of her magical war with Pasteur, or the result of her general involvement with the occult.

> Whether I brought it upon myself occultly by means of my projec-
> tions against Pasteur, which, not being sufficiently strongly impelled

or skillfully directed, recoiled upon myself – a supposition which I have some grounds for thinking probably correct – or whether the whole weight of my karma has fallen on me *en bloc* as a result of my entry upon a certain occult period of my career, matters not very much.[82]

Kingsford had first become involved in practical magic and occultism while studying in Paris. She met a fellow student there who Maitland describes as being a proficient occultist of black magic and sorcery, and to whom he refers as 'Professor O'.[83] This man took Kingsford on as a student of an undescribed course of study which, presumably, was the study of occultism. Shortly after commencing her studies with Professor O, Kingsford began to have unsettling visions and dreams in which male demons attempted to seduce her. The dominant figure in these dreams was a demon that Kingsford believed to be her instructor. Both Maitland and Kingsford thought that this man had somehow placed Kingsford in his power. When she finally managed to break free of this unwilling fascination, Professor O fell ill, a result, Maitland and Kingsford believed, of the rupture of his magical hold.[84]

As previously mentioned, Kingsford perceived herself to be responsible for the deaths of two scientists involved in vivisection. She believed that the attempt to project her will to destroy these men, and Pasteur, resulted in their deaths. Her first supposed victim was the French physiologist Claude Bernard, a scientist experimenting on animal heat. In 1878, during an argument with one of her professors over Bernard's methods, she 'invoked the wrath of God upon him [Bernard], at the same moment hurling her whole spiritual being at him with all her might, as if with intent then and there to smite him with destruction'.[85] Six weeks later, Bernard was dead. The official postmortem identified Bright's disease as the cause of death; a disease Bernard had been investigating by inducing it in animals. According to a mutual friend of Bernard and Kingsford, at the same moment which Kingsford hurled her spiritual wrath at Bernard he felt as if he had been struck with some poisonous substance.[86]

Kingsford's second victim was a casualty in her magical war against her primary foe Pasteur. Professor Paul Bert fell ill and died shortly after a sustained series of magical attacks made by Kingsford on both Bert and Pasteur. Pasteur himself appeared to remain impervious. He did become ill for a short time and retired to the Riviera in 1887 to recover and Kingsford claimed partial success in the matter.

In her use and understanding of magic Kingsford provides important historical links in two different capacities. First, she bridges the gap between a Neoplatonic comprehension of the role of the will in magic and the late nineteenth-century one, popularized by the Golden Dawn. She believed that the human will, when united with a divine will, can effect physical change. This is essentially the definition of theurgy drawn from Neoplatonic sources, namely from Iamblichus in his *On the Mysteries*. This form of magic was later perfected by the Golden Dawn and modified in that it was no longer necessary that the action to be carried out be perceived as divinely intended. It was enough that the individual magician intended the action and joined his or her will with a divine one to access the power to carry it out. Kingsford's understanding of magic is also an interesting departure from the traditional ritual magic of the era of Barrett, Hockley and Mackenzie in which intermediary spirits were invoked to carry out a magical task.

Kingsford also represents a fascinating link in the development of the role of women in marginalized intellectual and social movements. As Alex Owen has shown in her study on gender and power in Victorian spiritualism, nineteenth-century women had access to power through the passivity of their roles as mediums.[87] Kingsford, with her dreams and visions, is an example of this on the one hand, while on the other, she represents a role for women that developed more fully after her death. Victorian ritual magic offered women the opportunity to become practising magicians and to learn techniques to use their will as a creative and powerful force. This active role was enthusiastically embraced by dozens of women before the end of the century and resulted in some of the most talented female magicians including Annie Horniman, Florence Farr and Moina Mathers.

Both the Hermetic Society and the Theosophical Society, despite their differing foci, were important in that they offered an alternative religious and mystical philosophy to a world rapidly becoming devoid of mystery. And, most importantly, they offered this to both men and women. These societies were part of an underground movement that did not necessarily invade public intellectual life in a radical way. Yet as the end of the century approached, more and more artists, intellectuals and professionals signed up as they sought to understand the reinterpretation of existence that science was demanding, without losing the mystery and appeal of the unknown. The allure of an ancient knowledge and divine power existing outside the realm of science was attractive. At the same time, the appeal of developing the individual to its full potential was very much a product of this same scientific era and was another factor behind the attraction of esoteric societies. While members of these groups were reacting against the mainstream intellectual thought of the era, they were also influenced by it.

The Theosophical Society offered people an alternative to the mainstream by introducing a system based upon Eastern mysticism. This Eastern focus may have been perceived as a refuge for the validation that science was stripping from Western religion and mysticism. It could have appeared plausible that there existed an intellectual system beyond the domain of Western thought that could defy scientific domination. This Eastern focus, however, did not appeal to all. Many believed that the Western world need not be abandoned in the search for a universal religious and mystical system. For those people the Hermetic Society offered its predominantly Western approach. In this environment, in which Eastern and Western mysticism, Hermeticism, Neoplatonism and spiritualism flourished, practical magic found fertile ground. Interest in magic had always existed in the nineteenth century, as we have seen in individuals such as Barrett, Hockley, Mackenzie and Lévi and some of the societies with which they were associated. While later organizations such as the Theosophical Society and the Hermetic Society showed no apparent focus on magic, individuals involved with these groups, such as Kingsford, were certainly experimenting with occult techniques. The Theosophical Society and the Hermetic Society also provided the manpower to people the Golden Dawn. Both MacGregor Mathers and Westcott were associated with the Hermetic Society, as mentioned above, and W.B. Yeats was also a member. It has been suggested that the attraction of Theosophists to the ranks of the Golden Dawn is what spurred Blavatsky into starting up an esoteric section of the Theosophical Society in October 1888, just seven months after the Golden Dawn came into existence.[88] Van Egmond maintains that this esoteric section had been extant for quite some time, but without much success, and that Blavatsky revived it once her Theosophists began to abandon the Society.[89] Regardless as to whether the esoteric section was a new creation or a revival, Blavatsky was upset that members of her society were signing up with the Golden Dawn. In a private letter from Westcott it is suggested that Blavatsky went so far as to forbid members of her esoteric section from belonging to any other occult order.[90] The matter was settled to some degree with an appeal to Blavatsky who eventually withdrew her ultimatum and with Westcott being awarded honorary membership in the esoteric section. Westcott claimed in an address given to the Isis-Urania Temple in 1891 that he was selected to make peace in such a fashion between the two societies and the *Soc. Ros.* through an agreement with Blavatsky.[91]

With the members and founders of the Order holding memberships at various times in the wide selection of existing esoteric societies, the Order was bound to reflect the influence and doctrines of these other groups. In creating the Order, its founders intentionally drew upon their Masonic and Rosicrucian experiences. The Golden Dawn picked up the thread of Western magic, as it was introduced into the nineteenth century by Barrett and his *Magus*; then expanded upon by Hockley's spiritualism, Lévi's occultism and Mackenzie's bizarre blend of fringe Masonry and practical magic. To this, the Order added the 'Eastern' elements touted by Blavatsky, namely reincarnation, and the Neoplatonism and Hermeticism expressed in the esoteric Christian works of Kingsford. These last two also contributed to the final shaping of Victorian magic through their attempts to reconcile conflicting doctrines of nineteenth-century science and religion, and through their equal admission of men and women. Finally, Kingsford's perception of magic as an individually powered process of the imagination and the will, in conjunction with that of the divine, formed the basis of the Order's magical theory. The uniqueness of this theory will be the subject of a later chapter when we examine how and why this new Victorian occult synthesis went on to affect the course of magic into the next two centuries. First, however, we must return to our textual sources and take a glimpse at the literary influence on British occultism. This requires rummaging through the bookshelves of the Victorian occultists and discovering what magicians read.

5
Magical Libraries: What Occultists Read

This book has been concerned so far with the traditions, individuals, and to some extent the literature that were influential in shaping the revolutionary form of British occultism emerging at the end of the nineteenth century. The examination of textual sources, however, has so far been restricted to those produced by late-Victorian occultists. We must now turn our attention to what informed the creative process behind these primary sources. An investigation into the history of magic in any period would be incomplete without considering the texts that enlightened the individuals involved. Ceremonial magic had long been an elitist branch of magic and one requiring literacy. It is rare to find a magician, in history or fiction, without an accompanying magical book. Books had long been deemed crucial to the transmission of occult knowledge and the Victorian period was no exception. In fact, the Golden Dawn's institutionalization of magical learning ensured that the written word's place of importance was enshrined. We have seen which rituals and texts occultists used in their actual magical practice; what remains is an examination of the written sources these adepts used to inform and construct this unique brand of magic.

Occultists' libraries are treasure troves for such an investigation. It is here where we can identify which texts were held dear and regarded as vital enough to collect and preserve. By uncovering what topics were of most interest and made up the bulk of these collections, we can also reaffirm which individuals and traditions held sway over nineteenth-century magicians. In doing so we see the Victorian magical revival as part of a continuous invented tradition and we can further solidify the connections of certain individuals with the Golden Dawn itself and their role in revitalizing and repackaging British magic. The topics covered in these magical collections will delineate how Victorians differentiated between the various esoteric subjects and even between broader fields, namely those of science and magic. The occult libraries to be examined are two of the more prestigious ones of the century: the personal library of the mid-century occultist Frederick Hockley and the Golden Dawn's own library, the Westcott Hermetic Library.

As we have seen, some sources from Hockley's library were consulted by several members of the Golden Dawn, including A.E. Waite, Florence Farr, W.A. Ayton and Percy Bullock. Hockley's role in influencing the magic developed by the Order has already been clearly established. By examining his collection we can determine what books were deemed relevant and desirable by mid-century occultists and we can then compare these to the holdings of the later Golden Dawn library to see if there is any duplication and what the significance of this might be.

Hockley's personal library contained hundreds of books and manuscripts on topics such as astrology, mesmerism, cabala and magic. After his death, the library was catalogued by Covent Garden bookseller and publisher, George Redway, who acquired the massive collection.[1] This catalogue lists more than a thousand books and manuscripts, many of which ended up in the collection of another occultist, Walter Moseley, who was also a member of Kingsford's Hermetic Society.[2] Kingsford and Maitland both made use of Moseley's 'admirable library of old and rare books'.[3] Some of the more interesting magical works in Hockley's collection were manuscripts that he had personally transcribed on ceremonial magic, cabala and divination.[4] Several of these works are now in the Harry Price Collection at the University of London, including works on witchcraft, alchemy, and demon and ghost-lore.

While the original catalogue listed more than a thousand entries, the only copies I have discovered are incomplete and contain only 662 of the items.[5] The title of the catalogue, *List of Books Chiefly from the Library of the Late Frederick Hockley, Esq., Consisting of Important Works relating to the Occult Sciences, both in print and manuscript,* makes it somewhat doubtful that all of the books are from Hockley's collection. There is no way, however, to identify those which do not come from the occultist. The word 'important' is in bold and underlined in Redway's catalogue making it clear that this was perceived to be a significant collection. The list itself is arranged in a confusing manner. The organization is not alphabetical nor is there any particular order to the headings. Some books are introduced by the author's surname, some by their general topic and others by title. As this arrangement is likely the result of Redway's organization and not that of Hockley's, we cannot make any conclusions concerning how Hockley viewed his collection. As a publisher specializing in esoteric

works, however, it is not unreasonable to assume that Redway's categorization would have been rather coherent and would reflect how his cus-
tomers, namely Victorian occultists, distinguished between the various
esoteric subjects of the day. It is likely that the reason some texts were
introduced by author, others by title and yet others by topic, depended
upon the popularity of the book or author. Books that were well known
by title were listed by such and those penned by well-known authors
went by the surname of the author, such as the case of John Dee, Thomas
Taylor, Bulwer-Lytton and Hargrave Jennings. It could be argued that in
the case where neither the book nor its author was popular enough to be
readily recalled by most of Redway's clients, the publisher would classify
it according to topic. Sometimes, however, a book with an interesting
title would be listed according to that title, no doubt to highlight its
appeal to a potential purchaser. *How to Grow Handsome, or Hints towards
Physical Perfection* by D.H. Jacques is a perfect example of this type of
classification.[6]

The general topics used for the categorical arrangement are an eclectic
assortment. From astrology to witchcraft, with headings such as nasology,
hallucinations and secret societies in between, the catalogue covers the
myriad collection that represented esoteric and pseudo-scientific interests
of the nineteenth century. Other topics include druids, folklore, palmistry, Neoplatonism, mesmerism, mysticism and cabala. The list contains
books which date predominantly from the nineteenth century although
there is a healthy inclusion of sixteenth-, seventeenth- and eighteenth-
century works. Most of the nineteenth-century material, however, deals
with astrology, Freemasonry and spiritualism. We can take this to indicate
that nineteenth-century occult interests focused on these topics resulting
in more publications and more readership of such texts. Other categories firmly placed in the nineteenth century include the Rosicrucians,
druids, phrenology, somnambulism, occultism and occult fiction. Older
books are included under the topics of astrology, alchemy and witchcraft
alongside more contemporary works. Even older sources are found in
reprints of the works of or about Plato, Aristotle, Porphyry, Ptolemy,
Valentinus and Heliodorus of Alexandria. Here we start to see the inclusion of works not necessarily directly associated with occultism and we
can appreciate the scope of the Victorian magician's thirst for knowledge
and self-education. With regards to philosophy, along with the previously
mentioned Greek and Neoplatonic schools, Hockley's list includes works
by the eighteenth-century German philosopher Immanuel Kant and the
seventeenth-century English empiricist John Locke, as well as other texts
addressing utilitarianism and metaphysics.[7]

What is of particular interest when analysing the relationship between nineteenth-century occultism and science is the scientific content of these libraries. As we have seen, occultists were quite keen to link their art with scientific developments and argued that magical experimentation adhered to scientific standards. Current research into nineteenth-century occultism in both Britain and Germany has demonstrated the desire to provide the occult tradition with scientific respectability.[8] In looking at Hockley's library and that of the Golden Dawn, analysing how much reliance there is on scientific material is fruitful in assessing how concerned Victorian magicians were with understanding and linking nineteenth-century magic with nineteenth-century science. Beginning with the categories themselves, they do not necessarily lend themselves to the standards of scientific respectability of the period. Numerous journals, monographs and manuscripts about astrology, druids, palmistry, divination, spiritualism, phrenology, mesmerism, alchemy and Solomonic magic, firmly place this library both in the tradition of Western magic and in line with some of the more popular, but arguably marginal, scientific pursuits of the day. And, while most of the nineteenth-century works deal with astrology, Freemasonry and spiritualism, some exceptions to this are two works by Herbert Spencer,[9] one by Thomas Huxley on evolution,[10] and a response to John Tyndall on scientific materialism.[11] But these few are by far outweighed by the numerous volumes on esoteric subjects. There is an emphasis on works dealing with the occult and Hermetic sciences and a propensity for works on demonic magic. Overall, there is a mix of popular and learned magical texts and of natural and demonic magic. Hockley's library also included classical scientific works and some dating from the scientific revolution. However, these works – namely those of Aristotle, Ptolemy's *Tetrabiblios* or *Quadrapartite*, and Francis Bacon's *Sylva Sylvarum* – were considered sought after, and worthy of inclusion in an occultist's library, because of their discussions of occult powers and signs, and in the case of Bacon, of alchemy. While there is not merely an emphasis, but a primary focus on more occult subjects, there is only token representation of contemporary science in the works of Spencer and Huxley.

Regarding the religious content of Hockley's library, any seemingly religiously-oriented texts tend to deal with the religions of distant lands. Judging from some of the entries these seem to be incorporated more for their exotic, anthropological and mythological value than for any serious inquiry into the nature of faith. What sources there are do not identify the collector as following a particular faith. Several of the books with religious leanings also have strong Gnostic or Neoplatonic content, suggesting that they were acquired for that content rather than for a broad religious appeal. The variety of sources that could be labelled religious indicates no focus on a specific religion thus implying that Hockley was not intentionally collecting 'religious' texts. The broadness of his occult interests resulted in the inclusion of texts that could be deemed religious, but were probably included for their other concentrations.

Overall, Hockley's library has a definite occult bent but is quite inclusive of many peripheral topics. As this library was a personal one, such a wide-ranging collection would be expected. And, as has been previously emphasized, what we have in Redway's catalogue is Hockley's library plus additional texts from other sources, and sometimes identifying these extraneous texts as such can be difficult. It is tempting and perhaps correct to identify books with occult interest as Hockley's. This particular occult focus was certainly recognized through Redway's choice of title for the catalogue. This occult focus in the collection demonstrates the continuation of a Western magical tradition into the nineteenth century through the inclusion of certain core texts. This library shows that mid-nineteenth century magic was a compilation of ceremonial magic, cabala, Hermeticism, Neoplatonism, Rosicrucianism, Freemasonry, astrology and alchemy. Hockley's collection also demonstrates how early to mid-century occultism became entwined with some of the pseudo-scientific interests of the day such as mesmerism and some of the emerging pseudo-occult pursuits such as spiritualism and Theosophy. As we will soon see, this library also shows the early entry of the magic of John Dee into the Victorian magical system. Before going further, however, we need to delve into the contents of our second library.

The Westcott Hermetic Library was founded by Westcott in 1891. The revised rules of the library, dated 1897, state that while the library was open to 'Members of any College of the Rosicrucian Society', the 'Founder reserves the right to permit other persons, who are desirous of studying works on Egyptology, Magic, Alchemy and the Occult Sciences, to have access to the library'.[12] Located in West Kensington in a room 'suitable for study', the library welcomed donations of both printed books and manuscripts.[13] This collection of esoteric literature is rather different from that of Hockley's as it was intended to be used by others. The Hockley library, on the other hand, was very much a personal and private collection. Both libraries are nonetheless useful in piecing together the history of Victorian occultism by showing which texts and manuscripts were consulted by the men and women engaged in ritual magic during this period.

The organization of the Westcott Hermetic Library's catalogue is somewhat similar to that of Hockley's with more of an obvious effort made towards accessibility. Like the Hockley list, texts fall under headings according to author or topic; however, unlike that of Hockley, the Westcott library's catalogue is alphabetical making it that much more user-friendly. The Westcott catalogue begins with a list of the library's regulations outlining who can use the collection, under what conditions and what fines must be paid or action taken in the event that a book or manuscript was lost or damaged. We can assume or hope that the consequences were not as dire as those for breaking the Golden Dawn's oath of secrecy.

The Westcott library is much smaller than Hockley's, holding 286 books, manuscripts and journals. As for its contents, the Golden Dawn library's name, the Westcott Hermetic Library, suggests the focus. This library contains much more seventeenth and eighteenth-century material than Hockley's, with a dependence upon cabalistic, Rosicrucian, Hermetic and Neoplatonic texts. An increased contribution is also found from nineteenth-century sources, in particular, those dealing with Egyptian material, Rosicrucianism and Freemasonry. This is not surprising given the growing popularity of these three subjects in Victorian Britain and given the focus and founding influences of the Golden Dawn.

By comparing the contents of the libraries we can discover which texts and authors both libraries held in common and which subjects were exclusive to one or the other and thus determine how magical interests may have developed from earlier in the century to the full heyday of Victorian occultism. The areas in which we see direct overlap in text are astrology, mesmerism, Neoplatonism, Rosicrucianism, Egypt and the magic of John Dee.

There are several astrological sources which shared classification in both lists. This is not unusual given that books on astrology were overly abundant in Hockley's collection. While the Westcott library does not have much of a focus on astrology, since the magicians of the Golden Dawn were more inclined to incorporate astrological symbols into their unique blend of magic rather than look to the stars to determine their fate, it did have a few scattered sources on the subject and most of these were also found in Hockley's collection. They include Claudius Ptolemy's *Tetrabiblios* or *Quadrapartite,* which is one of the oldest manuals on the principles of astrology and is essentially an astrological bible. Originally written in Greek in the second century, the work consists of four books. Both libraries contained 1822 editions translated by J.M. Ashmead, although the Hockley catalogue also lists another edition, undated, and translated by James Wilson.[14] Other astrological standards of the period include *Celestial Philosophy, or the Language of the Stars* by Zuriel[15] and William Lilly's *Christian Astrology*.[16] Both collections also contain a history of Lilly's 'Life and Times' as written to Elias Ashmole.[17] Lilly's works contain descriptions of scrying crystals decorated with the names of archangels, which would have been of great interest and use to Hockley.[18] The most famous work of the seventeenth-century French astrologer Jacques Gaffarel is also found in both libraries. His *Curiositez inouyes sur la sculpture talismanique des Persans, horoscope des Patriarches et lecture des estoiles* from 1631 is found in the original French in the Westcott library and in a 1650 English translation in Hockley's.[19]

As with the astrological sources found in both collections, the works held in common on mesmerism were likely so, due to the overabundance of such material in the Hockley collection. Included here are the works of mid-nineteenth-century British physician and mesmerist Edwin Lee on animal magnetism and clairvoyance[20] and the work of French librarian and Professor of Natural History at the Jardin des Plantes in Paris, J.P.F. Deleuze.[21] Deleuze was responsible for reviving interest in mesmerism in both France and Britain with his *Histoire critique du magnétisme animal* (1813), which emphasized the role of the human will and introduced the idea of hypnotic suggestion.[22]

Most of the Hermetic texts listed in both catalogues are the translations of Thomas Taylor who was renowned for having translated into English the works of Aristotle, Plato and many of the Neoplatonists. In both of these collections there were translations of the hymns of Orpheus while Hockley's shelves also held Taylor's translations of Porphyry, Proclus, Plato, and Aristotle with some selections from Pythagorean sources.[23] The Westcott library's Taylor holdings also include translations of Iamblichus and Sallust.[24] The Neoplatonic material reflects the Victorian enthusiasm for classical literature and art and the growing popularity of perceived pagan practices spurred on by the emerging field of folklore. Taylor's translations would have been standard inclusions in many a book collector's library. The collection of an occultist however would require Taylor's more esoteric translations such as those of Iamblichus and of the orphic hymns.

The overlap of Rosicrucian material in both collections is to be expected given that both Hockley and Westcott, plus several members of the Golden Dawn, were associated with and were members of the many Masonic fraternities and pseudo-Rosicrucian societies of the mid-to-late century, for example the *Soc. Ros.* The two sources, however, held in both libraries which are blatantly identified as Rosicrucian are quite different. The first is *Le Comte de Gabalis, ou Entretiens sur les Sciences Secretes,* first published in 1670. The book was reported in the *New York Times* upon its entry into America as being 'a study in occultism [that] presents a mystic theory of the meaning of life and the evolution of the human soul'.[25] The article discusses how the book influenced the likes of Pope, Browning, Lytton and Southey. In fact, in Pope's dedication to *The Rape of the Lock* he lauds the book's author, the Abbé de Montfaucon de Villars, as the leading authority on sylphs and salamanders, which, in ritual magic circles, are elementals representing air and fire respectively.[26] *Le Comte de Gabalis* came to be associated with Rosicrucianism after its original publication. The book itself tells of the author's relationship with a great mystic who taught him the secrets of occultism. The inclusion of this text in both libraries is not unusual given the interests of Hockley and Westcott and the traditions upon which they both drew in formulating and cultivating Victorian occultism. The idea of secret knowledge being passed on from a great master to an initiate, lies at the heart of Western esotericism. It was the Golden Dawn's institutional structure that took this format of initiation and reshaped it into a more modern method with mass appeal and access as we will see in the following chapters.

The other shared text that clearly proclaims its Rosicrucian content is an edition of Thomas De Quincey's *Confessions of an English Opium Eater* which, in the Westcott library's copy, contained the author's article on Rosicrucians and Freemasons.[27] This article is De Quincey's 'Historico-Critical Inquiry into the Origin of the Rosicrucians and the Free-Masons', originally published in *London Magazine* in 1824. It is not clear whether the copy in Hockley's library contained the same article but it would not be surprising. In this article De Quincey concludes that the original Freemasons emerged out of Rosicrucian mania in the mid-seventeenth century with the goal of pursuing cabalistic magic or occult wisdom.[28] It is unlikely that Westcott or other members of the Golden Dawn would have agreed with this account of the origins of Freemasonry. While Westcott did discredit the notion that Freemasonry somehow developed out of Mithraism, he certainly believed it had greater antiquity than the seventeenth century. What Hockley would have thought is difficult to guess. However, he and Golden Dawn occultists would have most certainly concurred with De Quincey's assessment that one of the goals of such societies was to acquire and transmit occult knowledge under an oath of secrecy.

The growing interest in all things Egyptian during the nineteenth century only served to strengthen the already well-established role of

Egypt as the source of all occult knowledge. The significance of Egypt is demonstrated in both collections and the shared holdings included French artist and archaeologist Dominique Vivant Denon's account of his travels with Napoleon as a war artist during the Egyptian expedition, *Travels in Upper and Lower Egypt during the Campaigns of General Bonaparte,* an English version in Hockley's catalogue and a French edition in Westcott's.[29] We know that MacGregor Mathers most likely read this book as he thanks Gardner in a letter for 'Denon, which will be of great use to me'.[30] Arab scholar and traveller E.W. Lane's *Manners and Customs of the Modern Egyptians,* with, as stated in the Hockley list, illustrations of 'Dancing Girls' was prerequisite for most Victorian readers interested in the exotic and was listed in both catalogues.[31] In this book the author describes having witnessed an Arab magician experiment with scrying, using a boy seer. The magician drew symbols associated with the planet Saturn on the boy's hand and poured ink on it. In the subsequent vision the boy saw several things including the slaughter of a bull and a feast.[32] Also on the shelves of both collections was James Bruce's late eighteenth-century bestseller *Travels to Discover the Source of the Nile.*[33] All of these texts are mostly concerned with the exotic customs and culture of Egypt and the surrounding area and, while they would supplement an occultist's more particular interest in such matters, they would also have been in demand by the general public. All books did indeed sell well upon publication. As such, it is difficult to identify these texts as belonging to Hockley knowing that the catalogue listing his books included some from other collectors. Anyone could have owned copies of these texts; they would not have been exclusive to a magician's shelves.

One source which we find in both catalogues and a copy of which most certainly belonged to Frederick Hockley is the account of John Dee's communications with spirits through scrying sessions with Edward Kelley. Both libraries contained copies of the original 1659 edition of Meric Casaubon's *A True and faithful Relation of what passed for many years between Dr. John Dee and some spirits,* while the Westcott library also held a copy of Dee's private diary and a catalogue of his manuscripts held by the Ashmolean and Trinity College libraries as published in 1842 by James Orchard Halliwell-Phillips.[34] The shared inclusion of Dee's work points to a Victorian emphasis and continued interest in Enochian magic. While it was MacGregor Mathers who incorporated Dee's magic into the Golden Dawn synthesis, thus ensuring its place as an integral component of modern magic, the interest in and study of Dee's magical system was already firmly embedded in Victorian occultism before the Golden Dawn opened its doors. As Hockley held membership in so many earlier occult organizations it would not be unreasonable to suspect that Dee's magic may have been integrated even earlier into Victorian occultism and that MacGregor Mathers may have been finessing an adaptation begun before his time.

A further group of texts that deserves mention are the works of Eugenius Philalethes. The Hockley catalogue lists three such books and the Westcott contains five.[35] Philalethes is believed to have been the seventeenth-century alchemist and natural philosopher Thomas Vaughan, the twin brother of Henry Vaughan. His magical writings held immense importance to Golden Dawn members, particularly Waite, who went on to publish Vaughan's magical works with George Redway in 1888.[36] Waite describes Vaughan by quoting Anthony à Wood's *Athenae*, 'He was a great chymist, a noted son of the fire, a zealous brother of the Rosie-Crucian fraternity, an understander of some of the Oriental languages and a tolerable good English and Latin poet.'[37] Waite himself goes on to praise Vaughan as 'among the first of British mystics and Hermetic adepts'.[38] Golden Dawn member Rev. W.A. Ayton was greatly influenced by the works of Vaughan which he read at the British Museum and which helped to fuel his alchemical ambitions.[39] Vaughan's *Lumen de Lumine: or a Magicall Light discovered, and Communicated to the World* and his *The Second Wash or the Moore Scoured once more* were also found in both libraries.[40] The Hockley library also held a copy of *Anima Magica Abscondita: or a Discourse of the Universall Spirit of Nature* while the Golden Dawn library held a reprint of *Euphrates or the Waters of the East*.[41] The inclusion of Vaughan's work in these collections establishes an important link between English Renaissance occultism and Victorian magic; a connection already acknowledged through the continued interest in the magic of John Dee.

In both libraries we also see overlap in some fictional works. A closer look at who penned these works reveals that there is an underlying occult link with these sources. Both libraries boasted works by Edward Bulwer-Lytton and both held his 1871 science fiction novel *The Coming Race*.[42] In this novel the author writes about a subterranean world whose inhabitants harness the power of a fluid-like force called 'vril' in order to effect change, namely to heal and destroy, perhaps not such a far-fetched idea for the men and women of the Golden Dawn, nor for those fascinated by the subject of animal magnetism or mesmerism in mid-century Britain. *Zanoni* was the other novel by Bulwer-Lytton that we have already seen to be influential on Victorian occultism and that we find only in the Hockley library.[43]

Other books with shared ownership include Thomas Wright's collection of tales of witchcraft and sorcery, *Narratives of Sorcery and Magic* and the eighteenth-century French Benedictine abbot Antoine Augustin Calmet's, *The Phantom World,* which was found in both libraries in an 1850 English edition translated by the antiquarian Henry Christmas.[44] Calmet's work was originally published in 1746 as *Dissertations sur les apparitions, des anges, des démons et des esprits, et sur les revenants et vampires de Hongrie, de Boheme, de Moravie et de Silésie* and is a collection of various supernatural happenings throughout much of Europe, with a particular emphasis upon vampire legends.

An examination of the shared texts in both collections reveals certain things about the state of nineteenth-century occultism as it passed through the middle of the century, sharpening its focus and becoming more specialized. It is equally enlightening, however, to examine what was found in one library but not in the other. One such area is that of Freemasonry. While both catalogues list numerous nineteenth-century sources on this subject there is no overlap in actual texts. This gives rise to several questions. Was there no standard source used by occultists for the history of this tradition and for its rituals? This would not be surprising given that both Hockley and Westcott, and their fellow magicians, were primarily interested in more fringe Masonic activities. Perhaps there was no desire to seek out and adhere to a strict Masonic code in constructing their rituals and magic. Also, given their involvement in orthodox Masonic societies, Victorian occultists were already well familiar with Masonic ritual and were perhaps more interested in researching and reading about the ways in which Freemasonry had evolved and become embedded in other traditions. It is also of interest to note that the Westcott library held a copy of the founding Rosicrucian document, the *Fama Fraternitatis,* while the Hockley collection did not.[45] This document was of course essential in the formulation of the Golden Dawn's Second Order rituals. The Westcott library also included a manuscript of a ritual of the *Fratres Lucis*, Francis Irwin's mid-century occult society.[46] And while the Hockley catalogue contains no such manuscript, the crystal scryer belonged to the *Fratres Lucis* and so the inclusion of this ritual in the Westcott collection further establishes a connection between the earlier magical activities of Hockley's associates and the Golden Dawn.

The Redway catalogue lists several manuscripts which were, without question, Hockley's and while these manuscripts are not included in the Westcott library, some of them are of grave importance to the creation and legacy of the Golden Dawn. Hockley's collection included translations of some of the standard *grimoires* of ritual magic. They included three of the books of the *Lemegeton or the Lesser Key of Solomon*: the *Ars Notoria,* the *Goetia,* and the *Almadel*.[47] Two of these, the *Almadel* and *Goetia* were later translated and published by MacGregor Mathers. Golden Dawn historian R.A. Gilbert claims that while it is tempting to think that MacGregor Mathers actually had access to Hockley's manuscript, there is no proof.[48] Hockley's copy of *The Key of Solomon* is one of four of his manuscripts that are not accounted for.[49]

Other obvious omissions in the Westcott library fall under the categories of spiritualism and Theosophy. The Golden Dawn did try to separate itself from spiritualism, rejecting its passive nature and preferring the intense active and subjective involvement required by ceremonial magic. The lack of Theosophical works however is surprising given the connection of several prominent members of the Golden Dawn with the Theosophical Society. While Hockley's collection holds work by both Sinnett and Blavatsky there is a dearth of Theosophical material in Westcott's library. This does not necessarily indicate that Westcott or other Golden Dawn members did not read the works of their Theosophical colleagues, but rather points to the specialty of the Westcott library. As its title suggests, it was a library of Hermetic texts and as such suggests a Western focus. We have already seen the East–West divide emerge between Victorian occultists resulting in two camps. Westcott's library simply preserves the Western focus of the Hermetic camp further emphasizing the Western focus of Golden Dawn magic.

It is likely that this specialization of the Westcott library is also responsible for the paucity of texts on more general topics, such as those found in the Hockley catalogue. In focusing purely upon supposed 'Hermetic' sources the Westcott library has far less scientific and religious content than Hockley's. While this may be due to the more general nature of Hockley's collection it may also be indicative of a shift away from attempting to understand magic as scientific or justifying it as such. The complicated relationship between magic, science and religion is still quite evident in the varied sources collected by Hockley earlier in the century. The Westcott library, however, seems to abandon religious and scientific inspiration with the singular goal of the pursuit of occult knowledge.

As a mid-century occultist, Hockley concerned himself with the science, not just of antiquity, but of his own period. The Westcott Hermetic Library, however, contains few representatives of nineteenth-century science, with no copies of the works of mainstream scientists. Any seemingly scientific works are from much earlier periods and were likely to have been included for their occult content rather than their scientific advancements: works by the likes of pseudo-Albertus Magnus and Francis Bacon, the former undoubtedly for his references to natural magic and occult science, and the latter for his contribution to alchemy.[50]

By looking at the contents of these two libraries, certain texts, authors and topics stand out for demonstrating a continuation of certain traditions and authors from mid- to the late century. Hockley's collection represents what made it into the nineteenth century while a cross analysis with the Westcott library reveals which interests and writers endured. There is a continued reliance upon and preference for a Solomonic tradition of magic wedded with certain Hermetic and Neoplatonic principles. Freemasonry and Rosicrucianism remain constant in their magnitude, yet no single authoritative source dominates these traditions. Dee's Enochian magic remains a fixture and Egypt maintains its status as fountainhead of all occultism. What changes is the shedding of pseudo-scientific subjects and the casting off of pure science and religion. As the pared down holdings of the Westcott Hermetic Library demonstrates, nineteenth-century magic was being overhauled to face a new dawn, and a very modern one at that.

6
Revolutionizing Magic: The Will Conquers the Spirit

Victorian magic relied heavily on nineteenth-century occult and esoteric developments as well as upon an invented tradition of Western magic. The significance of these origins is demonstrated in the lasting status of the final creation. Victorian occultism was no passing fad. Its creative and odd conglomeration has resulted in a most enduring and suitable magical system; one that has been found appropriate and efficacious to occultists of the past two centuries. The Golden Dawn took this particular Victorian synthesis and moulded it into an instructional format that has proved to have both great appeal and applicability for modern magicians. There are some specific changes which Victorian magic made to the magical tradition it inherited that are responsible for its subsequent popularity.

The first of these changes is the shift from solitary magical practice to group participation in ritual. This shift was a radical one in the history of Western magic. In reflecting upon the forms of magic encountered so far, we can recount the solitary practice of the Egyptian priest/magician, the lone medieval ritual magician and his methods as outlined in *grimoires* such as the *Key of Solomon*, and even the expectations for magical practice expressed in Francis Barrett's *Magus* at the beginning of the nineteenth century. All refer to magic as an individual undertaking. In many of the texts translated by MacGregor Mathers, including the *Key of Solomon* and *The Book of the Sacred Magic of Abramelin the Mage*, this tradition of the lone magician is evident. The magical rituals in these books rarely refer to the presence of anyone but the magician, and when another is referred to, it is an assistant or a disciple whose role is minimal. These servants or disciples are a support staff for the magician or the 'Master of the Arts' and have no direct role in communicating with spirits. The language used in the following extracts from the *Key of Solomon* makes clear the relationship and status of these others.

The Master should afresh exhort his Disciples, and explain to them all they have to do and to observe; the which commands they should promise and vow to execute ... [1]

When the Master shall have arrived at the place appointed, together with his Disciples, he having lighted the flame of the fire, and having exorcised it afresh as is laid down in the Second Book, shall light the Candle and place it in the Lantern, which One of the Disciples is to hold ever in his hand to light the Master at his work.[2]

The status and role of these disciples is further clarified by the claim in MacGregor Mathers' translation of the *Key*, that they can easily be replaced by a 'faithful and attached dog'. In a section of this translation, titled 'How the Companions or Disciples of the Master of the Art Ought to Regulate and Govern Themselves', it is also suggested that a little boy or girl would also make an adequate substitute for a disciple or companion. If the magician does, however, make use of disciples, then they must be three, five, seven or nine in number and they must 'implicitly obey the orders of their Master; for thus only shall all things come to a successful issue'.[3]

As for the magic in *The Book of the Sacred Magic of Abramelin the Mage*, the only other person required in the rituals is a child or 'innocent being' of six, seven or eight years. The child's role is to see the guardian angel of the magician and to act as a go-between in the initial stage of the ritual, prior to the magician beholding his guardian angel himself.[4]

The solitary magician is not an image that disappears in Victorian occultism. Golden Dawn rituals such as those of the pentagram and hexagram were still described as individual exercises. It is in the Flying Rolls that examples of group magical practice can first be found. Flying Roll IV, illustrates a magical experiment in November 1892 of two Golden Dawn magicians, Florence Farr and Elaine Simpson, in which both shared the same vision. In the text, the authors recommend that such experiments be carried out with at least one or two others.[5]

In another manuscript in the Yorke Collection, a magical experiment in astral travel is described by Annie Horniman. Astral travel and its techniques were one of the more advanced forms of magical learning in the Golden Dawn. In astral travel the individual magician would concentrate on certain symbols in order to prepare the mind for the subsequent trip. These symbols would represent the desired 'location'. Horniman documents having visited, along with fellow Golden Dawn member Frederick Leigh Gardner, different astral planes through the invocation of the hexagram ritual. This series of experiments began in September 1898 and continued until December that year. During the course of this experimentation, the two travelled to astral planes invoked through the planets Saturn, Jupiter, Mars, Venus, Mercury and the Sun. Horniman describes their first port of call:

> we floated in a paler air but of a blue tint. We alighted on some great mountains where there was no life nor vegetation. The rock was the colour of dark slate but the texture and substance like granite. Passing a little further we saw a small glowing lake far below us ...[6]

Horniman goes on to describe how the group encountered a tall, male figure with large indigo wings who told them that they had come to an old and dying world. This figure took them on a flying tour to a gloomy city populated by psychic, sexless citizens who lived on yellow and blue fish, and coarse grain.[7] In all Gardner and Horniman went on seven trips to six locations; Jupiter proved to be such a draw a repeat visit was required.

Most astral travel was undertaken for the exploration of higher spiritual planes. Horniman and Gardner take this very theoretical and spiritual form of journeying to a more practical and physical purpose. While they are still using the same techniques practised by Golden Dawn magicians, they seem to have divorced it somewhat from its original goal: the development of one's higher being. Horniman and Gardner are using astral magic to visit the planets and while the form of transportation is in keeping with the more esoteric aspects of their voyages, on the surface, the purpose and nature of their trips are more in line with the average Victorian day-tripper. In practical terms, the way in which astral travel took place can be uncovered in the travel journals left by Horniman. The two travellers would carry out certain rituals of the Golden Dawn using the astrological symbols and talismans created to represent aspects of their desired destination. The travellers' astral bodies would then rapidly rise in rays of light eventually reaching their location or some in-between land where a guide would meet them to escort them on their tour.

Some departures were more pleasant than others as in the case of the trip to Venus on 26 November 1898: 'As we rose we saw each other in very bright robes, wearing green garlands on our heads. The sensation of passing through the green light was delightful.'[8] Whereas travel to Mars was less delightful and the actual motion more forceful: 'We ... rose with a great explosive force, as if from a cannon.'[9]

Once the travellers arrived, the next step in the journey was to meet their guide. These guides were inhabitants of the worlds they visited or guardians of the planet. As such their appearance and attire were in keeping with the astrological characteristics of each planet. Saturn's guide was a tall male form, with pale face, dark hair and eyes, and great indigo wings. Jupiter's was a tall, well-proportioned woman with rich, auburn hair and wore white, classical-looking drapery, edged with purple. The guide for Mars was a beautiful youth with red hair, dark flashing eyes, ruddy face, and carried a sword and spear. On Venus our travellers were shown the sights by a lovely woman with a star on her forehead from which descended a gauzy veil covering her body. Mercury's guide was a many-winged, delicately-proportioned male with rich, curly brown hair and bright, grey-green eyes. Despite the differing appearances, all guides were quite willing and eager to show the visitors the sights and to explain to them the culture and social practices of the world being visited.

On Saturn Gardner asked their dignified and courteous guide what the people ate and Horniman wished to see their place of worship. In her account, Horniman describes what the inhabitants of this dying world looked like, what they wore, and their cultural activities. 'There had never been what we should call nations or countries on Saturn, the inhabitants were all of the same stock ... they had become few and their lives very simple, but they were not at all savages. Their fewness made it impossible for them to have arts, sciences or luxuries.'[10] The landscape is described as mountainous and bare with deathly marshes and gloomy cities. The travellers visit a deserted temple, no longer used by the inhabitants. As for the people of Saturn, they are pale with dark hair and are highly psychic and sensitive to the invisible presence of the travellers. They have little difference of sex and their continual suspicion and fear prevents them from being happy. The inhabitants subsist on coarse grain made into cakes and blue and yellow coloured fish cut into strips.

The two travellers' desire to learn about the civilization, culture and inhabitants of other planets is also represented on their trips to Jupiter. Here, the two are very much impressed with the highly advanced civilization in which disease has died out, religion has no role and all inhabitants have achieved high levels of wisdom. They do visit an ancient temple on a holy mountain which reminds Horniman of the Matterhorn. Descriptions of the temple bring to mind the classical architecture of Greece – porticos of great marble pillars, bronze doors inlaid with gold and silver. Horniman asks their guide many questions about the inhabitants and their lifestyle. The guide tells them that the people live on fruit and they have no such thing as weather – rain and sun take their cues from what the environment needs. Jupitarian society resembles Victorian morality in its 'invariable rule that most trouble should be taken with the laggards so as to raise the general standard.'[11] Jupiter is reminiscent of both the glories of classical Greece and the glorious ambitions of Victorian reform. There is no idleness or over-work. The guide explains: 'There is nothing that we on earth could call "misery disease or vice", they have all learned how to live too well for these sorrows to touch them.'[12]

The people of Jupiter seem to have accomplished much of what Victorian morality and the drive for self-betterment desired. The inhab-itants are not ignorant of other planets and are well aware of the state of affairs on Earth. The guide tells them that Gardner and Horniman's 'miserable world' makes the people of Jupiter sad and they don't often go to look at Earth 'because to them, it appears to be a sort of hell'.[13]

The two travellers encounter a very different civilization on Mars. The landscape is typically dotted with volcanic mountains; however, the inhabitants live in towns in the hills with high walls and their main focus in life is warfare. Horniman claims that everything is 'as it was in Italy about the 13th century'.[14] Their beautiful red-haired guide tells them that the planet is made up of many small kingdoms at war with each other 'not for any particular purpose but for the love of it'.[15]

The main business in the life of Martian men is fighting. Both sexes quarrel continually when not engaged in physical battle. Their guide tells them that families are unknown on Mars, people live haphazard in their own castes and they wear themselves out quickly, never living to be old. Gardner inquires about the religion practised here and the guide responds by saying that the inhabitants worship nothing but their own ideal of energy and courage, and are governed by fear.

On Venus the travellers encounter a sparkling emerald planet dotted with lush woods, fertile valleys and sparkling lakes. Civilization on Venus reflects this beauty; there are no houses, government, nations, tribes or families, only perfect peace and harmony. With little distinction between body and soul the inhabitants develop on purely spiritual lines and sit about listening to great teachers pass on great wisdom. As primarily spirit-ual beings they do not eat but 'when various atoms in their bodies require renewal, they take unconsciously what is wanted from the atmosphere.'[16] Their guide tells them that all beautiful mental and artistic ideas originate from this place and fall to Earth where they are expressed.

It is on Mercury that we once again find reference to Earth's past civilizations. The picturesque market place, filled with groups of lively tunic-clad people, coming and going, reminds Horniman of 'Athens in its most intellectual days'.[17] Their winged guide explains that everyone is 'so intellectual and learned in causes and results that only what is necessary and healthy is eaten' and 'laws are obeyed from reason and not from fear'.[18] Arts and sciences are highly valued and practised by everyone as necessities of life. Inhabitants eat fruits, maize, and shining balls of dough which repair brain power. This account is incomplete and what remains does not include the return journey home. It ends after Gardner and Horniman sample a local delicacy: a fruit Horniman believes to resemble mistberries found in Norway.

On all of these planets Gardner and Horniman want to know about the culture and about the people. The two magicians, however, were probably not intending to visit the actual physical planets. As astral magic practised by the Golden Dawn involved a spiritual journey to higher planes of existence, it is more likely that the two were exploring astral planes which were represented by the astrological symbols and forces of these planets.

This interesting example of magical experimentation is but one of many that demonstrates that Victorian occultists practised their techniques together. Another such example is found in the activities of the Sphere Group, an extra-curricular offshoot of the Golden Dawn, headed by Florence Farr. As we have seen, the Sphere Group engaged in group ritual, focusing the wills of 12 magicians to project a successive series of spheres across a geographical space for the purpose of transmuting evil into good.[19]

These examples demonstrate that Victorian magicians were involved in group methods of magical ritual as well as the traditional method of solitary experimentation. This shift from individual magic to group magic is not only evident in specific magical ritual but also in the mere fact that the Golden Dawn was a society of practising magicians. Even if they were all practising solitary magic, that they associated with other magicians at all is itself a radical change from the established technique in Western magic. Moina Mathers presents at least one rationale behind this more social method.

One of the reasons we are told not to isolate ourselves is; that isolation tends to make a man egotistical. – It will become a habit to him to study and to pay too much attention to his own Microcosm, whereby he will neglect other Microcosms which together with his form part of the Macrocosm; and this Egotism of the Spirit ... will yet be a far greater snare to him, as being more subtle and therefore less easy to be perceived … It will be best, then for us to live amongst our fellows, and in our contact with them are we advised to avoid preaching and proselytising; which often leads also to a condition of self-righteousness in the Preacher, and is generally useless to the listener.[20]

There are other identifiable reasons for this shift in the study and practice of magic from a solitary nature to a social one and they can be found in both the Renaissance and nineteenth-century influences on Victorian magic.

First, the idea of a group of practising magicians initially gained popularity with the stories circulated concerning the legendary Rosicrucians. The lack of knowledge and certainty about this mythical fraternity led to all sorts of speculations about the Rosicrucians as a real, physical, magical fraternity, although it is obviously clear from the manifestos that this was not the intention of the author(s) who penned the original texts. We have seen how the legend of the Rosicrucians spread and influenced future fraternities, namely offshoots of the Freemasons. The shift from solitary to group magic can be interpreted as a result of the adaptation of Western magic to the social structure of the Freemasons.

This change towards group practice has continued to influence how people practise magic right up to the present day. In both Ronald Hutton and T.M. Luhrmann's valuable studies on modern paganism and magic in Britain, evidence of the irrevocability of this change is obvious. Modern magicians and other practitioners of ritual magic such as wiccans, druids and pagans continue to gather in groups in the performance of magical ritual. This is most obvious in the forms of covens and druidic orders, and also in the numerous magical orders, many of which claim either direct or indirect descent from the Golden Dawn. Most modern magical groups ultimately do descend, in some fashion, from the Golden Dawn. Luhrmann traces the continuity through the demise of the Order, the establishment of the *Stella Matutina* as a successor order, the foundation of the Society of the Inner Light by Dion Fortune and the many fraternities that have subsequently descended from this last which call themselves Western Mysteries.[21] Hutton also asserts that the Golden Dawn exerted immense influence upon modern magic and paganism particularly in its blending of Masonic structure with ritual magic and in its invocation of deities directly into the magician's mind and body. Hutton demonstrates the Order's role in twentieth-century witchcraft and paganism through the magical work and fiction of Golden Dawn protégées, Aleister Crowley and Dion Fortune. He reveals how the first known wiccan rituals were influenced by Golden Dawn rituals.[22] This is not to say that solitary pursuit of the techniques of practical magic does not exist. This more traditional method of practical magic continues. The group approach to magic, however, is just as, if not more, common in modern ritual magic and this approach owes its popularity to the introduction it received from Victorian magic.

The second important change made by Victorian occultism is a shift in how magical knowledge was transmitted. Abandoning the traditional method – from one individual – the Golden Dawn established an institutionalized format. This second change is closely associated with the first. By incorporating a social structure into the tradition, it was natural the transmission should take on a different format. Instead of a solitary magician learning the tricks of the trade through a *grimoire* or other similar text, members of the Golden Dawn were assigned lectures and homework in a school-type setting. In doing so the Golden Dawn developed its own magical canon, composed of traditional material drawn from *grimoires*, Renaissance texts, alchemical manuscripts, contemporary works, and the original lectures of its own members. The Order developed a system in which this material was learned at various stages, and students were expected to prove that they had studied the material before they could progress to the next level. Essentially, the Golden Dawn developed the first large-scale magical school.

Magic continues to be transmitted in this institutionalized format. In fact, the very method of Golden Dawn instruction is still taught in many current magical societies, rightly or wrongly associated with the Order. This institutionalized system is encouraged by the group practice of magic. The Golden Dawn's organization of magical knowledge into a school-like setting and format has become fundamental to much modern day magic with many individuals enrolling in such 'schools' or 'study groups'. Luhrmann's research on late twentieth-century magical societies demonstrates the continued reliance on this method of transmission.

Home study courses, advertised in books and magazines, offer the most structured forum for the training which most magicians assume a neophyte needs. Most of these courses are quite similar. They provide a series of fortnightly or monthly lessons for which the student does daily exercises, and writes short essays on assigned themes ... They are structured like English university courses. There are Directors of Studies, and supervisors, and revision essays. Each 'student' is assigned to a supervisor who comments on the 'lessons'. And upon finishing the course, the student is often initiated as having attained the first 'degree'.[23]

The next three changes that were carried out in Golden Dawn magic involve the actual theory and process of magic. The first of these concerns the number of agents engaged in the magical process. In Victorian occultism there is a shift from using an intermediary spirit in the magical process to directly communicating with the force invoked. This involves invoking or evoking it within oneself by drawing down that power from the microcosm, or bringing it forth from oneself. Medieval and early modern ritual magic traditionally required three parties; the magician, the god or divine entity whose power is invoked, and a spiritual intermediary. Depending upon the type of magic being practised, that intermediary could be angelic or demonic. Using the *Key of Solomon* again as an example of this traditional method, the major component in many of the rituals is the conjuring of spirits to do the magician's will.

> O ye Spirits, ye I conjure by the Power, Wisdom, and Virtue of the Spirit of God, by the uncreate Divine Knowledge, by the vast Mercy of God, by the Strength of God, by the Greatness of God, by the Unity of God; and by the Holy Name of God EHEIEH, which is the root, trunk, source, and origin of all the other Divine Names, whence they all draw their life and their virtue, which Adam having invoked, he acquired the knowledge of all created things.[24]

> I conjure ye anew, and I powerfully urge ye, O Demons, in whatsoever part of the world ye may be, so that ye shall be unable to remain in air, fire, water, earth, or in any part of the universe or in any pleasant place which may attract ye; but that ye come promptly to accomplish our desire, and all things that we demand from your obedience.[25]

The successful conjuring of these spirits or demons did not mark the end of the ritual. Once they appeared they were given tasks to carry out on behalf of the magician, such as finding treasure, finding love, discovering a thief, or becoming invisible. Once the request was made of the conjured spirit, another important part of the ritual was the licence to depart in which the spirit was safely disposed of, or returned to its own realm without fear of it breaking loose and wreaking havoc. The spirit was under the control of the magician from the moment it appeared in the ritual until it was given leave to depart.

This traditional method of conjuring spirits is not entirely abandoned in Victorian magic. Some of the texts associated with the Golden Dawn, particularly those translated by MacGregor Mathers, describe and use this process. MacGregor Mathers' translations of the *grimoires*, however, were not usually included in the Golden Dawn magical system and were thus not part of the Order's curriculum. One exceptional example, however, is the previously mentioned black magic ritual, 'Ritual for the Formation, Building and Consecration of a Body, wherein to Travel, manifest & act in freedom from the Bonds & limitation of matter', in which the magician invokes, all in one go, 'creatures of the flashing Fire, & rushing Air – Spirits of water & Earth & Hell', 'legions of Demons who manifest in the land of Twilight', 'shades of the living who are Dead', and 'shades of the Dead who live'.[26] This ritual, however, is not representative of regulation Golden Dawn magic. It is by observing the actual magic described in rituals and lectures associated with the different grades, particularly those of the Second Order, and the magic described in first-hand accounts of various members, that the workings of Golden Dawn magic can be perceived and, most importantly, in which a shift from the traditional process can be identified.

To begin with, the first magic ritual learned by members was the ritual of the pentagram in which the magician makes use of cabalistic symbolism, occult symbols and language, and angelic names in a process of meditation and preparation. There are no intermediary agents in this ritual and the magician's statement that he is surrounded by Raphael, Michael, Gabriel and Auriel is indicative of encouraging a state of being as opposed to direct invocation.[27] Many of the magical exercises and rituals of the Golden Dawn involved the altering of a mental state in preparation for travel on the 'astral plane' and for individual and group visions. This is in part due to the fourth change, which, as we shall see, involves a change from personal gain as the goal of magic, to that of personal transmutation.

A more illustrative example of the exclusion of an intermediary in magical ritual can be found in the Abramelin magic introduced to the Order through MacGregor Mathers' translation. In this ritual the magician's goal is to achieve direct communication with his guardian angel. There is no mediation between magician and angel. There is no higher power with which the magician wishes to communicate through the use of the guardian angel. The ritual simply involves two agents.

This brings us to the magical process of invocation and evocation, both of which were used by Victorian occultists in this direct method of magic, devoid of mediation. Invocation required the magician bringing the power or aspect of the deity, or spirit, into him/herself. Evocation involved the magician bringing the power or aspect of the deity, or spirit, up out of the corresponding region of him/herself. This latter method relies on the theory of universal interdependence whereby the magician as a microcosm has corresponding qualities to all that exists exterior to him/her, i.e., the macrocosm. This idea is inherent in the magical synthesis of the Renaissance magi and the Golden Dawn's adoption of this idea is nowhere more evident than in the instructional texts of the Second Order, the Flying Rolls. In Flying Roll XXI, an address by Moina Mathers to the first grade of the First Order entitled, 'Know Thyself', there are several references to the interdependence of the microcosm and the macrocosm, including the following:

> Perfect knowledge of Self is required in order to attain Knowledge of Divinity, for when you can know the God of yourself it will be possible to obtain a dim vision of the God of All, for *the God of the Macrocosm only reflects himself to Man through the God of Man's Microcosm.*[28]

Flying Roll XXV, 'Essay on Clairvoyance and Travelling in the Spirit Vision by *Sub.Spe* (J. W. Brodie-Innes)' also provides evidence of this idea:

> The best theory of the phenomenon of Clairvoyance seems to be founded on the relation between Man as the Microcosm and the Universe as the Macrocosm; regarding the former as a reflection in miniature of the latter, as in a grass field full of dewdrops each drop might present a perfect tiny image of trees and mountains, the sky, clouds, the sun and the stars.[29]

One final example will serve to demonstrate that the idea of correspondences is present throughout Golden Dawn teachings. This one is taken from Flying Roll XXVII, 'The Principia of Theurgia or the Higher Magic by L.O. (Percy Bullock)':

> Man as the most completely evolved Microcosm of the Macrocosm synthesizes in his own constitution the forces of the greater World of which he is a part: every entity is thus related to him, – and he to

them. The World is, as it were, a vast animal, and its parts respond, being moved by mutual sympathies: sympathies obtained through approximation to type, antipathies when the types are imperfect.[30]

It is through this belief in correspondences between a higher and lower world that the Golden Dawn formulated its process of invocation and evocation. This new system eliminated both the spiritual intermediary and the 'innocent' medium of ancient magic. This invocation or evocation was brought about by using the systems of symbolism synthesized in Victorian magic so that, for example, should the magician wish to invoke a power associated with healing, the symbolism and language used would be those which represented this power. By concentrating upon these symbols, a collection drawn from cabalism, astrology, tarot, Enochian magic, and Hermeticism, the magician would either draw down the appropriate force into him/herself or out of him/herself.

One further variation of this third change is evident when the magical process is intended to result in the magician actually becoming the power invoked, in a temporary, conscious-altering fashion. This is exemplified in the Graeco-Egyptian ritual described earlier in which the magician invokes a 'headless' spirit and in so doing, becomes that same spirit by the end of the ritual. This is the pinnacle of Victorian magic and the successful ritual enabled the magician to have knowledge and communication with his/her 'higher genius'.

The technique of drawing divinity into, or up out of, one's own being, bypassing the need for a spiritual intermediary in the magical process, is another change which has survived in the magical and pagan rituals of modern practitioners. Modern paganism is dependent upon the idea of drawing out the divinity within humans for the two-fold purpose of honouring the divinity without and developing the divinity within.[31] Victorian magicians were not responsible for developing this magical process. As we have seen, it is a re-interpretation of theurgy. The Golden Dawn was, however, responsible for reintroducing it into the Western magical corpus and for bringing it to the late nineteenth and twentieth centuries.

The loss of the intermediary agent in late nineteenth-century magic is largely due to the fourth change that Victorian occultists made to the tradition of magic they inherited. This fourth change concerns the goal of magic. Golden Dawn magic changed the direction of the magical tradition substantially by focusing upon personal transmutation and spiritual development as opposed to material gain. This is not to say that such a goal was novel. Certainly the Renaissance magi were the first to bring this goal to such prominence. Magic for personal gain is one of the dominant features of medieval ritual magic and one that remained central to the magical tradition right up to the nineteenth century. The Golden Dawn's emphasis upon spiritual development was a restatement of the Renaissance goal and it overshadowed the traditional goal of material gain.

One need only browse through the medieval *grimoires* to appreciate how important material gain was to the magician of the Middle Ages. Chapter headings such as 'How to render oneself invisible', 'How to render thyself master of a treasure possessed by the spirits', and 'Of the experiment of seeking favour and love', serve to illustrate this purpose.[32] In contrast, the four main goals of Golden Dawn magic are laid out in Flying Roll XIX by Westcott:

> the main object is what is called the Higher Magic or the develop-
> ment of the Spiritual sides of our natures in contradistinction to the
> purely intellectual. As regards Spiritual Development you promised
> in the Obligation to use every effort to purify and exalt the Spiritual
> Nature so that you may be able to unite yourself with what the
> Hermetist calls his 'Higher Genius'.
>
> A second aim we may say is the extension of our powers of per-
> ception so that we can perceive entities, events and forces upon the
> super-sensuous planes.
>
> Thirdly, and in connection with the other two, you are encour-
> aged to practice the system of divination of which there are several
> but which are only aids to your intuition and methods by which the
> intuition may be developed and encouraged.
>
> Fourthly, there is what may be called the procuring of the influ-
> ence of Divine Powers through the peculiar modes taught in our
> Order and Vibrating of Divine Names.[33]

In observing these goals the change in process noted above makes more sense. Magic is being performed not to conjure up a spirit to do some-thing for the magician, but rather to develop the magician's spirit to a more enlightened state in which the individual's powers of perception and intuition are heightened and access is gained to higher powers. No intermediary agent is needed for these goals. The magician must tap into the magical process directly.

This experience of transmutation, the belief that the individual can modify one's very being, is quite obvious in Victorian magic. In fact, it is the very purpose of Golden Dawn magic. In a lecture to members of the Second Order, Westcott reminds his audience that they promised to unite themselves with their 'Higher Genius' in the adeptus minor ritual. He refers to this process as spiritual development and identifies it as the main object of Golden Dawn magic. He goes on to explain what exactly this development entails:

> we mean by it that you perform or endeavour to perform the trans-mutation of the vital forces of life into higher currents of life or rather their transmutation out of the lower into the higher so that you can use them for the purposes of Theurgia. This transmutation of physi-cal force is what is discussed in many of the old alchemical books. A large proportion of these books which have come down to us refer to purely physical processes. But there was an opposite pole of thought of which the language referred entirely to man and by transmutation was meant the diverting of physical life and force into the channels of spiritual perception and the higher magical powers generally.[34]

In Flying Roll XXI, Moina Mathers further exemplifies the importance of spiritual development and transmutation by using cabalistic lan-guage to discuss the process of becoming 'Perfect Man' and getting in touch with one's 'Higher Self' through the different cabalistic planes of existence:

> We know that all the works of Nature are gradual in their growth, therefore must a man also be gradual in his growth, and before attaining to that more than human, that is to say, to the Yetziratic, Briatic and to the Aziluthic planes he must certainly be the Perfect Man in Assiah.[35]

In Flying Roll II, Percy Bullock writes that 'Spiritual power results from the transmutation of the gross animal nature'.[36] Alex Owen argues that this concept of a higher self and the desire to attain full understanding of one's 'self', expressed a modern desire for self-realization and served to provide the foundation for the notion of the 'modern enchanted self'.[37]

The aims of the Golden Dawn reflect to some degree, the intellectual environment of Victorian Britain. The religious doubt created in this new era of scientific empiricism resulted in a new responsibility being placed on the individual. For some, religion had worn out its welcome as a suitable mediator between man and existence. In his 'Modern

Pagan Witchcraft' Ronald Hutton discusses the two different ways in which scientific rationalism actually encouraged conditions for the appeal of magic and occultism.

> It could drive people to whom a sense of divinity was instinctually important to seek a more direct contact with the superhuman, replacing that offered by orthodox religions. To such people the mediation of the established faiths has been badly compromised by the errors which the progress of knowledge had revealed in their teachings. At the same time, the impulse towards a revival of magic could itself be scientific, addressing precisely those areas which the new sciences had most neglected, and applying their techniques of empirical study and experimentation.[38]

This duplication of the intellectual environment is an integral characteristic in examining the origins of Victorian magic. An historical pattern can be established in which it may be argued that periods dominated by an overly scientific and empirical intellectual trend can provide the appropriate cultural atmosphere for the expansion and expression of a magical and esoteric one. Such a period can be found in nineteenth-century Britain when the opportunity arose for more direct communication, a format which also increased the role and influence of the individual in such a relationship. This is evident in Golden Dawn magic and its precedent may be found in the Theosophy of Madame Blavatsky and in Anna Kingsford's Hermetic Society.

Another way in which these last two changes can be considered is in light of Victorian spiritualism, a phenomenon that was quickly losing credibility in late nineteenth-century culture. In spiritualism, the medium plays the main role. The medium, by definition, is an intermediary. The Golden Dawn was opposed to the methods used by spiritualists in which the medium acted as the passive recipient of a spiritual being. Westcott and MacGregor Mathers clearly did not want members of their order recruited from the ranks of the spiritualists. As we have seen, Westcott's distrust and disdain for the medium in spiritualism led him to describe such a person as 'a negative being, the prey of every evil influence, and of anyone with malign passion'.[39] This distaste for mediumship reflects three things: the exclusion of the intermediary in Victorian magic, the cultural climate in which spiritualism was gaining a reputation for fraudulence, and the importance of the will in Victorian occultism; a feature we will soon address as another major change brought about by nineteenth-century magicians.

The processes of invocation and of evocation are closely linked with the goal of Victorian magic which is the spiritual development of the individual. Just as these processes remain evident in modern magic so does this goal. In his study of over 20 British covens, Ronald Hutton discovered that the central goal of modern pagan witchcraft is to 'cultivate the personal powers of self-control and self-knowledge, and perhaps clairvoyance, prophecy, psychokinesis and psychic healing'.[40] In describing her experience with modern magic practitioners in the Western Mysteries, Luhrmann describes the goals of ritual as being abstract and morally lofty such as revitalizing a city, restoring peace and integrating paganism with Christianity.[41] A student of the Western Mysteries commits him/herself to 'the work', which is the regeneration of oneself and of the planet.

> By this is meant that magic involves the evolution of the self and the planet, and in order to bring through and carry the force to change the planet, you yourself must become a fit vessel to channel the force. Magic, then, is seen as a series of confrontations with oneself, with different archetypes that represent different aspects of the being. Through these symbolic confrontations, the magician's 'true' self is meant to emerge undeterred by any distortions acquired through the course of his life. The practice, then, is explicitly therapeutic. More than that, the reward of the transformation is power.[42]

This confrontation with the magician's 'true' self is certainly reminiscent of the Golden Dawn goal of union with one's higher genius. It is also evident that just as the goals of Victorian magicians have remained in modern magic, so have the resulting process and the loss of the intermediary spirit as the magician taps directly into the power of the divinity. In the passage above the magician alone brings through and carries the force. Luhrmann also describes Western Mystery initiates as perceiving themselves to 'draw in power, aided by the contacts, from a higher spiritual realm, and to channel it out to a physical reality as if their own material bodies brought the force to earth'.[43] Luhrmann and Hutton both describe pagan rituals in which the priestess or priest actually incarnates the goddess or god.

There is another interesting aspect of this change which has to do with the process of the magician bringing and carrying the magical power directly, and it lent itself to the intellectual environment of the nineteenth century with its scientifically derived emphasis upon the physical world. We have seen how the Theosophical movement introduced

Eastern techniques of meditation that influenced the content and language of Victorian magic. There is one significant difference between these traditional Eastern techniques and Golden Dawn magic that can also be found in some of the Western esoteric doctrines employed by the Order, including those associated with Gnosticism, Hermeticism and theurgy. Magic used for spiritual development in these traditional systems implied a rising of the soul away from the physical towards the divine. This imagery is found throughout Gnostic and Hermetic myth, and in Neoplatonism and Christian mysticism. This attraction to the divine as a desertion of the mundane is radically reversed in Victorian magic. In Golden Dawn ritual the purpose of making use of the divinity or force drawn into or out of the individual magician is to empower the individual in order to effect change in the physical world. Yeats expresses this sentiment best in a letter to Florence Farr from 1906.

> I have myself by the by begun eastern meditations of your sort, but with the object of trying to lay hands upon some dynamic and substantialising force as distinguished from the eastern quiescent and supersentualizing state of the soul – a movement downwards upon life not upwards out of life.[44]

This passage presents Victorian invocation as being an active and energizing process and it highlights the difference between the Golden Dawn's focus on practical magic with a Western emphasis, and Theosophy's theoretical focus with an Eastern emphasis. It also represents the reconciliation Victorian magic attempted to make between a scientific framework and a religious one by its focus on the physical world through spiritual development. This emphasis on bringing magical power into the earthly world is reflected in modern magic in the pagan emphasis on Nature. The Golden Dawn's refashioning of Renaissance cabalistic magic and Neoplatonic theurgy so that the goal of uniting with the divine was not to escape the physical world but rather to improve it, proved to be amenable to modern thought and this new focus features predominantly in contemporary magical ritual.

Tying in with this goal is the idea that nature is perceived to be a living being. This is one of the four essential characteristics developed by the French esotericist and scholar Antoine Faivre that a tradition or work must have in order to be considered esoteric within the context of Western modernity.[45] The other three are the idea of correspondences, the experience of transmutation and imagination and mediations. This idea of living nature is strongly linked with the process of invocation and evocation and is exemplified in the instructional texts of the

Golden Dawn. Westcott's lecture to the members of the Isis-Urania Temple 'Man, Miracle and Magic' calls nature:

> unseen, concealed, and existing as the shade or the type of all that is seen and known. Nature has a Spiritual Essence; behind the Astral form and the Material image lies the concealed Spirit, the Vis ab initio, the Energy from on high, from the exalted, from the divine essence.[46]

Later, in the same lecture, Westcott states that the world is moved by a vital energy that can be controlled by man.[47] This very much supports the argument that Golden Dawn magic entailed understanding nature as a living being that can be interpreted by the individual through a system of sympathies and antipathies between that individual and nature.

Despite these lofty goals and complex spiritual and psychological developments, modern magical ritual is still practised for personal gain and other practical ends as well. Luhrmann refers to rituals carried out to 'cure Jane's cold or to get Richard a job'.[48] The aim of spiritual development in magic, however, has flourished from the time of the Victorian magi and has since found fertile ground in the New Age movement and its mantra of self-improvement.

The fifth change was perhaps the Order's most important contribution. This is the dominance of the imagination and the will in the magical process. In conjunction with the will, the imagination functions as a creative power in Victorian magic. In some regards the imagination and the will can be considered as having replaced the intermediary agent. The magician uses both these tools in accessing the desired power or spiritual state. Flying Rolls I, II and V deal with the role of imagination and will. In Flying Roll I, 'A Subject for Contemplation by G.H. Frater *N.O.M.*', 1892–95, Westcott writes:

> To obtain Magical Power, one must strengthen the Will. Let there be no confusion between Will and Desire. You cannot Will too strongly, so do not attempt to Will two things at once: and while Willing one thing do not desire others.[49]

Florence Farr offers the following advice concerning the use of the will and imagination in magic in Flying Roll II, 'Three Suggestions on Will Power by *S.S.D.D.*':

> To want or desire a thing is the first step in the exercise of Will; get a distinct image of the thing you desire placed as it were in your heart, concentrate all your wandering rays of thought upon this image until

you feel it to be one glowing scarlet ball of compacted force. Then project this concentrated force on the object you wish to affect.[50]

In Flying Roll V, 'Some Thoughts on the Imagination', Edward Berridge writes that the will and the imagination must work together in magic:

> The Will unaided can send forth a current, and that current cannot be wholly inoperative; yet its effect is vague and indefinite, because the Will unaided sends forth nothing but the current or force. The Imagination unaided can create an image and this image must have an existence of varying duration; yet it can do nothing of importance, unless vitalized and directed by the Will. When, however, the two are conjoined – when the Imagination creates an image – and the Will directs and uses that image, marvellous magical effects may be obtained.[51]

In this text, the imagination is portrayed as an actual plane of reality: 'When a man imagines he actually creates a form on the Astral or even on some higher plane; and this form is as real and objective to intelligent beings on that plane, as our earthly surroundings are to us.'[52]

Westcott adds some supplementary remarks to this particular lecture which furthers this perception of the imagination. Westcott distinguishes imagination from fancy and associates the power of imagination with a term borrowed from the 'Esoteric Theosophists', *Kriya Sakti*, which denotes 'the mysterious power of thought which enables it to produce external phenomenal, perceptible results by its own inherent energy when fertilized by the Will'.[53] Westcott also associates this idea of the imagination with Hermetic doctrine which holds that ideas can be made manifest, and with cabalistic theory which claims that man has creative power through thought and will.[54] The linking of imagination with mediation is found in most Golden Dawn rituals in which different symbols associated with the systems of tarot, cabala, astrology, cabalistic and angelic magic, and alchemy are used in conjunction with the imagination of the magician in order to achieve perceptible results.

The roles of the will and imagination in magic have already been discussed in the context of Neoplatonic theurgy as described by Iamblichus. The union of the individual will with that of the divine is a crucial process in Iamblichus' theurgy. The human will in this process however, was under the control of the divine and the imagination was used by that divinity to produce visions.[55] In Victorian magic the individual will and imagination are not subordinate to a divine will.

Rather, the magical procedure is directed by the magician's will and imagination. This apparent shift in the roles of the will and imagination may be less salient when taking into account that Iamblichus was defending theurgy. His emphasis on the domination of the divine will renders the magician less accountable in any accusations of magical practice. Nonetheless, it was not until the Golden Dawn came along that the imagination and the will of the individual were to feature so prominently in Western magic. Not surprisingly, Yeats best expresses the importance of the imagination in Victorian magic as reflecting a cultural movement leading to the exaltation of this previously neglected faculty. In his 1895 essay entitled 'The Body of the Father Christian Rosencrux', Yeats compares the history of the imagination to the legend of Christian Rosenkreuz, by observing that both have been entombed and forgotten. Yeats perceives that a new age is dawning, an age in which imagination will once again be unearthed and scientific empiricism will no longer dominate intellectual society.

> I cannot get it out of my mind that this age of criticism is about to pass, and an age of imagination, of emotion, of moods, of revelation, about to come in its place; for certainly belief in a supersensual world is at hand again; and when the notion that we are 'phantoms of the earth and water' has gone down the wind, we will trust our own being and all its desires to invent; and when the external world is no more a standard of reality, we will learn again that the great Passions are angels of God, and that to embody them 'uncurbed in their eternal glory,' even in their labour for the ending of man's peace and prosperity, is more than to comment, however wisely, upon the tendencies of our time …[56]

Observations such as these, made by Golden Dawn magicians in their creative and ritual writing, are important in that they document an awareness of what Victorian magic was and how it differed from the traditional magic from whence it came. These writings provide insight that these men and women were fully aware of the cultural and social environment in which they lived and were intent on shaping their magic to reflect this environment and even to change it. Owen argues that this awareness, on the part of the magician, what she calls 'occult reality' is created by the individual's imagination or 'fictionalizing mind' and is further evidence of the modern nature of *fin de siècle* occultism.[57]

The prominence of the imagination has also remained a dominant feature of modern magic. Imagination is the key to contemporary ritual. It is the first step in performing any kind of magic ritual and indeed in any kind of intentional human action. Through her research, Luhrmann discovered that, for modern practitioners, magic works directly through the imagination.

> When one imagines, that imaginative act – in itself, as a mental image, regardless of its behavioral compulsion – can affect what we think of as unrelated 'material' reality. Magicians use this conception of dynamic interconnectedness to describe the physical world as the sort of thing that imagination and desire can affect. The magician's world is an interdependent whole, a web of which no strand is autonomous. Mind and body, galaxy and atom, sensation and stimulus, are intimately bound.[58]

The sixth and final change to be discussed in this chapter is the opening up of ritual magic to women and the acknowledgement of their equal status. This was completely unprecedented in the history of British magic. The inclusion of women appears to be a feature largely dependent upon the cultural environment of Victorian Britain. A sampling of references to women in magical texts and rituals will serve to demonstrate the traditional exclusion of women from magic.

In medieval magic the magician was male. Medieval ritual magic was text-based and only the literate (mostly men) would have had both access to the appropriate books and the ability to read such material. Medieval ritual magic was largely the domain of clerics and as such, was exclusive to men. The magical texts themselves speak of the inadequacy of women in performing ritual magic. In *The Book of the Sacred Magic of Abramelin the Mage*, there is an entire chapter devoted to describing the necessary qualities that the magician must hold in order to attempt the magic outlined in the text:

> his age ought not to be less than twenty-five years nor more than fifty; he should have no hereditary disease, such as virulent leprosy; whether he be free or married importeth little ... Among women, there be only Virgins who are suitable; but I strongly advise that so important a matter should not be communicated to them, because of the accidents that they might cause by their curiosity and love of talk.[59]

The traditional role for women in magic is as a medium, scryer or crystal-gazer in the magical procedures of clairvoyance, divination and crystal gazing. This has been observed in the context of ancient Egyptian magic, John Dee's angelic magic, and Frederick Hockley's experimentation with crystals. This seemingly passive role reached its glory in Victorian spiritualism. While the role of the Victorian medium has been acknowledged as providing empowerment for women in nineteenth-century America and England, its passive origins and nature remain all too obvious.[60] It was the Golden Dawn that provided the first opportunity for women to gain equality with men in magical ritual. The status of women in the Golden Dawn is evident first in the Order's admission policy of both women and men, a precedent set by the Theosophical Society, the Hermetic Society and some of the earlier fringe Masonic organizations of the late eighteenth and nineteenth centuries. Secondly, this equal status is emphasized in some of the writings of the members. In fact, in a footnote to the above quotation from *The Book of the Sacred Magic of Abramelin the Mage*, MacGregor Mathers wrote: 'Here comes another touch of prejudice. In the present day many of the profoundest students of the Qabalah are women, both married and single.'[61]

Many of the Second Order knowledge lectures were written by the women of the Golden Dawn, namely Florence Farr and Moina Mathers, both of whom, together with Annie Horniman, held some of the highest positions in the Order and were regarded as talented magicians. This equal status for women within the Order indicates that the people involved in the Golden Dawn were supportive of some of the ideas expressed by those at the forefront of the women's movement in late Victorian Britain. Certainly MacGregor Mathers and Westcott were influenced by the domineering personalities of Anna Kingsford and Helena Blavatsky and followed the open admission policies of the societies founded by those women. Yet it remains the privilege of the Golden Dawn to claim responsibility for opening up the world of practical magic to the female sex. Indeed, Alex Owen demonstrates that despite the Victorian perception of one of the primary tools of ritual magic, that of willpower, as belonging to a male temperament, the Golden Dawn made no distinction in their training of the sexes in honing this powerful instrument.[62]

It is rather interesting to note that while the women of the Golden Dawn made strides in their involvement in magical ritual, they did not necessarily abandon the more traditional magical roles for women. Moina Mathers functioned as a kind of scryer or medium for her husband as it was through her visionary capabilities that he communicated with the higher levels and the Order's unknown superiors or secret chiefs.

The equal status with men that women achieved as magicians within the Golden Dawn remains evident in modern magic. The Pagan

Federation maintains that its members must subscribe to the belief that divinity can be both masculine and feminine and the expression of this principle is the belief that women are at least as effective as men in holding religious and magical power.[63]

These six changes, either developed or re-emphasized through Victorian magic, continue to affect modern magical practitioners and doctrine. In fact, twentieth- and twenty-first-century magical groups are dependent on the Golden Dawn system for their magical theory and rituals. It is these very developments that have made the Order's magic so practical and functional for modern magicians. These characteristics were developed or recreated by the Order in light of the intellectual environment of the nineteenth century and the demands which that environment made on perceptions of the relationship between man and divinity and the role of the individual.

The modifications that the Order made to magic were primarily motivated by the cultural, social and intellectual factors of Victorian Britain. The lasting power of late nineteenth-century occultism and its enduring legacy to contemporary magicians have also been observed and its resilience has been associated with the changes that it made to Western magic. Not only was nineteenth-century thought primarily responsible for the intellectual origins of the Golden Dawn, but also for rendering it seemingly timeless in its suitability and adequacy for modern magic. Victorian magic has lasted so long because of the characteristics developed out of a response to the cultural atmosphere in which it developed.

The people involved in fashioning this magical system were by no means unaware of what they were doing. Westcott and MacGregor Mathers were not merely creating magical theory in a cultural and intellectual vacuum. Their awareness of what they were creating, and their reasons for this creation are evident in the following passage from a paper presented by Westcott to the *Soc. Ros.*

> Our England has in the Victorian age lost much of its faith in the spiritual world, and developed a grossly material view of the universe, and physical science reigned supreme in the minds of the learned. So there arose a great conflict between Christian Orthodoxy, Natural Science, the Theosophy of the Indian faith, and of the Rosicrucian and Hermetic doctrines and occult sciences. Even if Spirituality has not yet won a victory it has broadened the minds of materialists, made them more tolerant, and has induced a revival of research into the human environment and the relation of man to the beings,

powers and forces of the spiritual plane contiguous to man, acting and reacting upon him although invisible and unperceived in common life by our senses.[64]

By attempting to find a balance of principles and theories, the Golden Dawn was intentionally offering an alternative to the opposing camps of orthodox Christianity and scientific naturalism, and to the mixed camp of Theosophy, Rosicrucianism, Hermeticism and occultism. In doing so the Order added a new dimension to nineteenth-century intellectual history and a new chapter to the history of Western magic, by positioning Victorian magic as a worldview encouraged by the cultural and intellectual debates of the century in which it emerged. Its emergence repeated the process, to some degree, found in the development of cabalistic magic in the Renaissance in that both arose in response to the confrontation of opposing systems of thought, science and religion. Victorian magic had more success in retaining a prominent position in popular culture throughout the twentieth and twenty-first centuries than the Renaissance synthesis of magic had in the centuries following its formation for two reasons. First, Victorian magic did not meet with the same opposition from organized religion that Renaissance magic did, emerging in the midst of a secularized world. Second, by expelling the spiritual intermediary and focusing on bringing magical power into the physical world, the Golden Dawn brought magic back into the world, a development which agreed with the scientific mentality dominating nineteenth-century thought. Despite its dependency upon Renaissance magic, both in content and process, the Victorian magical system owes its resilience to its underlying rationale which was created out of nineteenth-century confrontations between opposing intellectual movements.

7
Middle-Class Magic

Victorian culture has been interpreted as the product of an internal rebellion against Anglican culture and the major values traditionally associated with it. In his exploration of Victorian intellectual life, historian Frank M. Turner describes how Roman Catholicism, romantic subjectivism, naturalism and materialism forced a recasting of culture, aiding in the destruction of Anglican culture, and leading to the creative culture of the Victorian period.[1] Turner refers to this process as 'cultural apostasy'. This new culture was characterized by naturalism, religious experiment and subjective aesthetic response.[2] It is in this climate of cultural change and out of the spirit of cultural rebellion that Victorian occultism emerged. But it was not alone. Many other developments and currents of thought flourished in this environment and subsequently had a hand in shaping the nature and development of late nineteenth-century magic.

One of the most striking developments in academic circles in the early decades of the century was the growing professionalization of all disciplines and primarily that of the sciences. As scientific method took the lead, the number of professional scientists and scientific societies increased dramatically in the 1830s. This trend continued for the next five decades during which membership in scientific societies almost tripled and the numbers of scientific faculties and professors also rose.[3]

Anthropology and folklore were two of the many disciplines affected by this growing professionalization and its related authority shift from religion to science. Before the emphasis on Darwinism in academic thought, anthropology was strongly directed by Christian belief. A previous preoccupation with uncovering the nature of human unity was transformed in the Darwinian environment into a preoccupation with the origin of civilization. The major issues addressed by the British Association of Anthropology in the middle of the century were the antiquity and descent of man, man's ultimate origin, and the progressive character of the growth of civilization.[4] With the loss of religious authority and belief in supernatural origins of man, anthropology began to seek the origin of religious truths within the myths of primitive cultures thus furthering the evolutionary view of religious thought and the scientific naturalist dismissal of religion and the supernatural as irrational and primitive. Another influencing factor on anthropological research was the archaeological findings of the nineteenth century which promoted interest in ancient civilizations and fostered the inherent Victorian fixation with the culturally exotic.

Not all academic research was focused on the distant and the primitive. The development of the British folklore movement advanced awareness of local history. Conscious of the effects of industrialization on local traditions, scholars began searching out and preserving folk customs and beliefs before they became irretrievable. British folklore evolved out of a sixteenth-century antiquarian tradition that came into its own in the nineteenth century and exerted great influence on other academic disciplines, in particular, anthropology. Folklore and anthropology shared similar interests in ceremonies and beliefs tied to the seasons and superstitions concerning witchcraft and magic.[5]

Anthropological interest in the exotic and in finding the one origin of civilization within the myths of earlier cultures is reflected in the doctrines of Theosophy, the writings of Anna Bonus Kingsford, nineteenth-century elaborations on the history of Freemasonry and Rosicrucianism, and in the magical theory of the Golden Dawn. The growing number of publications and research into the magical practices of earlier cultures nourished the increasing interest of spiritualists, theosophists and magicians seeking to establish the universality and the antiquity of their doctrines and beliefs. Folklore, on the other hand, does not appear to have had as much influence on the esoterically inclined with its emphasis upon nature-based religious rituals and folk custom and belief. The religious and philosophical focus of the Golden Dawn positions the order outside of any obvious influence from the folklore movement. The Golden Dawn revived supposed ancient rituals and researched earlier civilizations out of the belief that such knowledge would bring them even higher knowledge and spiritual development. In this context it is understandable that the folklore movement with its more recent historical focus and its seemingly 'quaint' character would hold less appeal for those in search of gnosis. It was not until later in the twentieth century when modern pagan witchcraft began to take shape that folk custom and belief would provide a rich source for the fashioning of that tradition.

Another development in academic circles concerned an obsession with classical culture and its application to, not only Victorian scholarship, but also literature, architecture and even social policy. This classical focus began earlier and is found throughout the eighteenth century in the numerous publications of classical writings, in Greek mythological influences on visual art, and in the use of myths and mythological thought in the works of the romantic poets well into the nineteenth century.[6] There were many aspects of Greek culture that appealed to the Victorians. The classical world provided a model of how to approach changing cultural and social institutions and it influenced nineteenth-century thought, political philosophy, religion and education.

One of the major Greek influences on Victorian culture is found in the works of Plato. His influence was ubiquitous from the incorporation of Platonic myth in the literary and poetic works of the era, to the adaptation of his ideas of social organization and community in British politics.[7] Plato's works and other classical writing also provided a religious role as a secular substitute for Christianity by providing a moral code composed of traditional Christian values outside the constraints of the religion itself. This adaptation of Greek philosophy to support Christian values was first embraced by German artists and literary critics in the middle of the eighteenth century who sought to sustain such values without the accompanying baggage of the Christian religion.[8] The Victorians followed this direction and forged an unusual alliance between Christianity and the study of the classics, unusual in that the two cultures are theologically incompatible. By ignoring the incompatibility of paganism with Christianity, the Victorians focused instead upon the social and moral values of both.

The desire to emulate classical society as well as the brotherhood Victorians felt with the Greeks was obvious in many social values and institutions. The parallels between Greek and Victorian notions of democracy, aesthetics, athletics and even gender roles were emphasized and promoted by the Victorians. The Victorian obsession with the classics, however, was nowhere more vividly expressed than in literature and art. The names of Greek gods and divine beings abound in Victorian anthologies of verse and in the middle of the century a trend developed of depicting elves and fairies in painting, the British equivalents of Greek nymphs.[9] In literature, the role of myth experienced a demotion of sorts during the height of scientific rationalism and empiricism, but by the end of the century, owing to the efforts of Golden Dawn member and poet William Butler Yeats, myth was repositioned as a form of experiential thought and not as a mere literary convention.[10]

It was during this earlier rationalistic period of Greek myth, however, that the link between the social sciences and the classics was forged, namely between myth and anthropology. The influential anthropologist James Frazer was responsible for making this connection and in his monumental *Golden Bough,* he formulated some of the fundamental definitions of magic and also examined the social origins of myth; an examination that inspired nineteenth-century theosophists and esotericists in their search for the unity of all myth, religion and magic.[11]

The Victorian admiration for Greek culture is found throughout the rituals and literature of the Golden Dawn. Greek titles were used in designating the officiating members of the First Order's rituals and the ritual content and structure was dependent upon nineteenth-century interpretations of Greek mystery religions. It is obvious, however, that Victorian magic placed more emphasis upon ancient Egyptian culture, as demonstrated in the later interests of some of the more prominent occultists. This is contemporaneous with the trend and findings of late nineteenth-century Egyptology. In the late Victorian period, Egyptian civilization no doubt held more mystery than the well-plumbed culture of classical Greece especially for occultists who were ever in search of the new (yet still ancient) and the obscure in fashioning a new magical tradition. And as the Greeks had long admired Egyptian civilization, Egypt was the appropriate source for an even more venerable wisdom with its more obscure gods and goddesses at a time when the Greek pantheon had become commonplace. Egypt also featured prominently throughout Madame Blavatsky's early work and her society's influence on Victorian magic was quite significant. The most obvious reason for the Golden Dawn's emphasis upon Egypt, was its long association as the birthplace of magic as developed in the Renaissance with the popularity of the writings of the legendary Hermes Trismegistus.

Despite its preoccupation with things Egyptian, Victorian magic was still influenced by the status of Greek culture as an artistic, social and intellectual idea throughout the period. Victorian admiration for the classics led to the formulation of one of the most influential philosophical developments of the late nineteenth and early twentieth centuries. British idealism was a reaction against empiricism and utilitarianism and involved the redirection of philosophical thought from modern thinkers to the philosophy of classical Greece. This philosophical movement, influenced largely by German idealism, was motivated by the need to establish some kind of religious belief that stood up to Darwinism and naturalism. Idealism emphasized the relationship between the individual and the community as defining individual worth and significance, the dependence of the individual upon membership in the community for one's rights and liberty, and the duty of the community to guarantee those rights.[12] Through the work of T.H. Green, one of the most influential proponents of idealism, and other philosophers such as F.H. Bradley and Bernard Bosanquet, idealism grew in popularity at Oxford and most of the other British universities and even went on to influence general thought and public policy between 1880 and 1914.[13] Much like the emergence of ritual magic, the appearance of idealism and its subsequent popularity and dominance for a brief period may be considered inconsistent with the way in which British thought had been developing before its emergence and after its demise. Idealism appeared in the midst of a general social, intellectual and even political preference for empiricism and scientific methodology.[14]

It is not just in its seemingly misplaced arrival in intellectual thought that idealism shares certain features with the revival of ritual magic. The very key concepts and ideas expressed in the works of Green, the most influential and popular of the idealists during this period, are found in the doctrines and literature of Victorian occultism, particularly the emphasis upon the will of the individual and the notion of self-realization. In his work, Green tried to show the development of human life as a gradual fulfilment of a universal spirit. The individual possessed great creative power and inherent goodness and the realization of these talents resulted in the liberation of the self, the highest achievement possible for man.[15] This self-realization is phrased, much as it is in Victorian magical theory, as a progressive event, taking place in stages that differentiated between the actual self and a higher, possible self, the equivalent of the Golden Dawn's higher genius.[16] This shared terminology and theory between the leading philosophical movement of the time and Victorian occultism points to a common intellectual trend. Both were reacting to and incorporating new standards of truths offered by science while using those very standards to argue for the existence of something other than the objectively sensual world, something with which the individual was very much connected to and to which the individual had a responsibility through progressive self-realization.

The same intellectual and cultural struggles that were central to the formation of idealism were also found in the more popular Victorian pursuits of spiritualism, astrology, mesmerism and phrenology. Spiritualism arrived in Britain from America in the middle of the century and offered believers the opportunity to communicate with spirits of the dead. Spiritualists believed that human survival after death was possible and that disembodied spirits could be contacted through the forum of a séance. Many mediums, ranging from the rank amateur to those who delivered performances of awe-inspiring theatricality, were frauds. There were many others, however, who truly believed in both their abilities and in the process. It was not just the spiritualists who were engaged in this kind of afterlife experimentation: their more sceptical counterparts, psychical researchers, undertook systematic examinations of spiritualist phenomena to establish their validity and exposed many of the frauds. These researchers were fellows of the Royal Society and university professors while the spiritualists themselves came from all segments of society. In the second half of the nineteenth century there were more than 200 spiritualist societies in operation all over Britain.[17]

Spiritualism was a forum for social and political expression and the different classes mixed their spiritualist beliefs with their class-based social agendas. Plebeian spiritualism, found predominantly in northern England and controlled by working and lower-middle class people, was hostile to Christianity and was associated with atheism, free thought, feminism, trade unionism and socialism.[18] Middle-class spiritualism, centred in London, was not opposed to Christian belief and had its own social agenda that included protesting against vivisection, capital punishment and alcohol use. Both embraced the notion that knowledge was accessible to all, the main democratic epistemology of the nineteenth century.[19]

The arrival of spiritualism and its subsequent popularity coincided with several intellectual, cultural and social factors. Dissatisfaction with Western science and a loss of conviction in orthodox religion caused many to look elsewhere for security and comfort. Thousands turned to spiritualism which offered a substitute religion for some and a substitute science for others. Christianity no longer functioned as a bridge to the next world but spiritualism did and for some it offered tangible proof. As a compromise between new scientific method and religious truths, spiritualism worked for many, although it by no means offered a complete alternative faith or scientific proof or methodology. Rather it acted as a buffer during a changing cultural and intellectual period. In examining spiritualism in the context of religious and scientific developments, we see many of the same concerns being addressed that were motivating factors in the works of other esotericists, namely Kingsford and Blavatsky, and in the establishment of other societies, such as the Golden Dawn, the Hermetic Society and the Theosophical Society. Despite the Golden Dawn's hostility towards spiritualism, its members joined the ranks of the Order for many of the same reasons spiritualists formulated their beliefs.

The Golden Dawn also shares with spiritualism a common method of education. The nineteenth century saw a widespread passion for self-education. With the growing belief in equal access to knowledge, growing popular interest in exotic subjects and the multiplication of scientific, scholarly and non-scholarly societies, people began to gather in groups to study topics of interest and to individually pursue such subjects on their own. By the middle of the century the Victorian museum movement had transformed the British Museum 'from a place intended only for the amusement of the curious and the rich into the largest and most popular educational centre in the kingdom',[20] providing much of the necessary resources for the self-education movement. People no longer felt restricted to education according to their class. Groups sprang up all over Britain, for the purpose of studying everything from anthropology to the analysis of the bumps on one's head to predict the future. It was in this context that many spiritualist groups formed and by 1865 some had evolved into spiritualist educational institutions where believers could not only witness spiritualist phenomena but could also learn the theories supporting it.[21] The structure of the Golden Dawn as a magical school simply followed a nineteenth-century model of an alternative educational institute stimulated by a middle-class preoccupation with self-education and exotic subject matter.

There was a certain segment of society for whom spiritualism had a particular appeal. With little or no access to university education or political power, women found an audience and a role for themselves among the spiritualists. Not only did women have a voice, quite literally, in spiritualist phenomena, but also in the social movements associated with spiritualism. Anna Kingsford found an audience for her protest against vivisection and promotion of vegetarianism. Annie Besant, a prominent Theosophist and women's and social rights activist, also used the spiritualist platform to further her causes. Even among women with no specific agenda, spiritualism provided a space where they had an important role to play. In her study on late Victorian spiritualism, Janet Oppenheim notes that the number of middle-class housewives who discovered powers of trance communication, clairvoyance, and furniture relocation during this period was particularly striking.[22] Mediumship offered the opportunity for both social acceptance and ascent, something particularly attractive to middle-class women and which we see again in the Golden Dawn's admission policy.

The final obvious feature of the role of spiritualism and its influence on the Golden Dawn is the relationship between spiritualism and magic. The strength of this relationship varied. From the perspective of the scientific community, spiritualism was dangerously close to exposing the skeletons in Western science's closet through reincorporating rejected aspects of magic into the supposed scientific system embraced by the spiritualists. These fears were unfounded in the minds of most spiritualists who rejected the secrecy and ritualistic aspects of occultism in preference for the open and rational method of inquiry established by modern science.[23] Nonetheless, there are obvious similarities between the magical worldview of the Golden Dawn and the way in which the spiritualists understood the functioning of the universe. These similar views are also consistent with the popularity enjoyed by Greek philosophy throughout the nineteenth century and the development of idealism. They include the Neoplatonic view of the world as being united by a cosmic soul or a universal spirit and the belief in a hierarchical structure through which the spirit evolves or progresses.

Followers of spiritualism frequently branched out into other esoteric interests such as crystal gazing, mesmerism and phrenology. As was the case with spiritualism, these practices were frequently found alongside certain social movements. One person who combined his working-class agenda with crystal gazing and the cabala was John George Henry Brown. In Nottingham in the 1850s the angel Gabriel revealed apocalyptic messages to Brown, which he printed and circulated to his more than a hundred followers. Some of these prophecies concerned issues of class oppression and predicted battles between the rich and the poor. Brown also used astral and cabalistic magic to conjure spirits and angels. References to Sibly and Dee in these prophecies indicate that Brown was influenced by the same magical tradition that produced Barrett, Hockley and the Golden Dawn.[24] In such cases it is clear that while Victorian spiritualism and its associated esoteric currents are unique and not forerunners of nineteenth-century ritual magic, all shared similar sources, influences and opponents and could not help but reflect these similarities in their structure and content.

In the 1830s, decades before spiritualism made its foray into British society, astrology was making a comeback as a curious form of entertainment and serious consultation among the urban middle-class.[25] Astrological journals such as *The Straggling Astrologer, Urania* and *Zadkiel's Almanac* boasted annual sales in the tens of thousands. Despite increasing hostility from the scientific community and mainstream educated opinion, and despite the criminalization of astrology under the Vagrancy Act,

London astrologers Raphael (Robert Cross Smith) and Zadkiel (Richard James Morrison) enjoyed overwhelming success among their middle-class clientele. Both Raphael and Zadkiel borrowed from crystal gazing, ceremonial magic, the cabala and alchemy in their writings, primarily from Barrett's *Magus,* in the case of the latter.[26] Such urban astrologers frequently moved freely between astrological circles and occult circles.

A move from rural to urban areas, a change in clientele from the uneducated working class to the professional middle class and the acceptance of women astrologers all characterized nineteenth-century astrology. It was also characterized by its adaptation of other esoteric movements such as ceremonial magic, crystal gazing, mesmerism and Theosophy. In terms of geographical location, demographics and syncretic nature, Victorian astrology mirrored other contemporary esoteric movements such as spiritualism, Theosophy and most importantly the Golden Dawn. It did succeed in outliving many of these contemporaries and it is claimed that to this day every practising modern British astrologer owns a copy of Raphael's *Astrological Almanac*.[27]

Nonetheless astrology remained somewhat marginalized and was never incorporated into Victorian magic in its nineteenth-century format. Astrology had already provided necessary components for the Western magical blend in the Renaissance when Marsilio Ficino used astrological symbolism and theory to develop his astral and spiritual magic. Astrology as a form of predestination was rejected by Western magic for its incompatibility with the notion of free will. Despite being found on the same pages of nineteenth-century astrological publications, magic and astrology remained quite separate currents of thought and the astrology of Raphael and Zadkiel never found its way into the theory or literature of Victorian magic.[28] It was far more likely for astrologists to branch out into other occult pursuits than for occultists to dabble in traditional astrology. Occultists did however freely incorporate astrological symbolism into their ritual practice.

Mesmerism and phrenology were two other nineteenth-century intellectual influences that frequently crossed over into the occult milieu, particularly in the first half of the century. Both of these unusual areas of study and practice were also often present in the domains of the spiritualists and astrologers. Mesmerism was named after Franz Anton Mesmer, a pioneer of hypnotism who developed the theory that a subtle fluid pervaded all entities and the universe that could be manipulated by magnets to affect the health of an individual. Mesmer professed to be able to cure a variety of illnesses through this unusual method and he attracted numerous believers, followers and patients in Paris in the late eighteenth century, some of whom apparently received miraculous cures under his care. Mesmer's techniques included inducing stages of hypnosis or lucid consciousness during which spiritualist phenomena could be channelled by the magnetized patient through the suggestion of the mesmerist. By the early 1850s, about the same time that spiritualism was making its appearance in Britain, mesmerism had become quite popular and numerous mesmeric publications and journals were being circulated. One of the most frequent associates of mesmerism was phrenology, the study of the structure and shape of the head in order to predict the conduct of the individual – a kind of astrology of the head, popular at the time because of the concurrent scientific empiricist belief that the brain was the organ of the mind.[29]

What mesmerism and phrenology shared with spiritualism were the influences of science, religion and the occult. All three blended these into an appropriate, accepted and desirable balance for the intellectual climate of the time. All classes, but predominantly the middle class, found in these scientifically-based theories rooted in an occult and/or magical past, a retreat from the threat of materialism and the demise of religion. Just as with spiritualism, however, both mesmerism and phrenology also had their critics. Science and medicine were moving away from the very theories that spiritualism and mesmerism promoted and their growing popularity met with hostility from much of the educated elite, or at least those that were not attending séances and mesmeric presentations themselves, out of curiosity, conversion, or scepticism.

From the beginning of the nineteenth century, people of all classes were presented with the opportunity to participate in numerous unusual activities whose theory and practices were developing in response to the cultural, social and intellectual environment. Not only did some of these movements offer desirable solutions to the necessary authority of science and the desire for some form of religious participation or content but they also played into much of the social issues of the time and catered to the agendas of different segments of society. They also offered the forum and audience for those who were excluded from both in academic and political circles.

Placed within this context we see Victorian magic as a successor of many of these movements. It is however, important to remember that late nineteenth-century occultism quite intentionally shunned spiritualism and astrology and did not incorporate any of the techniques of Mesmer or phrenology into its theories. In this conscious rejection Victorian magic isolated itself from the more obvious attempts at knitting together the unravelling threads of science and religion and also alienated itself from the passivity inherent in mediumship and the denial of free will that accompanied urban astrology. It is in these deliberate actions that Victorian occultism was more in line with certain developments in nineteenth-century philosophy and the ideas expressed in British idealism.

Victorian magic also appealed to the creatively inclined and had its share of artistic members. Actress Florence Farr and amateur visual artist Moina Mathers were some of the more prominent members of artistic bent. In no other member, however, can the artistic environment of the nineteenth century be shown to reflect the doctrines of Golden Dawn magic than in the person of W.B. Yeats. His interest in occultism followed a tradition of association of English artists with the occult sciences that began much earlier in the century. Such artists included William Blake, Samuel Palmer, John Varley and Richard Cosway.[30] The appeal of the Golden Dawn was part of an attraction to the occult that Yeats felt throughout most of his life. This interest was fostered by both his particular disposition and the contemporary popular interest in spiritualism, esotericism and the occult. In the last decades of the nineteenth century, Yeats was a member of many esoterically-oriented orders. He continued his membership in offshoot societies of the Golden Dawn well into the twentieth century. For Yeats, this interest proved to be more of a passing fad. In fact, next to poetry, he considered magic his most important area of study and perceived the two as connected, associating poetry with the world of myth, intuition and magic.[31]

The tension between science and religion was also a formulative factor in Yeats's attraction to the mystical. In his *Autobiographies*, he claims that the followers of Huxley and Tyndall had put him into a rage by their diminution of the subject in art and literature and in their having deprived him of the comfort of the 'simple-minded religion' of his childhood.[32] In search of a replacement for this lost religion and influenced early on by the symbolism and mysticism of Blake, Emmanuel Swedenborg and the French spiritualist Allan Kardec, Yeats readily fell into the esoteric circles of late nineteenth-century London.[33]

His membership in the esoteric section of the Theosophical Society and in another Theosophically-oriented group, the Adelphi Lodge, brought him into contact with members of the Golden Dawn. The Order won him over with its focus on practical magic and use of symbols to induce visions. The creative genius of the Golden Dawn, MacGregor Mathers, was immensely influential on Yeats, particularly in his apparent abilities to direct the visions of others. Yeats first met MacGregor Mathers in the British Museum reading room where MacGregor Mathers and those with similar interests spent much time researching obscure material with which to nourish emerging esoteric societies and rituals. Yeats was fascinated even before he knew of MacGregor Mathers' interests, describing him as a 'figure of romance'.[34] After discovering MacGregor Mathers' attraction to ritual magic, Yeats was even more intrigued and no doubt their common aspirations for a Celtic revival helped solidify their relationship and the two became close colleagues in mystical exploration. Through his studies with MacGregor Mathers and the Golden Dawn, Yeats became convinced that the individual, through the use of certain symbols, could produce images in the mind from a source deeper than the subconscious and he described such experiences with MacGregor Mathers:

> He gave me a cardboard symbol and I closed my eyes...there rose before me mental images that I could not control: a desert and a black Titan raising himself up by his two hands from the middle of a heap of ancient ruins. Mathers explained that I had seen a being of the order of Salamanders because he had shown me their symbol, but it was not necessary even to show the symbol, it would have been sufficient that he imagined it.[35]

Yeats's poetic imagination revelled in these discoveries and in the preoccupation with symbolism and an ancient tradition that was all part of the Golden Dawn. Not only did the Order provide Yeats with the magical and symbolic material to fuel his creative work, but it also provided some invaluable contacts who would go on to become key players in Yeats's other interests, most notably the actress Florence Farr and theatre benefactor, Annie Horniman. However, it was the world of magic which furnished him with the language, symbols and techniques to evoke the images found in his work. The Golden Dawn provided him with the possibility that the world of myth and magic found in his imagination, may indeed, exist elsewhere.[36]

Another thing that appealed to Yeats was the invention of tradition, something which came easy to him and which was central to the very essence of the Golden Dawn. This entire book, to some degree, has been an examination of the invention of tradition carried out by the Golden Dawn and, more generally speaking, the invention of tradition that lies at the heart of Western magic. Invented tradition refers to a set of practices of a ritual or symbolic nature governed by rules that seeks to establish certain values and standards of behaviour through repetition of these practices. This repetition also serves to solidify continuity with a suitable historic past.[37] The invention of tradition occurs during times of social transition when old traditions no longer function in a new cultural and intellectual climate. It is therefore of little surprise that the period between 1870 and 1914 saw the invention of numerous traditions.[38] Many of the traditions formed at this time were political and emphasized the role of ritual, ceremonial and myth.[39] Not only is the Golden Dawn itself a prime example of an invented tradition concerned with ritual, ceremonial and myth, but its very components, Freemasonry, Rosicrucianism, and Hermeticism are all also examples of this type of tradition. The process of inventing tradition frequently involved drawing on a social storehouse of historical ritual, symbolism, religion and folklore.[40] This is obvious in the Golden Dawn symbolism and its use of Egyptian, Greek, Neoplatonic, Hermetic, Masonic and Rosicrucian sources. The idea of the invention of tradition has come to be associated with the issue of authenticity. An invented tradition is somehow less worthy because of its appropriation. Recent scholarship has argued that such an interpretation of Hobsbawm is neither useful nor correct. Theologian Paul Post suggests that, in a more accurate interpretation of Hobsbawm '"inventing traditions" can be regarded as equal to construction, creation and innovation (in which the emphasis lies on the *novus*!) of traditions'.[41] Such an interpretation is more constructive in asserting the relevance of Hobsbawm's invented tradition for occultism. While other studies on nineteenth-century occultism have discussed the connection between invented tradition and occultism, such discussions rely on the interpretation of invented tradition as inauthentic. David Harvey Allen, in his study on French occultism, claims that the invention of tradition was employed by occultists to establish authority and legitimacy for their ideas and practices.[42] While this may be true, and may also be true of occultists on the other side of the Channel, such an interpretation disregards the more positive and progressive goals and effects of the process. Victorian occultists in particular were involved in more than mere appropriation in the construction of their rituals and tradition. In drawing upon older texts and rituals in the creation of a new and potent form of magic, the emphasis here is indeed upon the *novus*. In perceiving these older traditions, invented or real, as conduits to magical power, Victorian occultists were more engaged in a process of invoking tradition than inventing tradition.

Victorian magic was not only dependent upon British culture and domestic intellectual developments. Across the channel we have already seen that France contributed greatly not only in the influence of certain individuals but as a destination for the emigration of British occultism thanks to the Matherses and their Rites of Isis. We have seen the influence of French occultism on the Golden Dawn through the works of Eliphas Lévi and the importance of the city of Paris has been established as the site of the Order's fifth temple, the Ahathoor Temple. There are readily identifiable similarities between French and British occultism in the development of esoteric and occult activities leading up to the nineteenth-century and throughout that period. While Victorian magic was a distinctly British creation, some of the intellectual and cultural factors that contributed to its development overflow geographical boundaries.

The revival of occultism took place much earlier in France than in Britain and can even be traced back to the years leading up to the French Revolution.[43] While it was the nineteenth century that saw the most popular years of British occultism, its French counterpart enjoyed popularity throughout the eighteenth century as well as the nineteenth. If we are to take the argument that the belief in magic flourishes in a society undergoing great cultural change then the growing number of occult societies and writings makes sense in eighteenth-century France, a place of social and political upheaval. By the time the Revolution broke out, the ever-present companion of occultism, Freemasonry, had also made its presence felt in every corner of the country. More than 30 000 belonged to the 600 or 700 lodges that were operating throughout France.[44] Just as we have seen in nineteenth-century British occultism, the prominent occultists of eighteenth-century France were all influenced by Freemasonry. Some of these include Martines de Pasqually, the founder of the Order of the Elect Cohens in 1760, a rite in which members practised ritual magic based on the works of Agrippa and the Catholic mass, and Antoine-Joseph Pernety who, in the 1760s, founded the Illuminés d'Avignon, a Masonic society that focused upon alchemy.[45] Another interesting Masonic development in eighteenth-century French occultism was the establishment of Cagliostro's Egyptian Rite which, as we have seen, was open to women as well as men. Here we see another precedent for the Golden Dawn's all-inclusive admission policy and its interest in Egyptian magic.

Many other prominent esotericists and occultists predating Lévi left their mark on French occultism. Some of these men shared a similar influence on British esotericism and have already been mentioned briefly such as Swedenborg, Mesmer and Allan Kardec. Swedenborg's mysticism, Mesmer's theory of animal magnetism and Kardec's hierarchical spiritualism had a wide impact on the formation of esoteric belief throughout the eighteenth and nineteenth centuries. Interestingly, like their British counterparts, French spiritualists and occultists, despite several attempts, were unable to unite because of fundamental disagreements concerning the ability to communicate with the spirits of the dead.[46] Some of the other individuals who helped form early French occultism included Antoine Court de Gebelin, who contributed to the incorporation of the tarot as an Egyptian system of symbolism into the occult tradition; Jean-Baptiste Alliette or Eteilla and his popularization of cabala through fortune-telling; Hebraic occultist Antoine Fabre d'Olivet; and the cabalistic writer Lazare Lenain.

It was into this already well-established occult milieu that Lévi arrived in the middle of the nineteenth-century with his successful series of writings on magical theory. As discussed earlier, Lévi's great success was in tying the tarot to cabala and thus connecting it inextricably to the Western magical tradition. Lévi's connections with the British occult scene have also been briefly mentioned in the context of Mackenzie's visit and his transmission of Lévi's tarot-infused version of occultism. The French occultist, however, had other connections with British magical circles. He made two visits to London during his magical career, visiting his close friend the renowned author and suspected Rosicrucian, Bulwer-Lytton. In fact, it has been suggested that Lytton was the one responsible for leading Lévi into magic, which would weaken the argument for a French influence on English occultism and suggest the reverse.[47] Accounts of Lévi's visits make it clear that he was well-connected with magical circles in London and that there was interaction between the occult worlds of both countries. The French magus, however, was generally unimpressed with British occultists, finding them superficial, frivolous and far too interested in the practical aspects of magic.[48] Lévi influenced both countries' conceptions of magic by uniting the tarot with the magical tradition and by emphasizing the role of self-realization through the proper channelling of the will. His contribution elevated French and British magic from its understanding as the superstitious manipulation of the forces of nature to an almost religious and spiritual calling. His emphasis upon Catholicism and Christian principles helped to position this new idea of magic as a more spiritually based process.[49]

Where we see little of Lévi's influence is in the equal admission of men and women in British occult circles. Lévi argued that for a woman to become a magician, she would have to abdicate her sex and such a physically impossible task would result in the creation of a monstrous androgynous being. Allen explores the masculine nature of French occultism in his discussion of Lévi's sexism and the magus' belief that a female magician was a 'revolt against the natural order of things'.[50] Allen goes on to discuss Lévi's comparison of such a woman with the Greek mythological sorceress Medea, 'a bad mother who murdered her children'.[51]

We have already traced the progress of Lévi's British inheritors; by examining some of his fellow countrymen it will be possible to observe whether his contributions resulted in a similar refashioning of the magical tradition in both countries. Gérard Encausse, or Papus, furthered Lévi's association of the tarot with the cabala in his occult classic *Le Tarot des Bohémiens* (1889) and founded and participated in several of the occult societies of late nineteenth-century France. One of these was the Qabalistic Order of the Rosy Cross, founded the same year as the Golden Dawn in 1888, and headed by two important figures in French occultism, the Marquis Stanislas de Guaita, whom Yeats visited in Paris, and Joséphin Péladan (1850–1915). The Qabalistic Order of the Rosy Cross was similar to its British counterpart in that there were different grades of initiation according to Masonic structure, but the two orders were very different in purpose. The French order's goal was to study occultism, to achieve spiritual communion with the Divine through meditation and to spread the word among the uninitiated.[52] There are no indications that members practised ritual magic or learned such techniques in a school-like environment. By the late nineteenth-century French occultism had reached its peak and, as with British occultism, its influence was felt throughout artistic circles inspiring many of the literary and poetic works of the era demonstrated in the works of J.K. Huysmans, Arthur Rimbaud, Gérard de Nerval, Honoré de Balzac, and even Victor Hugo whose interest in spiritualism and the occult resulted in his having several conversations in verse with Shakespeare's spirit.[53]

The similarities between the development of French and British occultism are evident. The impact of a changing social and cultural environment, the influence of Masonic structure, the influence of spiritualism, mesmerism, and other eighteenth and nineteenth-century esoteric traditions, the emphasis on Egyptian mythology, the proliferation of esoteric societies towards the end of the nineteenth century, the positioning of ritual magic as a process of spiritual self-development and the mutually influential roles of occultism and the arts in both countries demonstrate these shared developments. Occultists in both countries were trying to formulate another form of knowledge through the re-reading of sacred texts and the reinterpretation of the new science with the goal of transforming the world through interior and subjective illumination.[54]

What remains unique to Britain is the development of ritual magic as part of a core curriculum in a school of magic. This and other unique characteristics of British occultism can be attributed to the country's unique social and cultural developments. Despite the similarities between French and British *fin de siècle* occultism, the two emerged in very different religious, social and intellectual milieus. Their similarities can be attributed to the general consistency of the development of the magical tradition within the Western world. What made Golden Dawn magic distinctly British, however, was the uniqueness of Victorian culture within that Western culture. Where France and Britain differed within that greater context was in France's characterization of the church as villainous or oppressive, while the British expression of religious doubt was less demonizing in its approach. Britain also differed in the development of an artisan class that responded to this religious doubt while satisfying its thirst for education and self-improvement.[55]

The Order exerted an appeal, not only on a magical level, but also on a social and cultural level, to the most influential and largest growing segment of Victorian society, the middle class. To quote Maud Gonne (who, in 1891, joined the Order through her friendship with Yeats and resigned shortly thereafter out of dismay with its Masonic connections), the members of the Golden Dawn, with the exception of MacGregor Mathers and Farr, were the 'very essence of British middle class dullness'.[56] A close look at the membership list demonstrates the middle-class appeal of the Order. The Order's founders themselves, Westcott, Woodman, and MacGregor Mathers, were all of middle-class origins. Both Westcott and Woodman were medical practitioners, Westcott a coroner and Woodman a doctor, while MacGregor Mathers was the son of a clerk. Lawyers and medical doctors were plentiful in the Order, with several clergyman signing up. And as we have seen, there was quite a strong representation of the artistic world. Many would-be writers and artists, as well as accomplished ones, were attracted to the theatrical and creative aspects of ritual magic.

The women of the Golden Dawn were no exception. They too came from middle-class backgrounds and tended to be involved in the arts. Annie Horniman, tea heiress and daughter of the founder of the Horniman Museum, went on to become an important patron of both the Irish and English theatre scenes. Florence Farr, daughter of medical practitioner William Farr, went on to pursue acting, George Bernard Shaw and the occult arts. And last but not least, Mina Bergson, sister to philosopher Henri Bergson, pursued her artistic dreams at the Slade School of Fine Art. Within the Order we see a healthy marriage of the Victorian middle class and the artistic world.

Middle-class ideals are also strongly expressed in the rituals of Victorian magic. The goal of Golden Dawn magic was personal transmutation as opposed to any material gain. Magic was performed not to conjure up a spirit to do something for the magician, but rather to develop the magician's spirit to a more enlightened state. In such a state, the individual's powers of perception were heightened and access was gained to higher powers. The aim of spiritual development in magic resonated with a middle-class ideology of self-betterment.

Gonne was not the only Golden Dawn member to assess the Order as a manifestation of the more unattractive elements of the middle class. The Order's most notorious progeny, Aleister Crowley described his fellow members as 'utterly undistinguished', 'vulgar and common place' and 'muddled middle-class mediocrities'.[57]

Such insults aside, the Golden Dawn did encompass many of the aspirations and ideals of middle-class Victorians. Very much of its time, Victorian magic tapped into the middle-class desire for moral and spiritual self-betterment and self-education in accordance with popular nineteenth-century themes of classical and folk mythology and Egyptology. The Golden Dawn was one of many societies offering a type of social participation that appealed to the middle class, although its particular focus on magic was a bit more unusual. Its more philosophical and religious focus and its creative potential attracted a particular segment of the middle class, the professional and the artistic. Its very formation can be interpreted as arising from a need for the artistic, religious and philosophical expression of the middle class in response to the cultural rebellion taking place around them. The emergence of the occult revival at the end of the nineteenth century is a rational and natural development not only in the context of the history of Western magic, but also in the history of Victorian intellectual life.

Conclusion

In response to social and cultural change, both individuals and institutions have played a crucial role in contributing to the eclectic collection that constitutes Victorian occultism. The cultural rebellion of the nineteenth century drastically changed many aspects of Victorian society and magic was no less affected. Certain adaptations made to the magical tradition resulted in a permanent change in direction for Western occultism. Other modifications were a result of the traditional and ongoing process of synthesis which was far less radical in the development of magical practice and belief.

The Golden Dawn's synthesis of secret societies, ceremonial magic, tarot, cabala, Enochian magic, Abramelin magic, Egyptology, theurgy, and pseudo-science represents one strand in the history of nineteenth-century magic while the drastic modifications examined in Chapter 6 represent another. These fundamental changes primarily concern the individual, particularly the individual's will and responsibility in the magical process, and of course, of utmost importance, the goal of that individual. These alterations reflect critical developments in Victorian society. They also reflect key cultural advances due to social and scientific progress.

While Golden Dawn members appear to have failed to convincingly ally their new magic with contemporary scientific developments, we have seen that there was, nonetheless, a concerted effort to do so. This was in keeping with a traditional conflation of magic and science and attempts to render occult beliefs more 'safe' or efficacious by associating them with this more respectable field. Nineteenth-century occultists were most concerned with comparing their magical methods with those of the natural and physical sciences. A shift occurs in the following century, however, when magicians such as Golden Dawn prodigies,

Aleister Crowley and Dion Fortune, begin to draw comparisons between magic and a new set of sciences. By turning to the social sciences, namely the emerging fields of psychology and psychoanalysis, occultists had a whole new system of terminology and methodology with which they could attempt to validate or rehabilitate their magic. It is debatable as to whether occultists were successful in this new endeavour and falls beyond the scope of this book. It is, however, of immense significance that there still remained this desire to be associated with cutting-edge scientific developments. What is also of considerable interest is that by attempting to associate their magic with these new sciences, we finally see, to some degree, the abandonment of efforts to link magic with a certain more traditional set of sciences. Magic had fallen in with a new crowd and one that may have proven to be more relevant.

The history of magic has only recently received proper recognition as a critical area of study alongside the histories of religion and science. Its integral role in European culture and society has long been established and its role in North America and other regions has more recently come to be explored in light of the proliferation of new magical orders into such places. MacGregor Mathers brought Victorian magic to France at the end of the century and on to America through his American initiates into the Rites of Isis. This diaspora of Golden Dawn magic continued into the twentieth century with Dr Felkin introducing its concepts to initiates in New Zealand. That same century saw Florence Farr moving to Ceylon, and Westcott to South Africa. Victorian occultism itself played a crucial role in enabling British magic to spread to these places, not merely by members of magical societies moving to far-off places and bringing their practices and beliefs, but also in its new format provided by these Victorian occultists. This new institutionalized magic and its accompanying curriculum resulted in a more portable and publicly accessible system. With even more recent technological advances, inventions such as the internet have furthered this accessibility, making it easy to become an adept with a click of a mouse from a home computer.

The nineteenth century witnessed a crucial turning point in modernizing magic. Victorian occultism took magic out of the dark laboratories of the medieval alchemists, and out of the hands of immortal legendary figures such as Cagliostro, enabling ordinary people to attend weekly meetings and attempt to encounter their higher geniuses. It can be argued, however, that in this process and modernized format magic has lost its 'magic'. Can modern magic retain its esoteric character in light of such public accessibility? In such a technologically progressive age, can the tradition of inventing, or rather, invoking tradition continue? As long as new discoveries are being made by archaeologists and astronomers, it would seem that modern magicians may continue to incorporate new knowledge of ancient and even contemporary theoretical civilizations into their corpus. The Victorian period marked a shift from looking solely to the old to looking towards the new. Nineteenth-century occultism incorporated the notions of progress and evolution into its synthesis. Such a reformulated magical system is no longer restrained by the necessity of having ancient foundations. By bringing an earthly focus into the magical process, not trying to free something, but rather ground it, modern magic has become of this world and of the present. What lies ahead for this constantly changing tradition remains to be seen.

Notes

Introduction

1. Alex Owen, *The Place of Enchantment: British Occultism and the Culture of the Modern* (Chicago: University of Chicago Press, 2004), 120.
2. Corinna Treitel, *A Science for the Soul: Occultism and the Genesis of the German Modern* (Baltimore: Johns Hopkins University Press, 2004), 3–4. Such scientists included Karl Friedrich Zöller, a well-respected professor of astrophysics at the University of Leipzig, physicists William Edward Weber and Gustav Theodor Fechner, mathematician Wilhelm Scheibner and the psychologist Wilhelm Wundt.
3. Owen, *The Place of Enchantment*.
4. Treitel, *A Science for the Soul*.
5. David Allen Harvey, *Beyond Enlightenment: Occultism and Politics in Modern France* (Dekalb: Northern Illinois University Press, 2005).
6. For a thorough discussion of the struggle by historians to establish the enchanted nature of the modern see Michael Saler 'Modernity and Enchantment: A Historiographic Review,' *American Historical Review*, 2006 111 (3): 629–716.
7. Nicola Bown, 'Esoteric Selves and Magical Minds,' *History Workshop Journal*, 2006 61 (1): 281–7, 284, 286. Similar criticism comes from Michael Saler. Michael Saler, review of *The Place of Enchantment: British Occultism and the Culture of the Modern*, by Alex Owen, *American Historical Review* 2005 110 (3): 871–2, 872.

1 A New Order

1. R.A. Gilbert, *Revelations of the Golden Dawn: The Rise and Fall of a Magical Order* (London: Quantum, 1997), 34.
2. Gilbert, *Revelations,* 45.
3. Ellic Howe, *The Magicians of the Golden Dawn: A Documentary History of a Magical Order 1887–1923* (London: Routledge and Kegan Paul, 1972; York Beach, Maine: Samuel Weiser, 1978). Gilbert, *Revelations*.
4. Howe, *Magicians of the Golden Dawn,* 36.
5. Antoine Faivre, *Access to Western Esotericism* (Albany: State University of New York Press, 1994), 90.
6. William Wynn Westcott, 'Data of the History of the Rosicrucians', in *The Magical Mason. Forgotten Hermetic Writings of William Wynn Westcott, Physician and Magus*. Ed. R.A. Gilbert (Wellingborough: Aquarian Press, 1983), 39.
7. Westcott, 'Data of the History of the Rosicrucians', 34–5.
8. Howe, *Magicians of the Golden Dawn,* 8–9.
9. In her biography of Mathers, Ithell Colquhoun, however, does not argue that this account is true as she also offers the explanation that Westcott

may have manufactured them. Ithell Colquhoun, *Sword of Wisdom. MacGregor Mathers and 'The Golden Dawn'* (New York: G.P. Putnam's Sons, 1975), 77.

10. Colquhoun, *Sword of Wisdom*, 75.
11. Howe, *Magicians of the Golden Dawn*, 2.
12. Howe, *Magicians of the Golden Dawn*, 5–25.
13. Colquhoun, *Sword of Wisdom*, 68–9.
14. Howe, *Magicians of the Golden Dawn*, 39 and Francis King, *Modern Ritual Magic. The Rise of Western Occultism* (Bridport, Dorset: Prism, 1989), 48.
15. Moina MacGregor Mathers, introduction to S.L. MacGregor Mathers' *Kabbala Denudata: The Kabbalah Unveiled* (London: Kegan Paul, Trench, Trubner & Co., Ltd., 1926), xii.
16. Howe claims that not even the most determined genealogist could have established Mathers' descent from the Macgregors of Glenstrae. Howe, *Magicians of the Golden Dawn*, 39.
17. Samuel Liddell MacGregor Mathers, *Practical Instruction in Infantry Campaigning Exercise* (London: City of London Publishing Company, 1884).
18. Mathers, *The Fall of Granada: A Poem in Six Duans* (London: Williams and Strahan, 1885).
19. Colquhoun, *Sword of Wisdom*, 73–4.
20. The publisher, George Redway, acquired the copyright of other works by Mathers, including *Fortune-telling Cards. The Tarot, its Occult Significance and Methods of Play*, 1888, and *The Key of Solomon the King: Clavicula Salomonis*, 1889. Redway paid Mathers £35 for the copyright of *The Kabbalah Unveiled*. Howe, *Magicians of the Golden Dawn*, 41.
21. For a complete account of these internal conflicts see Howe, *Magicians of the Golden Dawn*, 110–38. For a detailed discussion of the particular nature of Horniman's discontent see Alex Owen, *The Place of Enchantment*, 101–3.
22. William Wynn Westcott, A letter to Frederick Leigh Gardner as cited in Howe, *Magicians of the Golden Dawn*, 165.
23. Mathers, Letter to Florence Farr, Howe, *Magicians of the Golden Dawn*, 210.
24. Owen, *Place of Enchantment*, 79.
25. Gilbert, *Revelations*, 37.
26. Mathers, *The Grimoire of Armadel*, Ed. Francis King (New York: Samuel Weiser, 1980). King gained access to the original manuscript through the collection of Gerald Yorke and it now rests in the library of the Warburg Institute.
27. Owen, *Place of Enchantment*, 83.
28. Colquhoun, *Sword of Wisdom*, 94–5.
29. Colquhoun, *Sword of Wisdom*, 273.
30. Westcott, 'The Golden Dawn's Official History Lecture' in Francis King's *Modern Ritual Magic*, 217.
31. Golden Dawn member Frederick Leigh Gardner produced a catalogue of the Westcott Hermetic Library. This catalogue is reprinted in George Mills Harper, *Yeats's Golden Dawn* (London: MacMillan Press, 1974), 290–305.
32. Howe, *Magicians of the Golden Dawn*, 44.
33. John Watkins in Colquhoun, *Sword of Wisdom*, 172.

2   A New Magic

1. Wouter J. Hanegraaff, *New Age Religion and Western Culture: Esotericism in the Mirror of Secular Thought* (Leiden: E.J. Brill, 1990), 390.
2. James Hankins, *Plato in the Italian Renaissance* (Leiden, New York: E.J. Brill, 1990; 1994), 282.
3. See D.P. Walker's monumental work on Ficinian magic, *Spiritual and Demonic Magic from Ficino to Campanella* (London: Warburg Institute, 1958; Notre Dame: University of Notre Dame, 1975).
4. Walker, *Spiritual and Demonic Magic,* 52.
5. Hanegraaff proposes that Renaissance esotericism is made up of six components. These are the two philosophical traditions, Neoplatonism and Hermeticism, three traditional sciences of astrology, alchemy and magic, and one current of theosophical speculation, cabala. Hanegraaff, *New Age Religion and Western Culture,* 388.
6. Gershom Scholem provides the most comprehensive and exemplary scholarship on Jewish cabala and its historical transmission in his *Kabbalah* (New York: Quadrangle, 1974).
7. Scholem, *Kabbalah,* 182.
8. Scholem, *Kabbalah,* 182.
9. Scholem, *Kabbalah,* 183–4.
10. Scholem, *Kabbalah,* 197 and Frances A. Yates, *The Occult Philosophy in the Elizabethan Age* (London: Routledge & Kegan Paul, 1979), 19.
11. Pico della Mirandola, Conclusions 9.9 and 9.13 in *Syncretism in the West: Pico's 900 Theses (1486) The Evolution of Traditional Religious and Philosophical Systems,* trans. S.A. Farmer (Tempe, Arizona: Medieval & Renaissance Texts & Studies, 1998).
12. Eugenio Garin, *Astrology in the Renaissance. The Zodiac of Life,* trans. Carolyn Jackson and June Allen. Revised by Clare Robertson (London: Routledge & Kegan Paul, 1983), 44 and 45.
13. Yates, *The Occult Philosophy,* 20.
14. Moshe Idel in his introduction to Johannes Reuchlin's *On the Art of the Kabbalah De Arte Cabalistica,* trans. Martin and Sarah Goodman (Lincoln: University of Nebraska Press, 1993), vii and G. Lloyd Jones in his introduction to Johannes Reuchlin's *On the Art of the Kabbalah De Arte Cabalistica,* trans. Martin and Sarah Goodman (Lincoln: University of Nebraska Press, 1993), 10.
15. For the best biographies on Agrippa see Charles Nauert's *Agrippa and the Crisis of Renaissance Thought* (Urbana: University of Illinois Press, 1965) and Marc van der Poel's *Cornelius Agrippa, The Humanist Theologian and his Declamations* (Leiden: E.J. Brill, 1997).
16. Nauert, *Agrippa and the Crisis of Renaissance Thought,* 231.
17. Heinrich Cornelius Agrippa, *De Occulta Philosophia. Three Books of Occult Philosophy,* ed. Donald Tyson (St Paul: Llewellyn Press, 1992), Book One, chapter LX.
18. Agrippa, *De Occulta Philosophia,* Book Two, chapter XLII.
19. Agrippa, *De Occulta Philosophia* Book Three, chapter XXXII and XXXIII.
20. Christopher Marlowe, *Doctor Faustus,* 1604 edition, ed. Michael Keefer (Peterborough, Ontario: Broadview Press, 1991), 1.i.118–19. Interestingly,

one of the two magicians Faustus claims won him over to the practice of magic is named Cornelius.

21. Mary Shelley, *Frankenstein or the Modern Prometheus, the 1818 text* (London: W. Pickering, 1993), 22.
22. Agrippa, *Three Books of Occult Philosophy*, ed. Donald Tyson (St Paul: Llewellyn Press, 1992).
23. Percy Bysshe Shelley, *St. Irvyne, or the Rosicrucian* (London: J.J. Stockdale, 1811). Edward Bulwer-Lytton *Zanoni* (London: Saunders & Otley, 1842). For a fascinating discussion of the theme of Rosicrucianism in literature see chapter 11, 'The Rosicrucian Adept in Literature' in Christopher McIntosh, *The Rosicrucians: The History, Mythology, and Rituals of an Esoteric Order* (York Beach, Maine: Samuel Weiser, 1997).
24. Israel Regardie, *The Golden Dawn,* first edition (Aries Press, 1937–40); sixth edition (St. Paul: Llewellyn Publications, 1997).
25. Regardie, *The Golden Dawn,* introduction to the first edition.
26. Francis King, *Ritual Magic of the Golden Dawn* (Rochester, Vermont: Destiny Books, 1997); originally published as *Astral Projection, ritual magic, and alchemy* (London: Spearman, 1971).
27. R.G. Torrens, *The Secret Rituals of the Golden Dawn* (Wellingborough: Aquarian Press, 1973).
28. *The Complete Golden Dawn Cipher Manuscript*, ed. and trans. Darcy Küntz (Edmonds, WA: Holmes Publishing Group, 1996).
29. *The Complete Golden Dawn Cipher Manuscript.*
30. R.A. Gilbert, *The Golden Dawn Companion. A Guide to the History, Structure and Workings of the Hermetic Order of the Golden Dawn.* (Wellingborough: Aquarian Press, 1986), 176–98.
31. See Harper's *Yeats's Golden Dawn* for how Yeats's work was affected by Golden Dawn magic and symbolism.
32. Howe, *Magicians of the Golden Dawn;* Gilbert, *Golden Dawn Companion;* Gilbert, *Revelations.*
33. Gilbert, *Revelations,* 29.
34. Ellic Howe, private letter to Gerald Yorke, MS 2, Yorke Collection.
35. Howe, *Magicians of the Golden Dawn,* 27; Joscelyn Godwin, *The Theosophical Enlightenment* (Albany: State University of New York Press, 1994), 362.
36. Howe, *Magicians of the Golden Dawn,* 58.
37. *The Complete Golden Dawn Cipher Manuscript.*
38. Torrens, *Secret Rituals of the Golden Dawn,* 87.
39. William Wynn Westcott, private letter to F.L. Gardner, 1912, MS 2, Yorke Collection.
40. Gilbert, *Revelations,* 45–6.
41. Regardie, *The Golden Dawn,* 53–5.
42. Gilbert, *Revelations,* 68.
43. King, *Modern Ritual Magic,* 55.
44. Howe, *Magicians of the Golden Dawn,* 104.
45. Adeptus minor ritual, as printed in Regardie, *The Golden Dawn,* 230.
46. Lesser Ritual of the Pentagram, MS 64, Yorke Collection.
47. MS 64, Yorke Collection.
48. MS 64, Yorke Collection.
49. MS 64, Yorke Collection.

50. Aleister Crowley, *The Confessions of Aleister Crowley*, eds John Symonds and Kenneth Grant (London: Routledge & Kegan Paul, 1979), 177.
51. J.W. Brodie-Innes, 'Notes on the First Knowledge Lecture', 1895 as printed in Gilbert, *Revelations*, 63.
52. Flying Rolls, MS 57, Yorke Collection.
53. Flying Roll No. 34, MS 57, Yorke Collection.
54. Adeptus minor ritual, as printed in Regardie, *The Golden Dawn*, 230.
55. See King, *Modern Ritual Magic*, 54–5.
56. William Wynn Westcott, *Sepher Yetzirah, or Book of Formation*, (Bath: R.H. Fryar, 1887); Westcott, *The Isiac Tablet or The Bembine Table of Isis*, (Bath: R.H. Fryar, 1887); Westcott, *Numbers: Their Occult Powers and Mystic Virtue*, (London: Theosophical Publishing Society, 1890); Westcott, *Collecteana Hermetica*, 1893–6.
57. William Wynn Westcott, 'Christian Rosenkreuz and the Rosicrucians', in R.A. Gilbert's *The Magical Mason*, 13–27, 25. Reprinted from *Theosophical Siftings*, 6 (15), 3–14.
58. Howe, *Magicians of the Golden Dawn*, 33.
59. Westcott, 'Man, Miracle, Magic' in *The Magical Mason*, 66–70, 67. Found by Gilbert among A.E. Waite's papers.
60. Westcott, 'Man, Miracle, Magic', 68.
61. Benjamin Woolley, *The Queen's Conjuror: The Science and Magic of Dr. Dee* (London: HarperCollins, 2001), 71.
62. Harley MS 1879, British Library.
63. John Dee, *Dr. Dee's Conference with angels from Dec. 22 1581 to May 30 1583*, Sloane MS 3188, British Library. Meric Casaubon, *A True and Faithful Relation of what passed for many years between Dr. John Dee and some Spirits*, 1659. Elias Ashmole's copy of this account, complete with his own preface, is in the Bodleian Library. For Dee's dream to establish a universal religion see Peter J. French, *John Dee: The World of an Elizabethan Magus* (London: Routledge and Kegan Paul, 1972), 118.
64. Sloane MS 3191, *De Heptarchia mystica*, British Library.
65. Sloane MS 3191, *De Heptarchia mystica*, British Library.
66. Geraldine Pinch, *Magic in Ancient Egypt* (London: British Museum Press, 1994), 88.
67. Woolley, *The Queen's Conjuror*, 176.
68. Woolley, *The Queen's Conjuror*, 289 and 327.
69. French, *John Dee*, 96.
70. W.B. Yeats, 'Magic', 1901 in *Ideas of Good and Evil* (London: A.H. Bullen, 1903) 29–70.
71. W.B. Yeats, 'Magic', 42–3.
72. Sloane MS 3191, *48 Claves Angelicae*.
73. Sloane MS 3189, *The Book of Enoch revealed to Dr. John Dee by the Angels*.
74. Sloane MS 3191, *De heptarchia mystica*.
75. King, *Modern Ritual Magic*, Appendix B, 261–3, 261; Nicholas Clulee, *John Dee's Natural Philosophy* (London: Routledge, 1988), 210; Richard Deacon, *John Dee: Scientist, Geographer, Astrologer and Secret Agent to Elizabeth I* (London: Frederick Muller, 1968), 148.
76. John Dee, *A True & Faithful Relation of what passed for many Years Between Dr. John Dee and Some Spirits*, ed. Meric Casaubon, (London, 1659). For a

discussion of why Casaubon would have set out to slander Dee and present him in an unfavourable light, as well as the subsequent favourable light in which Elias Ashmole's interest in Dee placed him, see French, 11–13.

77. Gilbert, *Revelations*, 68–9.
78. Gerald Yorke in his introduction to Howe's *Magicians of the Golden Dawn*, xii.
79. Samuel Liddell MacGregor Mathers, *The Key of Solomon the King* (London: George Redway, 1889); reprint (York Beach, Maine: Samuel Weiser, 2000), xi. Mathers claims here that he used the following manuscripts in compiling his version: Add. MSS 10,862; Sloane MSS 1307 and 3091; Harleian MSS 3981; King's MSS 288; and Lansdowne MSS 1202 and 1203.
80. Mathers, *Key of Solomon*, x.
81. Mathers, *Key of Solomon*, 16.
82. R.A. Gilbert, preface to Mathers' *Key of Solomon*, 2000, vii.
83. Mathers, *Key of Solomon*, 120.
84. Aleister Crowley, prefatory note to Samuel Liddell MacGregor Mathers, *The Book of the Goetia of Solomon the King* (Boleskine: Society for the Propagation of Religious Truth, 1904), v. This edition is falsely attributed to Crowley.
85. Joseph H. Peterson, ed., in his introduction to Samuel Liddell MacGregor Mathers, *The Key of Solomon the King* (London: George Redway, 1889); reprint (York Beach, Maine: Samuel Weiser, 2000), xi and xiii.
86. Mathers, *The Book of the Goetia*, 18.
87. Mathers, *The Book of the Goetia*, 19–20.
88. Peterson, xiv. *The Lesser Key of Solomon*. The full title of this compilation is: *Henry Cornelius Agrippa his fourth book of occult philosophy. Of geomancie. Magical elements of Peter de Abano. Astronomical geomancie. The nature of spirits. Arbatel of magick. The species or several kindes of magick*, 1655.
89. King, *Modern Ritual Magic*, Appendix B, 194–200, 196.
90. *Bibliothèque de l'Arsenal*, Sc. et A. No. 88. King, introduction to Samuel Liddell MacGregor Mathers' *The Grimoire of Armadel* (New York: Samuel Weiser, 1980), 6.
91. King, introduction to *The Grimoire of Armadel*, 11.
92. King, introduction to *The Grimoire of Armadel*, 11–13.
93. Howe, *Magicians of the Golden Dawn*, 159n.
94. Mathers, *The Book of the Sacred Magic of Abramelin the Mage* (London: John M. Watkins, 1898); second edition 1900; reprint (New York: Dover Publications, 1975), xvi. Howe, *Magicians of the Golden Dawn*, 59.
95. Mathers, *The Book of the Sacred Magic of Abramelin the Mage*, xvi.
96. Pinch, *Magic in Ancient Egypt*, 49.
97. Yorke, introduction to Howe's *Magicians of the Golden Dawn*, xv.
98. Regardie, *The Golden Dawn*, 442–5.
99. See Howe for an account of this in Chapter 12 of his *Magicians of the Golden Dawn*.
100. Crowley, *Confessions*, 176.
101. Yorke, introduction to Howe's *Magicians of the Golden Dawn*, xvi.
102. Sphere Group Working in a notebook of Flying Rolls, Private Collection C.
103. Sphere Group Working in a notebook of Flying Rolls, Private Collection C.
104. King, *Modern Ritual Magic*, Appendix C, 200–2, 202.
105. Howe, *Magicians of the Golden Dawn*, 246–7.

106. Between 1893 and 1896, Westcott edited a series of nine short volumes, *Collectanea Hermetica*, to which Percy Bullock, Farr and Westcott contributed.
107. Florence Farr, *Egyptian Magic*, 1896. Reprint (Montana: Kessinger Publishing, 1997).
108. C.W. Goodwin, 'On a Graeco-Egyptian Papyri Preserved in the British Library' in *Antiquarian Communications: Being the Papers Presented at the Meetings of the Cambridge Antiquarian Society*, 1 (Cambridge, 1859), 37–42. In Farr, *Egyptian Magic*, 9, 10 and 12 there are references to the research of a M.M. Chabas on a translation of the Harris Magical Payprus and to Textor de Ravisis' contribution to the Congress of French Orientalists in 1875.
109. R.A. Gilbert, 'Seeking that which was Lost: More Light on the Origins and Development of the Golden Dawn', *Yeats Annual14: Yeats and the Nineties*, 14 (2001), 33–49, 44.
110. From the rituals of the Order of G.O.T.S., Private Collection C.
111. From a ritual of the S.O.S., Private Collection C.
112. Farr, *Egyptian Magic*, 12.
113. Frederick Lees, 'Conversations with the Hierophant Rameses and the High Priestess Anari', in *The Humanitarian*, 19 (2) (New York, February 1900); reprint www.tarot.nu/gd/isis.htm.
114. Lees, 'Conversations'.
115. Lees, 'Conversations'.
116. André Gaucher, 'Isis à Montmartre', in *L'Echo de merveilleux* (Paris, 1 and 15 December 1900).
117. Lees, 'Conversations'.
118. *Fragment of a Graeco-Egyptian Work upon Magic from a Papyrus in the British Museum*, ed. and trans. Charles Wycliffe Goodwin for the Cambridge Antiquarian Society (Cambridge: Deighton; Macmillan & Co., 1852). Regardie, 'The Bornless Ritual for the Invocation of the Higher Genius' in Regardie, *The Golden Dawn*, 442–6.
119. 'Ritual for the Formation, Building and Consecration of a Body, wherein to Travel, manifest & act in freedom from the Bonds & limitation of matter', 1899–1900, Private Collection C.
120. Yeats, 'Magic', 29.

3   Resurrecting the Past: Hiram, Isis and the Rosy Cross

1. These two misconceptions are addressed and corrected in both of Scottish historian David Stevenson's major works on Freemasonry, *The First Freemasons: Scotland's Early Lodges and their Members* (Aberdeen: Aberdeen University Press, 1988) and *The Origins of Freemasonry* (Cambridge: Cambridge University Press, 1988).
2. David Stevenson, *The Origins of Freemasonry* and *The First Freemasons*. Stevenson's account has been accepted by many historians including Ronald Hutton in *Triumph of the Moon*, and by Margaret C. Jacob in *Living the Enlightenment. Freemasonry and Politics in Eighteenth-Century Europe* (Oxford: Oxford University Press, 1991), 35–6.
3. Stevenson, *The Origins of Freemasonry*, 5–6.

4. Stevenson, *The First Freemasons*, 3.
5. Stevenson, *The Origins of Freemasonry*, 7.
6. Stevenson, *The Origins of Freemasonry*, 8.
7. Stevenson, *The Origins of Freemasonry*, 153.
8. Hutton, *Triumph of the Moon*, 56.
9. Hutton, *Triumph of the Moon*, 56–7.
10. Stevenson, *The Origins of Freemasonry*, 82.
11. Frances Yates, *Giordano Bruno and the Hermetic Tradition* (London: Routledge & Kegan Paul, 1964), 273–4.
12. Stevenson, *The Origins of Freemasonry*, 233.
13. John Hamill, *The Craft – A History of English Freemasonry* (Wellingborough: Aquarian Press, 1986), 15.
14. Hamill, *The Craft*, 16.
15. Hutton, *Triumph of the Moon*, 57.
16. Thomas Marryat, *The Philosophy of Masons in Several Epistles from Egypt, to a Nobleman* (London: J. Ridgway, 1790).
17. John A. Weisse, *The Obelisk and Freemasonry* (New York: J.W. Bouton, 1880), 3, 39.
18. Marryat, *The Philosophy of Masons*, 72–3.
19. Walton Hannah, *Darkness Visible, A Christian Appraisal of Freemasonry* (London: Augustine Press, 1952; 17th reprint Saint Austin Press, 1998).
20. Hannah, *Darkness Visible*, 26, 41.
21. Hannah, *Darkness Visible*, 45.
22. Walter Burkert, *Ancient Mystery Cults* (Cambridge, Mass.: Cambridge University Press, 1987), 7.
23. Burkert, *Ancient Mystery Cults*, 28.
24. Westcott, 'The Resemblances of Freemasonry to the Cult of Mithra', in *Ars Quatuor* Coronatorum, 29 (1916), 1–9. Reprinted in *The Magical Mason*, 244–55.
25. Westcott, 'Freemasonry and its Relation to the Essenes', in *Ars Quatuor Coronatorum*, 28 (1915), 67–74. Reprinted in *The Magical Mason*, 233–43.
26. Westcott, 'The Resemblances of Freemasonry to the Cult of Mithra', 245, 255.
27. Hutton, *Triumph of the Moon*, 64.
28. Westcott, 'Freemasonry and its Relation to the Essenes', 235.
29. Cipher Manuscript, printed in *The Complete Golden Dawn Cipher Manuscript*.
30. Hutton, *Triumph of the Moon*, 78.
31. Yates, *The Rosicrucian Enlightenment* (London: Routledge & Kegan Paul, 1972), 41. Yates provides both the *Fama* and the second manifesto, the *Confessio* in the appendix. They are both 1652 English translations by Thomas Vaughn and are the translations used here.
32. *Fama Fraternitatis*, 1652 English translation by Thomas Vaughn of the 1614 German text. Reprinted by Yates, *Rosicrucian Enlightenment*, 242.
33. *Fama Fraternitatis*, Yates, *Rosicrucian Enlightenment*, 249.
34. *Confessio*, 1652 English translation by Thomas Vaughn of the 1615 Latin text. Reprinted in Yates, *Rosicrucian Enlightenment*, 260.
35. Yates, *Rosicrucian Enlightenment*, 49.
36. See Yates, *Rosicrucian Enlightenment*, for an exploration of these arguments and the people who put them forth.

37. McIntosh, *The Rosicrucians*, 24, 29–30.
38. Yates, *Rosicrucian Enlightenment*, 207.
39. McIntosh, *The Rosicrucians*, 22–3.
40. Julius Sperber, *Echo der von Gott hocherleuchteten Fraternitet* (Danzig, 1615). McIntosh points out this text and its elaboration on the Rosicrucian myth with biblical associations. McIntosh, *The Rosicrucians*, 32.
41. As identified in McIntosh, *The Rosicrucians*; Yates, *Rosicrucian Enlightenment*; and Stevenson, *The Origins of Freemasonry*.
42. Stevenson, *The Origins of Freemasonry*, 104.
43. Stevenson, *The Origins of Freemasonry*, 105.
44. Anonymous, *Text Book of Advanced Freemasonry*, 1873 as reprinted in McIntosh, *The Rosicrucians*, 141–4.
45. Kenneth Mackenzie, *The Royal Masonic Cyclopaedia* (London, 1877. Reprint, Wellingborough: Aquarian Press, 1987), 610.
46. From a manual of the order, *Eingang zur ersten Classe des preisswürdigsten Ordens vom Goldenen Rosen Creutze nach der letzten Haupt- und Reformations-Convention*, Leipzig 1788. Reproduced in McIntosh, *The Rosicrucians*, 31.
47. Godwin, *The Theosophical Enlightenment*, 121.
48. McIntosh, *The Rosicrucians*, 71.
49. Westcott, 'Data of the History of the Rosicrucians', 34.
50. Mackenzie, *The Royal Masonic Cyclopaedia*, 616. Mackenzie refers to the *Soc. Ros.* as the Rosicrucian Society of England.
51. Howe, *Magicians of the Golden Dawn*, 33.
52. King, *Modern Ritual Magic*, 38.
53. Westcott, 'Christian Rosenkreuz and the Rosicrucians', 26.
54. Westcott, 'Data of the History of the Rosicrucians', 33.
55. Godwin, *The Theosophical Enlightenment*, 122.
56. Westcott, 'The Rosicrucians, Past and Present, at Home and Abroad', in *The Magical Mason*, 40–7, 44.
57. Mathers, *The Book of the Sacred Magic of Abramelin the Mage*, xvi.
58. This catalogue is reprinted in George Mills Harper, *Yeats's Golden Dawn* (London: Macmillan Press, 1974), 290–305.
59. Franz Hartmann, *In the Pronaos of the Temple of Wisdom, Containing the History of the True and False Rosicrucians* (London: Theosophical Publishing Society, 1890), 70–4.
60. Hartmann, *In the Pronaos of the Temple of Wisdom*, 80.
61. John Robison, *Proofs of a Conspiracy against all the Religions and Governments of Europe carried on in the Secret Meetings of Free Masons, Illuminati, and Reading Societies* (London: Printed for T. Cadell, W. Davies, and W. Creech, 1797), 67.
62. Westcott, 'Christian Rosenkreuz and the Rosicrucians', 13.
63. Westcott, 'The Rosicrucians, Past and Present', 40.
64. Westcott, 'Christian Rosenkreuz and the Rosicrucians, 22.
65. McIntosh, *The Rosicrucians*, xviii.
66. Westcott, 'Data of the History of the Rosicrucians', 34.
67. Howe, *Magicians of the Golden Dawn*, 56.
68. Westcott, 'Man, Miracle, and Magic', 68–9.
69. Howe, *Magicians of the Golden Dawn*, 84 and McIntosh, *The Rosicrucians*, 101.

70. Howe, *Magicians of the Golden Dawn*, 84 and McIntosh, *The Rosicrucians*, 101.
71. Godwin, *The Theosophical Enlightenment*, 219.
72. Godwin, *The Theosophical Enlightenment*, 219.
73. Godwin, *The Theosophical Enlightenment*, 220–1.
74. Godwin, *The Theosophical Enlightenment*, 222.
75. *The Divine Pymander of Hermes Trismegistus* (Bath: Robert Fryar, 1884). Reprinted in Godwin, *The Theosophical Enlightenment*, 347.
76. For more on this scandal and the history of the Hermetic Brotherhood of Luxor see Godwin, *The Theosophical Enlightenment*, 347–61.
77. Pinch, *Magic in Ancient Egypt*, 12.
78. Pinch, *Magic in Ancient Egypt*, 9.
79. Pinch, *Magic in Ancient Egypt*, 29.
80. Pinch, *Magic in Ancient Egypt*, 16 and 46.
81. Pinch, *Magic in Ancient Egypt*, 16.
82. P. Le Page Renouf, *The Hibbert Lectures* (London and Edinburgh: Williams and Norgate, 1880), 192. Farr lists the work of Renouf in a glossary at the end of a manuscript on the rites of Osiris the Saviour in Private Collection C.
83. Lewis Spence, *Myths and Legends of Ancient Egypt* (London: George G. Harrap, 1915), 261. Farr also lists Spence in the glossary mentioned above.
84. E.A. Wallis Budge, *Egyptian Magic* (London: Kegan Paul, Trench, Trübner & Co., 1899) and *The Book of the Dead* (London: Kegan Paul, Trench, Trübner & Co., 1898).
85. Alfred Wiedemann, *Religion of the Ancient Egyptians* (London: H. Grevel & Co., 1897), 269.
86. Erik Hornung, *The Ancient Egyptian Books of the Afterlife*, trans. David Lorton (Ithaca and London: Cambridge University Press, 1999), 17–21.
87. Pinch, *Magic in Ancient Egypt*, 163.
88. Pinch, *Magic in Ancient Egypt*, 170.
89. Such as Hartmann's *In the Pronaos of the Temple of Wisdom*.
90. Iamblichus, *De mysteriis Aegyptorium – On the Mysteries*, ed. Stephan Ronan, trans. Thomas Taylor and Alexander Wilder (Hastings: Chthonios Books, 1989), III.6.112–14.
91. Iamblichus, III.14.133.3–8.
92. Emma C. Clarke, *Iamblichus's De mysteriis. A Manifesto of the Miraculous* (Aldershot, Hampshire: Ashgate, 2001), 119.
93. Petra Pakkanen, *Interpreting Early Hellenistic Religion* (Helsinki: Foundation of the Finnish Institute at Athens, 1996), 133.
94. Pakkanen, *Interpreting Early Hellenistic Religion*, 55–6.
95. Marvin W. Meyer, ed. *The Ancient Mysteries – A Sourcebook – Sacred Texts of the Mystery Religions of the Ancient Mediterranean World* (San Francisco: Harper & Row, 1987), 158.
96. Pakkanen, *Interpreting Early Hellenistic Religion*, 79.
97. Burkert, *Ancient Mystery Cults*, 102.
98. Burkert, *Ancient Mystery Cults*, 3–4.
99. Burkert, *Ancient Mystery Cults*, 38.
100. Apuleius, *The Golden Ass*, trans. E.J. Kenney (London: Penguin, 1998), 11.21, 21–8.

101. Apuleius, *The Golden Ass,* 11.22–3, 19.
102. Apuleius, *The Golden Ass,* 11.23, 20–34.
103. Apuleius, *The Golden Ass,* 11.27, 6–8.
104. Fritz Graf, *Magic in the Ancient World,* trans. Franklin Philip (Cambridge, Mass.: Harvard University Press, 1997), 203.
105. Graf, *Magic in the Ancient World,* 185.
106. Mircea Eliade, *Rites and Symbols of Initiation. The Mysteries of Birth and Rebirth,* trans. Willard R. Trask (New York: Harper & Row, 1965).
107. I am grateful to Owen Davies for this reference. Iain McCalman, *The Last Alchemist: Count Cagliostro, Master of Magic in the Age of Reason* (New York: Harper Collins, 2003. Reprint, Perennial, 2004), 41–2, 52.
108. The following description is taken from André Gaucher, 'Isis à Montmartre' in *L'Echo de merveilleux* (Paris, 1 and 15 December 1900).
109. Jean-Pascal Ruggiu and Nicolas Tereshchenko believe that Gaucher meant the goddess Hathor rather than Thor and was confusing the Egyptian pantheon with the Scandinavian one. 'Introduction Historique du Temple Ahathoor No. 7 de Paris', www.tarot.nu/gd/ahathoor.htm.
110. A glossary containing a list of texts Farr used in compiling her rites of Osiris is provided at the end of the described rituals in a manuscript version in Collection C.

4 Preservation and Improvisation: Nineteenth-Century Magicians

1. See Peter J. Bowler, *Reconciling Science and Religion* (Chicago: University of Chicago Press, 2001) for an examination of the resurgence of support for religious values in Victorian England in the face of the extreme philosophy of scientific naturalism. See also Frank Miller Turner, *Between Science and Religion* (New Haven and London: Yale University Press, 1974) for a detailed study of some of the individuals who opposed scientific naturalism.
2. Hanegraaff, *New Age Religion and Western Culture,* 444.
3. See Chapter 5 in Owen Davies, *Witchcraft, Magic and Culture 1736–1951* (Manchester: Manchester University Press, 1999).
4. See Davies again, *Witchcraft, Magic and Culture* and King, *Modern Ritual Magic,* 19–21.
5. Godwin, *The Theosophical Enlightenment,* 93–4.
6. Godwin, *The Theosophical Enlightenment,* 107.
7. Ellic Howe, *Urania's Children* (London: William Kimber and Co., 1967), 25; Godwin, *The Theosophical Enlightenment,* 107.
8. Godwin, *The Theosophical Enlightenment,* 107.
9. For a detailed discussion on the merits of Barrett's work see my article, 'Beyond Attribution: The Importance of Barrett's *Magus*', *Journal for the Academic Study of Magic,* 1 (2003), 7–32.
10. Francis King, *The Flying Sorcerer: Being the magical and aeronautical adventures of Francis Barrett author of The Magus* (Oxford: Mandrake Books, 1992), 40.
11. King, *The Flying Sorcerer,* 29.
12. Frances Barrett, *The Magus or Celestial Intelligencer* (London: Lackington, Allen, 1801. Reprint, Leicester: Vance Harvey, 1970), v.

13. The *British Museum General Catalogue of Printed Books* actually dates this work at 1640 in Brussels under the title *E. Mohyi Pulvis Sympatheticus, quo vulnera sanantur, absque medicamenti ad partem affectam applicatione & sine superstitione* ... Two more editions were printed in 1660 and 1662. As the work is in Latin it is doubtful that Barrett actually used this book and it is more likely that he is name dropping from the best-known treatises on this subject.
14. Godwin, *The Theosophical Enlightenment*, 118.
15. For a discussion of this and an analysis of the influence of clergy on magical texts, see Richard Kieckhefer's *Forbidden Rites: A Necromancer's Manual of the Fifteenth Century* (University Park: Pennsylvania State University Press, 1998), 4–17.
16. Barrett, *The Magus*, Book Two, 69.
17. In their survey books on magical literature, E.M. Butler and Golden Dawn member Arthur Edward Waite provide instructions given in various medieval grimoires on how to made a *Liber Spirituum*. E.M. Butler, *Ritual Magic* (Cambridge: Cambridge University Press, 1949. Reprint, University Park: Pennsylvania State University Press, 1998). Arthur Edward Waite, *The Book of Ceremonial Magic*. First printed as *The Book of Black Magic and of Pacts* (London, 1898. Reprint, Secaucus: Carol Publishing, 1997).
18. Waite, *The Book of Ceremonial Magic*, 90.
19. Barrett, *The Magus*, Book One, 27.
20. Barrett, *The Magus*, Book Two, 16.
21. Barrett, *The Magus*, Book Two, 140.
22. Godwin, *The Theosophical Enlightenment*, 116.
23. 'Directions for the Invocation of Spirits', MS 1073, 1802, Wellcome Institute. Another manuscript in the Wellcome Institute title 'On Spiritual Vision' also makes reference to Barrett's *Magus* in its instructions on working rituals with crystals and circles. MS 3770, 1802, Wellcome Institute.
24. Montague Summers, *Witchcraft and Black Magic* (London: Rider, 1946. Reprint, Detroit: Omnigraphics, 1990), 225. King, *The Flying Sorcerer*, 26.
25. E.M. Butler, *Ritual Magic*, 254.
26. E.M. Butler, *Ritual Magic*, 254.
27. Donald Tyson, ed. in his introduction to *Three Books of Occult Philosophy*, trans. James Freake, (St Paul: Llewellyn, 1998), xl.
28. Godwin's *The Theosophical Enlightenment* being an important exception.
29. King, *Modern Ritual Magic*, 194–5.
30. Frederick Hockley, 'On the Ancient Magic Crystal and its Connexion with Mesmerism', *The Zoist*, 27 (October 1849), 251–66 and 252n. John Hamill claims that Hockley may have been employed by Denley in the copying and even manufacturing of occult manuscripts. Hamill's information comes from original papers written by Hockley and copied by Gerald Yorke. *The Rosicrucian Seer: Magical Writings of Frederick Hockley*, 11, 21.
31. Godwin, *The Theosophical Enlightenment*, 169.
32. Godwin, *Theosophical Enlightenment*, 172.
33. Hockley, 'On the Ancient Magic Crystal', 256–7.
34. I have identified one such account in *The Zoist*, 27 (October 1849), 251–66, 264–5. Here Hockley includes a diary entry recording an experiment with crystal scrying and a speculatrix.
35. Hockley (ed. Hamill), *The Rosicrucian Seer*, 22.

36. Westcott, 'The Golden Dawn's Official History Lecture', Private Collection A.
37. Gilbert, 'Secret Writing: The Magical Manuscripts of Frederick Hockley', 27–8.
38. Gilbert, 'Secret Writing' 29.
39. Mackenzie's works include: *Burmah and the Burmese* (London: Routledge and Co., 1853), articles on Peking, America and Scandinavia in T.A.W. Buckley, *The Great Cities of the Ancient World, in Their Glory and their Desolation* ... (London: Routledge, 1852); a biography of Hans Christian Andersen in C. Boner's translation of *The Shoes of Fortune and Other Fairy Tales* (London: John Hogg, 1883); and a novel *Zythagala; or Borne by the Sea* (London and Paris, 1872). His translations include a biography of Bismark, *The Life of Homer* attributed to Herodotus, and Alfred Crowquill's *Eulenspiegel: The marvellous adventures and rare conceits of Master Tyll Owlglass*. Along with these publications, Mackenzie also contributed articles to *The Biological Review* and the *Masonic Directory Series*.
40. Kenneth Mackenzie, *Royal Masonic Cyclopaedia*, 649.
41. Gilbert, *Revelations*, 5.
42. Mackenzie, *Royal Masonic Cyclopaedia*, 309 and 344. Hamill and Gilbert, Introduction to *Royal Masonic Cyclopaedia*, vii.
43. Private letter from Mackenzie to F.G. Irwin. Documented in Ellic Howe, *The Magicians of the Golden Dawn*, 31.
44. Howe, 'Fringe Masonry in England 1870–85' in *Ars Quatuor Coronatorum*, September 1972. Gilbert, *Revelations*, 5–6.
45. Ronald Decker, Thierry Depaulis and Michael Dummett, *A Wicked Pack of Cards: The Origins of the Occult Tarot* (New York: St Martin's Press, 1996), 174.
46. Jean-Pierre Laurant, 'The Primitive Characteristics of Nineteenth-Century Esotericism', in *Modern Esoteric Spirituality*. Eds Antoine Faivre and Jacob Needleman (New York: Crossroad, 1992), 277–87, 280.
47. Westcott, 'The Golden Dawn's Official History Lecture'.
48. Howe, *Magicians of the Golden Dawn*, 9.
49. I am grateful to Owen Davies for this reference. Éliphas Lévi, *Transcendental Magic: Its Doctrine and Ritual* (London: Rider & Co., 1896. Reprint, New York: Samuel Weiser, 1974), 249.
50. Howe, *Magicians of the Golden Dawn*, 28.
51. King, *Modern Ritual Magic*, 32.
52. Westcott, 'The Golden Dawn's Official History Lecture'.
53. Godwin, *The Theosophical Enlightenment*, 185.
54. Private letter from Hockley as printed in Hamill and Gilbert, Introduction to *Royal Masonic Cyclopaedia*, vi.
55. Parchment Roll, Private Collection A.
56. King claims Kingsford was an addict and that her addiction was the source of these visions although he insists that this in no way diminished the significance of her remarkable 'dreams'. King, *Modern Ritual Magic*, 48n.
57. Edward Maitland, *Anna Kingsford: Her Life, Letters, Diary and Work*, 2 vols. (London: George Redway, 1896).
58. Anna Kingsford and Edward Maitland, *The Perfect Way, or, The Finding of Christ* (London, 1882; revised edition 1887. Reprint, Montana: Kessinger Publishing Company, 1997), 50.

59. For more on Kingsford's role in the nineteenth-century intellectual debate between science and religion see Alison Butler, 'Anna Kingsford: Scientist and Sorceress', in David Clifford, Elisabeth Wadge, Alex Warwick, Martin Willis (eds), *Repositioning Victorian Sciences: Shifting Centres in Nineteenth-Century Scientific Thinking* (London: Anthem Press, 2006), 59–69.
60. Compilations of these writings are found in *The Credo of Christendom and other Addresses and Essays on Esoteric Christianity.* Ed. Samuel Hapgood Hart (London: J.M. Watkins, 1916. Reprint, Montana: Kessinger, 1997) and *Clothed With the Sun.* Ed. Edward Maitland (London: 1889. Reprint, Montana: Kessinger, 1999).
61. Mrs Algernon Kingsford, *Violationism: or sorcery in science* (Bath, 1887), 1.
62. Maitland, *Anna Kingsford*, ii. 268.
63. Kingsford, *Violationism*, 1.
64. Anna Kingsford, *Pasteur: His Method and its Results* (Hampstead, 1886), 28.
65. Maitland, *Anna Kingsford*, ii. 271.
66. Advertisement found in Kingsford's *How the World Came to and End in 1881* (London: Field & Tuer [The Perfect Way Shilling Series], 1, 1884).
67. Advertisement found in Kingsford's *Dreams and Dream-Stories,* ed. Edward Maitland (London: George Redway, 1888).
68. Advertisement found in Kingsford's *Dreams and Dream-Stories,* ed. Edward Maitland (London: George Redway, 1888).
69. Mathers, dedication in *The Kabbalah Unveiled* (London: George Redway, 1887. Reprint, New York: Samuel Weiser, 1978).
70. Daniël van Egmond, 'Western Esoteric Schools in the Late Nineteenth and Early Twentieth Centuries', 321.
71. Blavatsky, *The Secret Doctrine*, 2 vols (London: Theosophical Publishing Company, 1888. Reprint, 1925), i, xviii–xix.
72. Samuel Hapgood Hart, preface to *The Credo of Christendom*, 11.
73. Maitland, *Anna Kingsford*, ii, 168.
74. Kingsford and Maitland, *The Credo of Christendom*, 25.
75. These lectures are compiled and published in *The Credo of Christendom.*
76. Maitland, *Anna Kingsford*, ii, 233.
77. Harper, *Yeats's Golden Dawn*, 9.
78. Godwin, *The Theosophical Enlightenment*, 224.
79. Westcott, 'The Golden Dawn's Official History Lecture'.
80. Moina Mathers, preface to *The Kabbalah Unveiled.*
81. Maitland, *Anna Kingsford*, ii, 246.
82. Maitland, *Anna Kingsford,* ii, 292. Diary entry from Kingsford, 14 April 1887.
83. Maitland, *Anna Kingsford,* ii, 168.
84. For a full account of this incident see Maitland, *Anna Kingsford,* ii, 182–248.
85. Maitland, *Anna Kingsford,* ii, 259.
86. Maitland, *Anna Kingsford,* ii, 261.
87. Alex Owen, *The Darkened Room: Women, Power and Spiritualism in Late Victorian England* (London: Virago Press, 1989).
88. Howe, *Magicians of the Golden Dawn*, 55. Gilbert, *The Golden Dawn and the Esoteric Section* (London: Theosophical History Centre, 1987), 6–7.
89. Van Egmond, 'Western Esoteric Schools in the Late Nineteenth and Early Twentieth Centuries', 325.

90. Private letter from Westcott, 1889, Yorke Collection.
91. Address to the Fratres of Isis Urania Temple at the Equinox 1891. From Private Collection C as documented in Gilbert, *The Golden Dawn and the Esoteric Section*, 8.

5   Magical Libraries: What Occultists Read

1. *List of Books Chiefly from the Library of the Late Frederick Hockley, Esq., Consisting of Important Works relating to the Occult Sciences, both in print and manuscript* (London: George Redway, 1887).
2. *A Catalogue of a Portion of the Valuable Library of the late Walter Moseley, Esq.* (London: George Redway, 1889).
3. Maitland, *Anna Kingsford*, ii, 212.
4. R.A. Gilbert traces which of Hockley's manuscripts survived and which ones are as yet unaccounted for in his essay 'Secret Writing: The Magical Manuscripts of Frederick Hockley' in *The Rosicrucian Seer: Magical Writings of Frederick Hockley* ed. John Hamill (Wellingborough: Aquarian Press, 1986), 26–33.
5. One copy is at the Bodleian Library in Oxford and the other at the British Library.
6. *List of Books Chiefly from the Library of the Late Frederick Hockley*, 15. The full entry reads *HOW to GROW HANDSOME, or Hints towards Physical Perfection*, by D.H. Jacques, *cuts*, sm. 8vo, *cloth, New York*, 1879, 7s 6d.
7. *List of Books Chiefly from the Library of the Late Frederick Hockley*, 6, 7, 16 and 19. These works are listed as follows: *On the Conduct of Understanding, by John Locke, edited by Bolton Corney*, 1859; *Essay Concerning Human Understanding, by John Locke*, 1731; *The Philosophy of Kant lectures by Victor Cousin, translated from the French with a Sketch of Kant's Life and Writings*, 1854; *The Conduct of the Understanding to which is added an Abstract of Mr. Locke's Essay on Human Understanding*, 1781; and *Essay concerning Human Understanding, written by John Locke, to which is added an Analysis of Mr. Locke's Doctrine of Ideas, a Treatise on the Conduct of Understanding*, 1796.
8. Owen, *The Place of Enchantment* and Treitel, *A Science for the Soul*.
9. *List of Books Chiefly from the Library of the Late Frederick Hockley*, 8 and 19. The entries read: Herbert Spencer, *Essays, Scientific, Political and Speculative, 1858: Contains articles on Manners and Fashion, The Philosophy of Style, Transcendental Physiology, Personal Beauty etc.*; Spencer, *First Principles, Vol. I of a System of Synthetic Philosophy*, 1870.
10. *List of Books Chiefly from the Library of the Late Frederick Hockley*, 17 and 23. The entries read: Thomas H. Huxley, *American Addresses on Evolution, with a lecture on the Study of Biology*, 1877; and *Articles on the Methods and Results of Ethnology by T.H. Huxley*.
11. *List of Books Chiefly from the Library of the Late Frederick Hockley*, 8. The entry reads: *Scientific Materialism considered, a reply to Professor Tyndall's Address delivered before the British Association, 1874 by G. Sexton*.
12. 'The Westcott Hermetic Library' in George Mills Harper, *Yeats's Golden Dawn* (London: MacMillan Press, 1974), 290.
13. 'The Westcott Hermetic Library', 290.

14. *List of Books Chiefly from the Library of the Late Frederick Hockley,* 1, 3; 'The Westcott Hermetic Library', 302. The Westcott edition spells the translator's name 'Ashmand'.
15. *List of Books Chiefly from the Library of the Late Frederick Hockley,* 22. The entry reads: *Celestial Philosophy, or the Language of the Stars, Lectures by 'Zuriel',* 1835. 'The Westcott Hermetic Library', 292. The entry reads: *Lectures on the Science of Celestial Philosophy by Zuriel,* 1835.
16. *List of Books Chiefly from the Library of the Late Frederick Hockley,* 13. The entry reads: William Lilly, *Christian Astrology,* 1647. 'The Westcott Hermetic Library', 299.
17. 'The Westcott Hermetic Library', 292. The entry reads: Elias Ashmole, *Mr. Wm. Lilly's History of his Life and Times, from 1602 to 1681,* (London, 1715). Hockley's list has an 1822 edition. *List of Books Chiefly from the Library of the Late Frederick Hockley,* 6.
18. Godwin, *The Theosophical Enlightenment,* 169.
19. *List of Books Chiefly from the Library of the Late Frederick Hockley,* 13; 'The Westcott Hermetic Library', 297.
20. *List of Books Chiefly from the Library of the Late Frederick Hockley,* 11 and 18. 'The Westcott Hermetic Library', 299. The entries read: Edwin Lee, *Animal Magnetism,* (London, 1843); Lee, *Animal Magnetism and Magnetic Lucid Somnambulism,* (London, 1866).
21. *List of Books Chiefly from the Library of the Late Frederick Hockley,* 11. 'The Westcott Hermetic Library', 295. The entry reads: J.P.F. Deleuze, *Practical Instruction in Animal Magnetism or Mesmerism,* trans T.C. Hartshorn, (London, 1843).
22. Godwin, *The Theosophical Enlightenment,* 154.
23. *List of Books Chiefly from the Library of the Late Frederick Hockley,* 2, 6, 9, 15, 19 and 24. 'The Westcott Hermetic Library', 304.
24. 'The Westcott Hermetic Library', 304.
25. 'Mystic Book which Inspired Famous Men Done into English', *New York Times,* 19 July 1914.
26. *New York Times,* 19 July 1914.
27. 'The Westcott Hermetic Library', 295.
28. Thomas De Quincey, 'Historico-Critical Inquiry into the Origin of the Rosicrucians and the Free-Masons' in *The Collected writings of Thomas De Quincey* ed. David Masson vol. XIII (London: A. & C. Black, 1897), 426.
29. *List of Books Chiefly from the Library of the Late Frederick Hockley,* 17. 'The Westcott Hermetic Library', 295.
30. As cited in Howe, *Magicians of the Golden Dawn,* 155.
31. *List of Books Chiefly from the Library of the Late Frederick Hockley,* 17. 'The Westcott Hermetic Library', 299.
32. Godwin, *The Theosophical Enlightenment,* 181.
33. *List of Books Chiefly from the Library of the Late Frederick Hockley,* 20. 'The Westcott Hermetic Library', 293.
34. *List of Books Chiefly from the Library of the Late Frederick Hockley,* 2. 'The Westcott Hermetic Library', 295. John Dee, *The Private Diary of Dr. John Dee And the Catalog of His Library of Manuscripts,* ed. James Orchard Halliwell-Phillips (London, 1842).

35. *List of Books Chiefly from the Library of the Late Frederick Hockley*, 9–10. 'The Westcott Hermetic Library', 291, 301–2 and 303.
36. Arthur Edward Waite, *The Magical Writings of Thomas Vanghan (Eugenius Philalethes) A Verbatim reprint of his First Four Treatises; Anthroposophia Theomagia, Anima Magica, Abscondita, Magia Adamica, and the True Coelum Terra* (London: George Redway, 1888).
37. As cited in Waite, *The Magical Writings*, vii–viii.
38. Waite, *The Magical Writings*, viii.
39. Gilbert, *Revelations*, 151.
40. *List of Books Chiefly from the Library of the Late Frederick Hockley*, 9–10. 'The Westcott Hermetic Library', 302.
41. *List of Books Chiefly from the Library of the Late Frederick Hockley*, 9. 'The Westcott Hermetic Library', 302.
42. *List of Books Chiefly from the Library of the Late Frederick Hockley*, 8. 'The Westcott Hermetic Library', 299.
43. *List of Books Chiefly from the Library of the Late Frederick Hockley*, 7.
44. *List of Books Chiefly from the Library of the Late Frederick Hockley*, 12 and 13. 'The Westcott Hermetic Library', 293 and 305.
45. The Westcott Hermetic Library', 296.
46. The Westcott Hermetic Library', 297.
47. *List of Books Chiefly from the Library of the Late Frederick Hockley*, 5.
48. Gilbert, 'Secret Writing', 26.
49. Gilbert, 'Secret Writing', 27.
50. The Westcott Hermetic Library' 291 and 292. The entries read: Albertus Magnus, *De Secretis mulierum*, 1625 and Bacon, F., *Novum organum scientiarum*, 1660.

6 Revolutionizing Magic: The Will Conquers the Spirit

1. Mathers, *Key of Solomon*, 15.
2. Mathers, *Key of Solomon*, 16.
3. Mathers, *Key of Solomon*, 86–7.
4. Mathers, *The Book of the Sacred Magic of Abramelin the Mage*, 45–6.
5. Florence Farr and Elaine Simpson, 'An Example of Mode of Attaining to Spirit Vision and What was seen by Two Adepti – S.S.D.D. and F. on November 10th 1892', MS 57, Notebook containing Golden Dawn Flying Rolls, Yorke Collection.
6. Annie Horniman, 1898, MS 11[GD MSS 5], Yorke Collection.
7. Horniman, 1898, MS 11[GD MSS 5], Yorke Collection.
8. Horniman, 1898, MS 11[GD MSS 5], Yorke Collection.
9. Horniman, 1898, MS 11[GD MSS 5], Yorke Collection.
10. Horniman, 1898, MS 11[GD MSS 5], Yorke Collection.
11. Horniman, 1898, MS 11[GD MSS 5], Yorke Collection.
12. Horniman, 1898, MS 11[GD MSS 5], Yorke Collection.
13. Horniman, 1898, MS 11[GD MSS 5], Yorke Collection.
14. Horniman, 1898, MS 11[GD MSS 5], Yorke Collection.
15. Horniman, 1898, MS 11[GD MSS 5], Yorke Collection.
16. Horniman, 1898, MS 11[GD MSS 5], Yorke Collection.
17. Horniman, 1898, MS 11[GD MSS 5], Yorke Collection.

18. Horniman, 1898, MS 11[GD MSS 5], Yorke Collection.
19. Manuscript of a Sphere Group Working, Private Collection C.
20. Mina Mathers, 'Know Thyself', MS 57, Yorke Collection.
21. Luhrmann, *Persuasions of the Witch's Craft*, 41 and 56.
22. Hutton, *Triumph of the Moon*, 10, 38 and 49.
23. Luhrmann, *Persuasions of the Witch's Craft*, 181.
24. Mathers, *Key of Solomon*, 26.
25. Mathers, *Key of Solomon*, 27.
26. 'Ritual for the Formation, Building and Consecration of a Body, wherein to Travel, manifest & act in freedom from the Bonds & limitation of matter', 1899–1900 in Private Collection C.
27. 'Ritual of the Lesser Pentagram', as printed in Regardie, *The Golden Dawn*, 53–4.
28. Mina Mathers, 'Know Thyself. Address to the Zelator Adepti Minores of the Order *R.R. et A.C.* By *Vestigia Nulla Retrorsum* 6°=5°', 1893. MS 57, Notebook containing Golden Dawn Flying Rolls, Yorke Collection.
29. J.W. Brodie-Innes, 'Essay on Clairvoyance and Travelling in the Spirit Vision By *Sub.Spe* – Zelator Adeptus Minor', 1892–5, MS 57, Notebook containing Golden Dawn Flying Rolls, Yorke Collection.
30. Percy Bullock, 'The Principia of Theurgia or the Higher Magic By L.O.', 1892–95, MS 57, Notebook containing Golden Dawn Flying Rolls, Yorke Collection.
31. Hutton, *Triumph of the Moon*, 301.
32. Mathers, *Key of Solomon*.
33. William Wynn Westcott, 'The Aims and Means of Adeptship By *N.O.M.*', 1892–95, MS 57, Notebook containing Golden Dawn Flying Rolls, Yorke Collection.
34. Westcott, 'The Aims and Means of Adeptship By *N.O.M*', 1892–95, MS 57, Yorke Collection.
35. Mina Mathers, 'Know Thyself', MS 57.
36. Percy Bullock, 'Remarks upon Subject for Contemplation By V.H. Fra *Levavi Oculos*', 1892, MS 57, Notebook containing Golden Dawn Flying Rolls, Yorke Collection.
37. Owen, *The Place of Enchantment*, 147.
38. Hutton, 'Modern Pagan Witchcraft', 10.
39. Westcott, 'Man, Miracle, and Magic', 68–9.
40. Hutton, *Triumph of the Moon*, 76.
41. Luhrmann, *Persuasions of the Witch's Craft*, 65–6.
42. Luhrmann, *Persuasions of the Witch's Craft*, 57 and 250.
43. Luhrmann, *Persuasions of the Witch's Craft*, 60.
44. William Butler Yeats, Letter to Florence Farr, 1906, MS 30585, Yeats Collection, National Library of Ireland.
45. Antoine Faivre, 'Renaissance Hermeticism and Western Esotericism', in *Gnosis and Hermeticism: From Antiquity to Modern Times*. Eds Roelof van den Broek and Wouter J. Hanegraaff (Albany: State University of New York Press, 1998), 109–23; 119–20.
46. Westcott, 'Man, Miracle and Magic', 67–8.
47. Westcott, 'Man, Miracle and Magic', 69.
48. Luhrmann, *Persuasions of the Witch's Craft*, 47.

49. William Wynn Westcott, 'A Subject for Contemplation by G.H. Frater *N.O.M.*', 1892–95, MS 57, Notebook containing Golden Dawn Flying Rolls, Yorke Collection.
50. Farr, 'Three Suggestions on Will Power by *S.S.D.D.*', MS 57, Yorke Collection.
51. Dr E. Berridge, 'Some Thoughts on the Imagination. By V.H. Fra. *Resurgam*', 1893, MS 57, Notebook containing Golden Dawn Flying Rolls, Yorke Collection.
52. Berridge, 'Some Thoughts in the Imagination. By V.H. Fra. *Resurgam*', 1893, MS 57, Yorke Collection.
53. William Wynn Westcott, 'Supplementary Remarks by G.H. Fra. *N.O.M.*', 1892–95, MS 57, Notebook containing Golden Dawn Flying Rolls, Yorke Collection.
54. Westcott, 'Supplementary Remarks by G.H. Fra. *N.O.M.*', 1892–95, MS 57, Yorke Collection.
55. Iamblichus, *De mysteriis Aegyptorium – On the Mysteries*, ed. Stephan Ronan, trans. Thomas Taylor and Alexander Wilder (Hastings: Chthonios Books, 1989), III.6.112–14, and III.14.133.3–8.
56. William Butler Yeats, 'The Body of the Father Christian Rosencrux', 1895. Reprinted in *Ideas of Good and Evil* (London: A.H. Bullen, 1903), 308–11, 310.
57. Owen, *The Place of Enchantment*, 184.
58. Luhrmann, *Persuasions of the Witch's Craft*, 118.
59. Mathers, *The Book of the Sacred Magic of Abramelin the Mage*, 55–6.
60. Owen, *The Darkened Room*.
61. Mathers, *The Book of the Sacred Magic of Abramelin the Mage*, 55n.
62. Owen, *The Place of Enchantment*, 88.
63. Hutton, *Triumph of the Moon*, 390.
64. Westcott, 'A Recent Spiritual Development', reprinted from *SRIA, Transactions of the Metropolitan College*, 1917, 18–25, in *The Magical Mason*, 287–95, 290.

7 Middle-Class Magic

1. Frank M. Turner, *Contesting Cultural Authority: Essays in Victorian Intellectual Life* (Cambridge: Cambridge University Press, 1993), 45–9.
2. Turner, *Contesting Cultural Authority*, 72.
3. George W. Stocking, *Victorian Anthropology* (New York: Free Press, 1987), 243 and Turner, *Contesting Cultural Authority*, 175 and 179.
4. Stocking, *Victorian Anthropology*, 44, 76, and 258.
5. Stocking, *Victorian Anthropology*, 53–4.
6. Frank M. Turner, *The Greek Heritage in Victorian Britain* (New Haven: Yale University Press, 1981), 77.
7. Jose Harris addresses the use of Platonic notions of community and collective social action by late nineteenth-century social theorists and social scientists in 'Platonism, positivism and progressivism: aspects of British sociological thought in the early twentieth century' in *Citizenship and Community: Liberals, radicals and collective identities in the British Isles, 1865–1931*, ed. Eugenio F. Biagini (Cambridge: Cambridge University Press, 1996), 343–60.
8. Turner, *The Greek Heritage in Victorian Britain*, 2–3.

9. Richard Jenkyns, *The Victorians and Ancient Greece* (Cambridge, Mass.: Harvard University Press, 1980), 160, 187, 215, and 283–4.
10. Turner, *The Greek Heritage in Victorian Britain,* 77.
11. Turner, *The Greek Heritage in Victorian Britain,* 119–21.
12. Ernest Barker, *Political Thought in England, 1848–1914* (London: Oxford University Press, 1959), 4.
13. Melvin Richter, *The Politics of Conscience: T.H. Green and his Age* (Cambridge, Mass.: Harvard University Press, 1964), 13–14.
14. Richter, *The Politics of Conscience,* 14.
15. John Bowle, *Politics and Opinion in the Nineteenth Century* (London: Jonathan Cape, 1963), 278–80.
16. Richter, *The Politics of Conscience,* 104 and 106.
17. Janet Oppenheim, *The Other World: Spiritualism and Psychical Research in England, 1850–1914* (Cambridge: Cambridge University Press, 1985), 7, 9, and 49.
18. Logie Barrow, *Independent Spirits: Spiritualism and English Plebeians, 1850–1910* (London: Routledge & Kegan Paul, 1986), 98 and Oppenheim, *The Other World,* 88–9.
19. Barrow, *Independent Spirits,* 146–7.
20. Stocking, *Victorian Anthropology,* 263.
21. Barrow, *Independent Spirits,* 194.
22. Oppenheim, *The Other World,* 9.
23. Oppenheim, *The Other World,* 159.
24. Brown's activities are thoroughly examined in Barrow, *Independent Spirits,* 36–66. For a detailed description of the content of Gabriel's prophecies see Barrow, *Independent Spirits,* 36–55.
25. Patrick Curry, *A Confusion of Prophets: Victorian and Edwardian Astrology* (London: Collins and Brown, 1992), 11.
26. Curry, *A Confusion of Prophets,* 50.
27. Curry, *A Confusion of Prophets,* 60.
28. Curry, *A Confusion of Prophets,* 160.
29. Oppenheim, *The Other World,* 205.
30. Godwin, *The Theosophical Enlightenment,* 131–48.
31. Laurence W. Fennelly, 'W.B. Yeats and S.L. MacGregor Mathers' in *Yeats and the Occult.* Ed. George Mills Harper (Toronto: Macmillan, 1975), 285–306, 285 and 297.
32. William Butler Yeats, *Autobiographies* (London: Macmillan, 1961), 115 and 190.
33. William Butler Yeats, *Explorations* (London: Macmillan, 1962), 54.
34. Yeats, *Autobiographies,* 182–3.
35. Yeats, *Autobiographies,* 185–6.
36. R.F. Foster, *W.B. Yeats: A Life,* vol. i (Oxford: Oxford University Press, 1997), 106.
37. Eric Hobsbawm, 'Introduction: Inventing Traditions' in *The Invention of Tradition.* Eds Eric Hobsbawm and Terence Ranger (Cambridge: Cambridge University Press, 1983), 1–14; 1.
38. Eric Hobsbawm, 'Mass-Producing Traditions: Europe, 1870–1914' in *The Invention of Tradition.* Eds Eric Hobsbawm and Terence Ranger (Cambridge: Cambridge University Press, 1983), 263–307; 263.

39. Hobsbawm, 'Mass-Producing Traditions', 283.
40. Hobsbawm, 'Inventing Traditions', 6.
41. Paul Post, 'Rituals and the Function of the Past' in *Journal of Ritual Studies,* 1996 10, 85–107, 94.
42. Allen, *Beyond Enlightenment,* 89.
43. Christopher McIntosh, *Eliphas Lévi and the French Occult Revival* (London: Rider, 1972), 12.
44. McIntosh, *Eliphas Lévi and the French Occult Revival,* 19.
45. McIntosh, *Eliphas Lévi and the French Occult Revival,* 20 and 26–9.
46. Nicole Edelman, *Voyantes, Guérisseuses et Visionnaires en France 1785–1914* (Paris: Albin Michel, 1995), 154–8.
47. Godwin, *The Theosophical Enlightenment,* 196.
48. Thomas A. Williams, *Eliphas Lévi: Master of Occultism* (Alabama: University of Alabama Press, 1975), 89 and McIntosh, *Eliphas Lévi and the French Occult Revival,* 101.
49. McIntosh, *Eliphas Lévi and the French Occult Revival,* 141–52.
50. Allen, *Beyond Enlightenment,* 104.
51. Allen, *Beyond Enlightenment,* 104.
52. McIntosh, *Eliphas Lévi and the French Occult Revival,* 170.
53. Alain Mercier, *Eliphas Lévi et la pensée magique au XIXe siècle* (Paris: Seghers, 1974), 143–53 and McIntosh, *Eliphas Lévi and the French Occult Revival,* 195 and 202.
54. Edelman, *Voyantes, Guérisseuses et Visionnaires en France,* 149.
55. Godwin, *The Theosophical Enlightenment,* 67.
56. Maud Gonne MacBride, *A Servant of the Queen, her own story* (Dublin: Standard House, 1950), 248.
57. Crowley, *Confessions,* 169–70.

Bibliography

Primary sources

Unpublished sources

Barrett, Francis. *The Magus or Celestial Intelligencer*, 1801, MS 1072, Wellcome Institute.

Barrett, Francis. 'Directions for the Invocation of Spirits', 1802, MS 1073, Wellcome Institute.

Berridge, Dr E. 'Some Thoughts in the Imagination By V.H. Fra. *Resurgam*', 1893, MS 57, Yorke Collection.

Brodie-Innes, J.W. 'Essay on Clairvoyance and Travelling in the Spirit Vision By *Sub.Spe* – Zelator Adeptus Minor', 1892–95, MS 57, Yorke Collection.

Bullock, Percy. 'The Principia of Theurgia or the Higher Magic By L.O.', 1892–95, MS 57, Yorke Collection.

Bullock, Percy. 'Remarks upon Subject for Contemplation By V.H. Fra *Levavi Oculos*', 1892, MS 57, Yorke Collection.

Dee, John. *Dr. Dee's Conference with angels from Dec. 22 1581 to May 30 1583*, BL MS Sloane 3188.

Dee, John. *A True and Faithful Relation of what passed for many years between Dr. John Dee and some Spirits*. Ed. Dr Meric Casaubon, 1659.

Dee, John. *De heptarchia mystica*, BL MS Sloane 3191.

Dee, John. *48 Claves Angelicae Cracow April 13 – July 13, 1584*, BL MS Sloane 3191.

Farr, Florence and Elaine Simpson, 'An Example of Mode of Attaining to Spirit Vision and What was seen by Two Adepti – S.S.D.D. and F. on November 10th 1892', MS 57, Yorke Collection.

Farr, Florence. 'Three Suggestions on Will Power by *S.S.D.D.*', MS 57, Yorke Collection.

Gardner, Frederick Leigh. MS 11[GD MSS 5], 1898, Yorke Collection.

Howe, Ellic. Letter to Gerald Yorke, MS 2, Yorke Collection.

Kelley, Edward. *The Book of Enoch Revealed to Dr. John Dee by the Angels*, BL MS Sloane 3189.

'Lesser Ritual of the Pentagram', MS 64, Yorke Collection.

Mathers, Mina. 'Know Thyself. Address to the Zelator Adepti Minores of the Order R.R. et A.C. By *Vestigia Nulla Retrorsum* 6°=5°', 1893, MS 57, Yorke Collection.

Parkins, John. 'On Spiritual Vision', 1802, MS 3770, Wellcome Institute.

'Ritual for the Formation, Building and Consecration of a Body, wherein to Travel, manifest & act in freedom from the Bonds & limitation of matter', 1899–1900, Private Collection C.

Ritual of the S.O.S, Private Collection C.

Rituals of the Order of G.O.T.S., Private Collection C.

Sphere Group Ritual, Private Collection C.

Westcott, William Wynn. 'Supplementary Remarks by G.H. Fra. *N.O.M.*', 1892–95, MS 57, Yorke Collection.
Westcott, William Wynn. 'The Aims and Means of Adeptship By *N.O.M.*', 1892–95, MS 57, Yorke Collection.
Westcott, William Wynn. Letter to F.L. Gardner, 1912, MS 2, Yorke Collection.
Yeats, W.B. Letter to Florence Farr, 1906, MS 30585, Yeats Collection, National Library of Ireland.

Published sources

Agrippa, Heinrich Cornelius. *Three Books of Occult Philosophy. De Occulta Philosophia.* 1533. Reprint, Ed. Donald Tyson. St Paul: Llewellyn, 1992.
Apuleius. *The Golden Ass.* Trans. E.J. Kenny. London: Penguin, 1998.
Barrett, Francis. *The Magus or Celestial Intelligencer.* London: Lackington, Allen, 1801. Reprint, Leicester: Vance Harvey, 1970.
Blavatsky, Helena Petrovna. *The Secret Doctrine.* London: Theosophical Publishing Company, 1888. Reprint, 1925.
Blavatsky, Helena Petrovna. *Isis Unveiled.* London: 1877. Reprint, Pasadena: Theosophical University Press, 1998.
Brodie-Innes, J.W. 'Notes on the First Knowledge Lecture', 1895, in R.A. Gilbert, *Revelations of the Golden Dawn.* London: Quantum, 1997, 63.
Budge, E.A. Wallis, ed. and trans. *The Book of the Dead,* 3 vols. London: Kegan Paul, Trench, Trübner & Co., 1898.
Crowley, Aleister. *The Confessions of Aleister Crowley.* Eds John Symonds and Kenneth Grant. London: Routledge & Kegan Paul, 1969. Reprint, 1979.
Della Mirandola, Pico. *Syncretism in the West: Pico's 900 Theses (1486) The Evolution of Traditional Religious and Philosophical Systems.* Trans. S.A. Farmer. Tempe, Arizona: Medieval & Renaissance Texts & Studies, 1998.
Farr, Florence. *Egyptian Magic.* London, 1896. Reprint, Montana: Kessinger, 1998.
Frazer, Sir James George. *The Golden Bough,* abridged. London: MacMillan, 1922. Reprint, Oxford: Oxford University Press, 1994.
Gaucher, André. 'Isis à Montmartre', *L'Echo de merveilleux,* Paris, December 1 and 15, 1900.
Gilbert, R.A., ed. *The Magical Mason. Forgotten Hermetic Writings of William Wynn Westcott, Physician and Magus.* Wellingborough: Aquarian Press, 1983.
Goodwin, C.W. 'On a Graeco-Egyptian Papyri Preserved in the British Library', *Antiquarian Communications: Being the Papers Presented at the Meetings of the Cambridge Antiquarian Society,* 1 (1859), 37–42.
Goodwin, Charles Wycliffe, ed. and trans. *Fragment of a Graeco-Egyptian Work upon Magic from a Papyrus in the British Museum.* Cambridge: Deighton; Macmillan & Co., 1852.
Hockley, Frederick. 'On the Ancient Magic Crystal, and its Connexion with Mesmerism', *The Zoist,* 27 (October 1849), 251–66.
Hockley, Frederick. *The Rosicrucian Seer: Magical Writings of Frederick Hockley.* Ed. John Hamill. Wellingborough: Aquarian Press, 1986.
Higgins, Godfrey. *Anacalypsis.* London, 1863.
Iamblichus. *De mysteriis Aegyptorium – On the Mysteries.* Ed. Stephan Ronan. Trans. Thomas Taylor and Alexander Wilder. Hastings: Chthonios Books, 1989.

King, Francis. *Ritual Magic of the Golden Dawn.* Vermont: Destiny Books, 1997. First published as *Astral Projection, ritual magic, and alchemy.* London: Spearman, 1971.

Kingsford, Anna. *Pasteur: His Method and its Result.* Hampstead, 1886.

Kingsford, Anna and Edward Maitland. *The Perfect Way, or, The Finding of Christ.* London, 1882. Revised edition 1887.

Kingsford, Anna and Edward Maitland. *Clothed with the Sun.* Ed. Edward Maitland. London, 1889. Reprint, Montana: Kessinger, 1999.

Kingsford, Anna and Edward Maitland. *The Credo of Christendom and other Addresses and Essays on Esoteric Christianity.* Ed. Samuel Hapgood Hart. London: J.M. Watkins, 1916. Reprint, Montana: Kessinger, 1997.

Kingsford, Anna and Edward Maitland. *How the World Came to an End in 1881.* London: Field & Tuer, 1884.

Kingsford, Anna and Edward Maitland. *Dreams and Dream-Stories.* Ed. Edward Maitland. London: George Redway, 1888.

Kingsford, Anna and Edward Maitland. *Physiology of Vegetarianism.* Manchester: Vegetarian Society, 1886.

Kingsford, Mrs Algernon. *Violationism: or Sorcery in Science.* Bath, 1887.

Küntz, Darcy, ed. and trans. *The Complete Golden Dawn Cipher Manuscript.* Edmonds, WA: Holmes Publishing, 1996.

Lees, Frederick. 'Conversations with the Hierophant Rameses and the High Priestess Anari', *The Humanitarian,* 16 (2) (New York, February 1900).

Lévi, Éliphas. *Transcendental Magic: Its Doctrine and Ritual.* London: Rider & Co., 1896. Reprint, New York: Samuel Weiser, 1974.

MacBride, Maud Gonne. *A Servant of the Queen, her own story.* London: Gollancz, 1938, Reprint, Dublin: Standard House, 1950.

Mackenzie, Kenneth. *Royal Masonic Cyclopaedia.* London, 1877. Reprint Wellingborough: Aquarian Press, 1987.

Maitland, Edward. *Anna Kingsford: Her Life, Letters, Diary and Work.* 2 vols. London: George Redway, 1896.

Marlowe, Christopher. *Doctor Faustus.* 1604 version edition. Ed. Michael Keefer. Peterborough, Ontario: Broadview Press, 1991.

Marryat, Thomas. *The Philosophy of Masons in Several Epistles from Egypt, to a Nobleman.* London: J. Ridgway, 1790.

Mathers, Samuel Liddell MacGregor, trans. *Kabalah Unveiled.* London: George Redway, 1887. Reprint, New York: Samuel Weiser, 1978.

Mathers, Samuel Liddell MacGregor, ed. *The Book of the Goetia of Solomon the King.* Boleskine: Society for the Propagation of Religious Truth, 1904.

Mathers, Samuel Liddell MacGregor, ed. and trans. *The Book of the Sacred Magic of Abramelin the Mage.* London: John M. Watkins, 1898. Reprint New York: Dover, 1975.

Mathers, Samuel Liddell MacGregor, ed. *The Grimoire of Armadel.* New York, 1980.

Mathers, Samuel Liddell MacGregor, ed. *The Key of Solomon the King.* London: George Redway, 1889. Reprint, York Beach, Maine: Samuel Weiser, 2000.

Meyer, Marvin M., ed. *The Ancient Mysteries – A Sourcebook – Sacred Texts of the Mystery Religions of the Ancient Mediterranean World.* San Francisco: Harper & Row, 1987.

Paban, Gabrielle de. *Histoire des Fantomes et des Démons.* Paris, 1820.

Perkins, William. *A Discourse of the Damned Art of Witchcraft.* Cambridge, 1608.

Peterson, Joseph, H., ed. *The Lesser Key of Solomon*. Maine: Samuel Weiser, 2001.

Redway, George. *List of Books Chiefly from the Library of the Late Frederick Hockley, Esq., Consisting of Important Works relating to the Occult Sciences, both in print and manuscript*. London: George Redway, 1887.

Redway, George. *A Catalogue of a Portion of the Valuable Library of the late Walter Moseley, Esq*. London: George Redway, 1889.

Regardie, Israel. *The Golden Dawn*. First edition 1937–40; sixth edition, St Paul, Minnesota: Llewellyn, 1997.

Renouf, P. Le Page. *The Hibbert Lectures*. London and Edinburgh: Williams and Norgate, 1880.

Reuchlin, Johannes. *On the Art of the Kabbalah. De Arte Cabalistica*. Trans Martin and Sarah Goodman. Lincoln: University of Nebraska Press, 1993.

Robison, John. *Proofs of a Conspiracy against all the Religions and Governments of Europe Carried on in the Secret Meetings of Free Masons, Illuminati, and Reading Societies*. London, 1797.

Shelley, Mary. *Frankenstein or the Modern Prometheus*. 1818 edition. London: W. Pickering, 1993.

Sibly, Ebenezer. *A Key to Physic and the Occult Sciences*. London, 1794.

Sinnett. A.P. *Esoteric Buddhism*. London: Trübner & Co., 1883. Reprint, Theosophical Publishing House, 1972.

Torrens, R.G. *The Secret Rituals of the Golden Dawn*. Wellingborough: Aquarian Press, 1973.

Waite, Arthur Edward. *The Book of Ceremonial Magic*. Secaucus: Carol Publishing, 1997. First published as *The Book of Black Magic and of Pacts*. London, 1898.

Westcott, William Wynn. 'A Recent Spiritual Development'. *S.R.I.A. Transactions of the Metropolitan College* (1917), 18–25. Reprinted in *The Magical Mason. Forgotten Hermetic Writings of William Wynn Westcott, Physician and Magus*, ed. R.A. Gilbert. Wellingborough: Aquarian, 1983, 287–95.

Westcott, William Wynn. 'Man, Miracle, and Magic'. Paper read to members of the Isis-Urania Temple of the Golden Dawn at an unrecorded date. Printed in *The Magical Mason. Forgotten Hermetic Writings of William Wynn Westcott, Physician and Magus*, ed. R.A. Gilbert. Wellingborough: Aquarian, 1983, 66–70.

Westcott, William Wynn. 'Christian Rosenkreuz and the Rosicrucians'. *Theosophical Siftings*, 6 (15), 3–14. Reprinted in *The Magical Mason. Forgotten Hermetic Writings of William Wynn Westcott, Physician and Magus*, ed. R.A. Gilbert. Wellingborough: Aquarian, 1983, 13–27.

Westcott, William Wynn. 'The Resemblances of Freemasonry to the Cult of Mithra'. *Ars Quatuor* Coronatorum, 29 (1916), 1–9. Reprinted in *The Magical Mason. Forgotten Hermetic Writings of William Wynn Westcott, Physician and Magus*, ed. R.A. Gilbert. Wellingborough: Aquarian, 1983, 244–55.

Westcott, William Wynn. 'Freemasonry and its Relation to the Essenes'. *Ars Quatuor Coronatorum*, 28 (1915), 67–74. Reprinted in *The Magical Mason. Forgotten Hermetic Writings of William Wynn Westcott, Physician and Magus*, ed. R.A. Gilbert. Wellingborough: Aquarian, 1983, 233–43.

Westcott, William Wynn. 'Data of the History of the Rosicrucians', published for the *SRIA*, second edition (1916). Reprinted in *The Magical Mason. Forgotten Hermetic Writings of William Wynn Westcott, Physician and Magus*, ed. R.A. Gilbert Wellingborough: Aquarian, 1983, 29–39.

Westcott, William Wynn. 'The Rosicrucians, Past and Present, at Home and Abroad', in *The Magical Mason. Forgotten Hermetic Writings of William Wynn Westcott, Physician and Magus,* ed R.A. Gilbert. Wellingborough: Aquarian, 1983, 40–7.

Yeats, W.B. *Autobiographies.* London: Macmillan Press, 1955. Reprint, London: Macmillan Press, 1961.

Yeats, W.B. *Explorations.* London: Macmillan Press, 1962.

Yeats, W.B. 'Magic', 1901. Reprint in *Ideas of Good and Evil.* London: A.H. Bullen, 1903, 29–70.

Yeats, W.B. 'The Body of the Father Christian Rosencrux', 1895. Reprint in *Ideas of Good and Evil.* London: A.H. Bullen, 1903, 308–11.

Secondary sources

Allen, David Harvey. *Beyond Enlightenment: Occultism and Politics in Modern France* Dekalb: Northern Illinois University Press, 2005.

Barker, Ernest. *Political Thought in England 1848 to 1914.* London, 1915. Reprint, London: Oxford University Press, 1959.

Barrow, Logie. *Independent Spirits: Spiritualism and English Plebians 1850–1910.* London: Routledge & Kegan Paul, 1986.

Beitchman, Philip. *Alchemy of the Word. Cabala of the Renaissance.* Albany: State University of New York Press, 1998.

Bowle, John. *Politics and Opinion in the Nineteenth Century.* New York: Oxford University Press, 1954. Reprint, London: Jonathan Cape, 1963.

Bowler, Peter J. *Reconciling Science and Religion.* Chicago: University of Chicago Press, 2001.

Bown, Nicola. 'Esoteric Selves and Magical Minds', *History Workshop Journal,* 61 (1) (2006), 281–7.

Budge, E.A. Wallis. *Egyptian Magic.* London: Kegan Paul, Trench, Trübner & Co., 1899.

Burkert, Walter. *Ancient Mystery Cults.* Cambridge, Mass.: Harvard University Press, 1987.

Butler, Alison. 'Making Magic Modern: Nineteenth-Century Adaptations', *The Pomegranate: The International Journal of Pagan Studies* 6, II (2004), 212–30.

Butler, Alison. 'Anna Kingsford: Scientist and Sorceress', *Repositioning Victorian Sciences: Shifting Centres in Nineteenth-Century Scientific Thinking.* Eds David Clifford, Elisabeth Wadge, Alex Warwick, Martin Willis, 2006, 59–69.

Butler, Alison. 'Beyond Attribution: The Importance of Barrett's *Magus'*, *Journal for the Academic Study of Magic,* 1 (2003), 7–32.

Butler, Alison. 'The Golden Dawn and the Victorian Revival of Ritual Magic', *Limina: A Journal of Historical and Cultural Studies,* 9 (2003), 78–95.

Butler, E.M. *Ritual Magic.* Cambridge: Cambridge University Press, 1949. Reprint, University Park: Pennsylvania State University Press, 1998.

Clarke, Emma C. *Iamblichus's De mysteriis. A Manifesto of the Miraculous.* Aldershot, Hampshire: Ashgate, 2001.

Clulee, Nicholas. *John Dee's Natural Philosophy.* London: Routledge, 1988.

Colquhoun, Ithell. *Sword of Wisdom. MacGregor Mathers and 'The Golden Dawn'.* New York: G.P. Putnam's Sons, 1975.

Curry, Patrick. *A Confusion of Prophets: Victorian and Edwardian Astrology*. London: Collins and Brown, 1992.

Davies, Owen. *Witchcraft, Magic and Culture 1736–1951*. Manchester: Manchester University Press, 1999.

Deacon, Richard. *John Dee: Scientist, Geographer, Astrologer and Secret Agent to Elizabeth I*. London: Frederick Muller, 1968.

Decker, Ronald, Thierry Depaulis and Michael Dummett. *A Wicked Pack of Cards: The Origins of the Occult Tarot*. New York: St Martin's Press, 1996.

Edelman, Nicole. *Voyantes, Guérisseuses et Visionnaires en France 1785–1914*. Paris: Albin Michel, 1995.

Edighoffer, Roland 'Rosicrucianism: From the Seventeenth to the Twentieth Century', in *Modern Esoteric Spirituality*. Eds Antoine Faivre and Jacob Needleman. New York: Crossroad, 1992, 186–209.

Eliade, Mircea. *Rites and Symbols of Initiation. The Mysteries of Birth and Rebirth*. Trans. Willard R. Trask. New York: Harper & Row, 1965.

Faivre, Antoine. *Access to Western Esotericism*. Albany: State University of New York Press, 1994.

Faivre, Antoine. 'Renaissance Hermeticism and Western Esotericism', in *Gnosis and Hermeticism: From Antiquity to Modern Times*. Eds Roelof van den Broek and Wouter J. Hanegraaff. Albany: State University of New York Press, 1998, 109–23.

Fennelly, Laurence W. 'W.B. Yeats and S.L. MacGregor Mathers', in *Yeats and the Occult*. Ed. George Mills Harper. Toronto: Macmillan Press, 1975, 285–306.

Foster, R.F. *W.B. Yeats: A Life*. Oxford: Oxford University Press, 1997.

French, Peter J. *John Dee: The World of an Elizabethan Magus*. London: Routledge & Kegan Paul, 1972.

Garin, Eugenio. *Astrology in the Renaissance. The Zodiac of Life*. Trans. Carolyn Jackson and June Allen. Trans. and revised by Clare Robertson. London: Routledge & Kegan Paul, 1983.

Gilbert, R.A. *The Golden Dawn Companion. A Guide to the History, Structure and Workings of the Hermetic Order of the Golden Dawn*. Wellingborough: Aquarian Press, 1986.

Gilbert, R.A. 'Secret Writing: The Magical Manuscripts of Frederick Hockley' in *The Rosicrucian Seer: Magical Writings of Frederick Hockley*. Ed. John Hamill. Wellingborough: Aquarian Press, 1986, 26–33.

Gilbert, R.A. *The Golden Dawn and the Esoteric Section*. London: Theosophical History Centre, 1987.

Gilbert, R.A. *Revelations of the Golden Dawn: The Rise and Fall of a Magical Order*. London: Quantum, 1997.

Gilbert, R.A. 'Seeking that which was Lost: More Light on the Origins and Development of the Golden Dawn', *Yeats Annual 14: Yeats and the Nineties*, 14 (2001), 33–49.

Godwin, Joscelyn. *The Theosophical Enlightenment*. Albany: State University of New York Press, 1994.

Graf, Fritz. *Magic in the Ancient World*. Trans. Franklin Philip. Cambridge, Mass.: Harvard University Press, 1997.

Hamill, John. *The Craft – A History of English Freemasonry*. Wellingborough: Aquarian Press, 1986.

Hanegraaff, Wouter J. *New Age Religion and Western Culture: Esotericism in the Mirror of Secular Thought*. Leiden: E.J. Brill, 1996.

Hankins, James. *Plato in the Italian Renaissance*. Leiden, New York: E.J. Brill, 1990. Reprint, 1994.

Hannah, Walton. *Darkness Visible, A Christian Appraisal of Freemasonry*. London: Augustine Press, 1952; 17th reprint Saint Austin Press, 1998.

Harper, George Mills. *Yeats's Golden Dawn*. London: Macmillan Press, 1974.

Harper, George Mills. *Yeats and the Occult*. Toronto: Macmillan Press, 1975.

Harris, Jose. 'Platonism, positivism and progressivism: aspects of British sociological thought in the early twentieth century', in *Citizenship and Community: Liberals, radicals and collective identities in the British Isles, 1865–1931*. Ed. Eugenio F. Biagini. Cambridge: Cambridge University Press, 1996.

Hartmann, Franz. *In the Pronaos of the Temple of Wisdom Containing the History of the True and False Rosicrucians*. London: Theosophical Publishing Society, 1890.

Hobsbawm, Eric. 'Introduction: Inventing Traditions', in *The Invention of Tradition*. Eds Eric Hobsbawm and Terence Ranger. Cambridge: Cambridge University Press, 1983, 1–14.

Hobsbawm, Eric. 'Mass-Producing Traditions: Europe, 1870–1914', in *The Invention of Tradition*. Eds Eric Hobsbawm and Terence Ranger. Cambridge: Cambridge University Press, 1983, 263–307.

Hornung, Erik. *The Ancient Egyptian Books of the Afterlife*. Trans. David Lortun. Ithaca: Cornell University Press, 1999.

Howe, Ellic. *The Magicians of the Golden Dawn: A Documentary History of a Magical Order 1887–1923*. London: Routledge and Kegan Paul, 1972. Reprint, York Beach, Maine: Samuel Weiser, 1978.

Howe, Ellic. 'Fringe Masonry in England 1870–85', *Ars Quatuor Coronatorum*, (September 1972).

Howe, Ellic. *Urania's Children*. London: William Kimber and Co., 1967.

Hutton, Ronald. *The Pagan Religions of the Ancient British Isles*. Oxford: Blackwell, 1991; Reprint, 1992.

Hutton, Ronald. 'Modern Pagan Witchcraft', in *Witchcraft and Magic in Europe in the Twentieth Century*. Eds Bengt Ankarloo and Stuart Clark. London: Athlone Press, 1999, 1–80.

Hutton, Ronald. *The Triumph of the Moon. A History of Modern Pagan Witchcraft*. Oxford: Oxford University Press, 1999.

Idel, Moshe. Introduction to Johannes Reuchlin's *On the Art of the Kabbalah. De Arte Cabalistica*. Trans. Martin and Sarah Goodman. Lincoln: University of Nebraska Press, 1993.

Jacob, Margaret C. *Living the Enlightenment. Freemasonry and Politics in Eighteenth-Century Europe*. Oxford: Oxford University Press, 1991.

Jenkyns, Richard. *The Victorians and Ancient Greece*. Cambridge, Mass.: Harvard University Press, 1980.

Jones, G. Lloyd. Introduction to Johannes Reuchlin's *On the Art of the Kabbalah. De Arte Cabalistica*. Trans. Martin and Sarah Goodman. Lincoln: University of Nebraska Press, 1993.

Kieckhefer, Richard. *European Witch Trials: Their Foundations in Popular and Learned Culture*. London: Routledge & Kegan Paul, 1976.

Kieckhefer, Richard. *Magic in the Middle Ages*. Cambridge: Cambridge University Press, 1989. Reprint, 1997.

Kieckhefer, Richard. *Forbidden Rites: A Necromancer's Manual of the Fifteenth Century*. University Park: Pennsylvania State University Press, 1998.

King, Francis. *Modern Ritual Magic. The Rise of Western Occultism.* Bridport, Dorset: Prism, 1989. First published as *Ritual Magic in England.* London: Neville Spearman, 1970.

King, Francis. *The Flying Sorcerer: Being the magical and aeronautical adventures of Francis Barrett author of the Magus.* Oxford: Mandrake Books, 1992.

Knight, Gareth. *Magic and the Western Mind.* London: Averill & Kahn, 1991.

Laurant, Jean-Pierre. 'The Primitive Characteristics of Nineteenth-Century Esotericism', in *Modern Esoteric Spirituality.* Eds Antoine Faivre and Jacob Needleman. New York: Crossroad, 1992, 277–87.

Luhrmann, T.M. *Persuasions of the Witch's Craft. Ritual Magic in Contemporary England.* Cambridge, Mass.: Harvard University Press, 1989.

McCalman, Iain. *The Last Alchemist: Count Cagliostro, Master of Magic in the Age of Reason.* New York: Harper Collins, 2003.

McIntosh, Christopher. *The Rosicrucians: The History, Mythology, and Rituals of an Esoteric Order.* York Beach, Maine: Samuel Weiser 1997.

McIntosh, Christopher. *Eliphas Lévi and the French Occult Revival.* London: Rider, 1972.

Mercier, Alain. *Eliphas Lévi et la pensée magique au XIXe siècle.* Paris: Seghers, 1974.

Nauert, Charles G. *Agrippa and the Crisis of Renaissance Thought.* Urbana: University of Illinois Press, 1965.

Oppenheim, Janet. *The Other World: Spiritualism and Psychical Research in England 1850–1914.* Cambridge: Cambridge University Press, 1985.

Owen, Alex. *The Darkened Room: Women, Power and Spiritualism in Late Victorian England.* London: Virago Press, 1989.

Owen, Alex. *The Place of Enchantment: British Occultism and the Culture of the Modern.* Chicago: University of Chicago Press, 2004.

Pakkanen, Petra. *Interpreting Early Hellenistic Religion.* Helsinki: Foundation of the Finnish Institute at Athens, 1996.

Pinch, Geraldine. *Magic in Ancient Egypt.* London: British Museum Press, 1994.

Richter, Melvin. *The Politics of Conscience: T.H. Green and his Age.* Cambridge, Mass.: Harvard University Press, 1964.

Saler, Michael. 'Modernity and Enchantment: A Historiographic Review' in *American Historical Review,* 111 (3) (2006), 629–716.

Saler, Michael. Review of *The Place of Enchantment: British Occultism and the Culture of the Modern,* by Alex Owen, *American Historical Review* 110 (3) (2005), 871–2.

Scholem, Gershom. *Kabbalah.* New York: Quadrangle, 1974.

Spence, Lewis. *Myths and Legends of Ancient Egypt.* London: George G. Harrap, 1915.

Stevenson, David. *The Origins of Freemasonry.* Cambridge: Cambridge University Press, 1988.

Stevenson, David. *The First Freemasons: Scotland's Early Lodges and their Members.* Aberdeen: Aberdeen University Press, 1988.

Stocking, George W. *Victorian Anthropology.* New York: Free Press, 1987.

Summers, Montague. *Witchcraft and Black Magic.* London: Rider, 1946. Reprint, Detroit: Omnigraphics, 1990.

Treitel, Corinna. *A Science for the Soul. Occultism and the Genesis of the German Modern.* Baltimore: Johns Hopkins University Press, 2004.

Turner, Frank Miller. *Between Science and Religion. The reaction to scientific naturalism in late Victorian England.* London and New Haven: Yale University Press, 1974.

Turner, Frank Miller. *Contesting Cultural Authority: Essays in Victorian Intellectual Life.* Cambridge: Cambridge University Press, 1993.

Turner, Frank Miller. *The Greek Heritage in Victorian Britain.* New Haven: Yale University Press, 1981.

Van der Poel, Marc. *Cornelius Agrippa: The Humanist Theologian and his Declamations.* Leiden: E.J. Brill, 1997.

Van Egmond, Daniël. 'Western Esoteric Schools in the Late Nineteenth and Early Twentieth Centuries', in *Gnosis and Hermeticism from Antiquity to Modern Times.* Eds Roelef van den Broek and Wouter J. Hanegraaff. Albany: State University of New York Press, 1998, 311–46.

Walker, D.P. *Spiritual and Demonic Magic From Ficino to Campanella,* London: Warburg Institute, 1958; Notre Dame: University of Notre Dame, 1975.

Weisse, John A. *The Obelisk and Freemasonry.* New York: J.W. Bouton, 1880.

Wiedemann, Alfred. *Religion of the Ancient Egyptians.* London: H. Grevel & Co., 1897.

Williams, Thomas A. *Eliphas Lévi: Master of Occultism.* Alabama: University of Alabama Press, 1975.

Wirszubski, Chaim. *Pico della Mirandola's Encounter with Jewish Mysticism.* Cambridge, Mass.: Harvard University Press, 1989.

Woolley, Benjamin. *The Queen's Conjuror: The Science and Magic of Dr. Dee.* London: Harper Collins, 2001.

Yates, Frances A. *The Occult Philosophy in the Elizabethan Age.* London: Routledge & Kegan Paul, 1979.

Yates, Frances A. *The Rosicrucian Enlightenment.* London: Routledge & Kegan Paul, 1972.

Yates, Frances A. *Giordano Bruno and the Hermetic Tradition.* London: Routledge & Kegan Paul, 1964.

Index